They Call t

MW00827691

They Call the Horses

*Eleven Race Announcers at
American Thoroughbred Tracks*

EDIE DICKENSON

Foreword by Michael Blowen

McFarland & Company, Inc., Publishers
Jefferson, North Carolina, and London

Photographs otherwise uncredited are from the author's collection.

LIBRARY OF CONGRESS CATALOGUING-IN-PUBLICATION DATA

Dickenson, Edie, 1949–
    They call the horses : eleven race announcers at American
thoroughbred tracks / Edie Dickenson ; foreword by Michael
Blowen.
        p.   cm.
    Includes bibliographical references and index.

    ISBN 978-0-7864-4769-5
    softcover : 50# alkaline paper ∞

    1. Racetrack announcers — United States — Anecdotes.
    2. Horse racing — United States — Anecdotes.   I. Title.
    SF336.A2D53   2010
    798.40092' 2 — dc22
                                                    2010014213

British Library cataloguing data are available

Front cover: top — Kurt Becker's idyllic view from the best seat
in the house (credit: Edie Dickenson); bottom — horses ©2010
Shutterstock. Back cover image ©2010 Shutterstock.

Manufactured in the United States of America

*McFarland & Company, Inc., Publishers
  Box 611, Jefferson, North Carolina 28640
  www.mcfarlandpub.com*

To my son,
Michael Charles

Acknowledgments

Eleven extraordinary track announcers generously gave me their time and memories. They ensured that my dream became a reality. Many thanks go to Kurt Becker, Larry Collmus, Trevor Denman, John Dooley, Tom Durkin, Dave Johnson, the late Luke Kruytbosch, Dave Rodman, Terry Wallace, and Michael Wrona. Robert Geller gave me insight, support, and his loyal friendship.

I hit the Pick Six with my family. My parents, Charles and Rosemary Atwell, showered unconditional love upon their only child. My late husband, Eric Dickenson, gave me a lifetime of happiness in three short years. My son, Michael Dickenson, is as passionate about writing as he is about life. He encouraged me by saying, "Persistence will get you published, Mom." Nicole Jenkins was always there for me at the other end of the phone with computer and fax advice and a sense of humor with my impatience. My adopted sister, Judy Wilson Wessling, was a part of my life for 56 years, and I miss her every day.

Michael Blowen, in the midst of welcoming more champion stallions to Old Friends, took the time to write the foreword. I appreciate his words, and he is my hero for the work he does with retirees.

Siblings, wives, parents, trainers, jockeys, owners, and racing enthusiasts took time away from their busy lives to talk to me about the race callers. They were courteous and generous with their anecdotes.

Friends and relatives knew that if they wanted to see me, they would have to join me at the racetrack. Teresa McAllister outdid herself coming to six meets. Jillian Abbott; Pat Brice; Bob Dickenson; Michael Dickenson; Chance, Kayla and Sherry Hecht; Matt, McKenzie, Nicole, and Seth Jenkins; Bob and Nancy Dickenson Jones; Ken and Mary Kennedy; Bob and

Caroline McKay; Pat Sheehan; Charlie Stevenson; and Greta Stock showed up to play the ponies, whether it was the Elko County Fair or the Breeders' Cup.

Many other friends listened to me talk on and on about horse racing. Those who listened endlessly until their eyes glazed over and still managed to encourage me were Pami Briggs, Dorothy Dickenson, Riva Grant, Mary Ellen Guenther, Carole Handt, Marilyn Janka, Gerrie Kath, Anita Kennedy, Father Brian Kennedy, Marilee Kuhl, Anna Maderis, Rama Paris, Lisa Schaffer, Bob and Linda Vasey, Jack and Irene Walther, and Nancy Wood.

Cheryl and Peter Denton are as passionate about this sport as I am. Here's to Operation Bluegrass #2! Only a true fan like Tom Ferry would drive 11 hours round-trip to spend 30 minutes with Peppers Pride! I am so grateful for the gift of his terrific pictures throughout the book.

Warmest thanks to Karen Green whose friendship came first followed by her offer to put together my Web page.

Sherry Hecht got me out of the gate and down the homestretch with her total conviction that this book was a winner. Friends don't come any better!

Finally, in over three years there have been hundreds of special experiences. However, the Eclipse Award–winning Moment took place at sunrise at Santa Anita, where I got to listen to Hall of Fame trainer Ron McAnally share his memories of the one and only John Henry!

Contents

Foreword

by Michael Blowen

At Old Friends, we listen to the stirring calls of classic races every day with the visitors who come to pay tribute to these magnificent athletes. There's Tom Durkin's breathtaking call of Awad's record-breaking performance in the 1997 Sword Dancer at Saratoga: "And here comes the old pro Awad ... and he DEMOLISHED the track record." Trevor Denman's breathless description of Ruhlmann's victory in the 1990 Big 'Cap at Santa Anita when Jerry and Ann Moss's black beauty went wire to wire to beat the likes of Criminal Type and Bayakoa: "Gary Stevens is riding for his life on Ruhlmann." And, one of my all-time favorites from one of the greatest announcers ever, Jim Hannon, when his voice got hoarser and hoarser calling the 1987 MassCap: "It's a ding-dong battle to the wire ... Waquoit ... Broad Brush ... Waquoit ... Broad Brush."

The great narrators of our sport, the artists who paint such varying, dramatic portraits of these spectacular competitions, have long been afterthoughts. There were many who objected when Keeneland finally added an announcer. Many handicappers, disappointed by their own poor judgment, take it out on the announcers ... even at the simulcasts. All you need to do is listen to a tired, dull, monotonous race call where the only thing that matters are the numbers and the payoffs to realize how much great announcers add to the magnificent experience that is horse racing.

These oral interpreters are our guides. We not only depend on them to be accurate — even on the foggiest days at Suffolk Downs and Aqueduct — but we also need them to operatically build the drama from start to finish. And, God help them if they make one mistake in one thousand races.

Years ago, I wrote about the movies and covered stand-up comedy for the *Boston Globe*. And, at least from a semiprofessional point of view, these track announcers can proudly stand along some of the best actors in the world. Think of it. They are their own writers, directors, producers and actors. Each race is a minidrama, and they must create at least nine a day. Whether it's a bunch of $3,500 claimers on a Wednesday afternoon in February or the first Saturday in May, they must treat every race as if it was the most important in history.

Until now, these artists have remained fairly anonymous. But, through Edie Dickenson's sympathetic ear and thorough research, we can see there is so much more to them than a chorus of disembodied voices. I've known Larry Collmus since he started calling races at Suffolk Downs ages ago, but I never knew he had lost both his parents by the time he was 22. It's great to read about Trevor Denman's campaign to abolish the whip, Dave Rodman's ideas about housing some retired racehorses at the track so their fans can see the old champs, or, on a more trivial note, that the late Luke Kruytbosch was born on the same day as Northern Dancer. In fact, Dickenson's detailed profiles provide so much flesh and bones to these artists that it makes you wonder why no one has written about them before.

Michael Blowen is the president and founder of Old Friends, a Thoroughbred retirement farm in Georgetown, Kentucky.

Preface

"Secretariat is blazing along! The first three-quarters of a mile in 1:09⅘.
Secretariat is widening now. He is moving like a tremendous machine!"

Secretariat won the Belmont by 31 lengths and captured the first Triple Crown championship in 25 years. It was a record-breaking performance, and track announcer Chic Anderson gave an unforgettable call. Years later whenever fans heard those words, they were immediately transported back to June 9, 1973, and the race of a lifetime.

Kurt Becker, Keeneland's track announcer, reflected, "Chic Anderson's call of the Belmont; I don't know if any other announcer that I've ever known could have described that the way he did. But somehow, he nailed it. He described it in a way that when the time came down the stretch, you still kept your focus on the horse. It wasn't like he was trying to insert himself into the equation."

Top track announcers know that the race call is not about them. It is about the horses, for they are the stars. These premier race callers inform the fans and describe the races without taking attention away from the Thoroughbreds. For 60 years after Keeneland opened in 1936, the regal racetrack did not have a track announcer. The patrons at this Lexington fixture had been raised around racehorses. They felt they could follow the races without any outside help. But even these well-informed fans and horsemen accepted Kurt when he became the first and only track announcer that Keeneland has known.

Look at racing forums on the Internet, and you will find members with quite strong opinions about the current race callers. They argue incessantly about who are the best announcers. They refer often to calls that they enjoyed. Fans mention announcers who are so grating on the telecast that they must hit the "mute" button. Posts inquire about which finalist will be Churchill's new announcer. Today's track announcers are an integral part of the horse race.

Articulate and accurate announcers take the races to the highest level. These men impart information with drama and excitement. The outstanding ones paint a picture of the race using precise terminology. They are passionate about the racing industry. These announcers are perfectionists; their stresses come from within as they strive to give each race the best description possible. They have reached the pinnacle of their profession by hard work, enthusiasm, energy, and some luck.

The track announcer has no "second take" available to him if he makes a mistake. He does not have the luxury of spotters. He is often alone in his announcer's booth; visitors are distracting. There are no hour-long lunch breaks. He has to create a circuit that enables him to call enough races each year to afford him a living. This often forces the caller to relocate one or more times during the year as he follows the race meets. This nomadic lifestyle is extremely hard on relationships; unofficially, the divorce rate for track announcers is much higher than the national average.

As a relative newcomer to racing, I was privileged to talk to 11 men at the top of the profession: Tom Durkin, Kurt Becker, Dave Rodman, Michael Wrona, Terry Wallace, Larry Collmus, John Dooley, the late Luke Kruytbosch, Dave Johnson, Robert Geller, and Trevor Denman. These men were courteous and classy. They invited me up to the "best seat in the house" and gave me hours of their valuable time.

I realize this list of premier track announcers is subjective, and there are certainly other very good ones in the United States. Not all of these first-class men work at first-class racetracks. And like most things, the dynamics and racetrack venues and participants are constantly changing. So let us begin. It's post time!

Introduction

Horse racing in America began before the turn of the 20th century. And the first track announcer followed shortly behind when, according to *Sports on New York Radio*, Clem McCarthy was hired to call races at Arlington Park in 1927.

That was in the days of radio, and fans relied heavily upon the race callers to tell them what was taking place with the horses racing on the tracks. On November 1, 1938, 40 million men, women, and children listened intently to McCarthy call the match race between Seabiscuit and War Admiral at Pimlico. McCarthy's call of the "Biscuit" triumphing over the Triple Crown winner War Admiral was a popular one that day. Nine years later in the 1947 Preakness Stakes, again at Pimlico, Clem's call was not as well received. He called the wrong horse the winner but later apologized profusely and was forgiven.

Chic Anderson suffered a similar fate in the 1975 Kentucky Derby when he claimed that three-year-old Prince Thou Art had won the race. The winner was Foolish Pleasure, whose jockey wore similar silks. He too apologized and was forgiven.

Keeneland's Kurt Becker grew up listening to Chic Anderson, and he said, "Probably a guy that just always amazed me was the late Chic Anderson. He was gifted with a voice that naturally drew you to the television set. To me, he had a quality about the race that made you want to rush into the room to see what was happening. What a loss to our sport when he died at a fairly young age!"

Television arrived in the middle of the century, and horse racing flourished. Its popularity continued, and the 1970s witnessed three Triple Crown winners: Secretariat in 1973, Seattle Slew in 1977, and Affirmed in 1978. As of 2009, no other horse has achieved the Triple Crown.

Track announcing has evolved over the years. In 1959 "The Voice of Chicago Racing" Phil Georgeff was the first to call the finish of a race. Today announcers are required to call the first three finishers, and often the fourth for those gamblers who bet the superfecta (picking the first four finishers in the correct order in a race). And while many men called the races over the public address systems at the tracks, only the top announcers called the big races on television.

The process of track announcing is memory and delivery. Track announcers use various methods involving rote memorization, crayons, and repetition during the approximately ten-minute post parade before the horses are loaded into the gate. Earlier race callers were often unemotional chroniclers relating the position of the horses as they advanced in the race. Over the years, the delivery has changed to a more exciting and descriptive race call. Four men pioneered this: Chic Anderson, Dave Johnson, Tom Durkin, and Trevor Denman.

I wish very much that I could have interviewed the late Chic Anderson. I thrilled to his call of Secretariat's record-breaking Kentucky Derby win in 1973. However, it was not until I attended my first Breeders' Cup at Santa Anita Park in 2003, that I was completely and totally captivated by the Sport of Kings. I embraced Thoroughbred racing completely and have become passionate about every aspect of it: its greatness along with its growing problems.

In the last six years I have read over 100 books about the horses, trainers, jockeys, and every facet of horse racing in general. But I have found only three books about the men who call the races. *And They're Off* is written by Phil Georgeff, who called races in Chicago from 1959 to 1992. *The Untold Story of Joe Hernandez: The Voice of Santa Anita* by Rudolph Alvarado relates the life of a man so dedicated to his profession that the only thing that stopped him was his collapse in the booth in 1972 and his death within the week.

The third book is *London to a Brick On* by Steve Cairns, which was recommended to me by the late Luke Kruytbosch. He explained that the book was about Australian race callers who were much more popular and well-known than announcers in the United States. I wanted to change that.

In October 2005 my mission began. In the next three years I earned lots of frequent flier miles visiting the 11 track announcers I interviewed for this book. I diligently researched before the interviews, but most of what I learned came from the men themselves. I discovered that there is much more to the job than the announcing. There is voice-over work. Arlington and Fair Grounds race caller John Dooley explains, "I just did a v.o. yesterday between races for an Earlie Fires promo for Sunday. Voice-overs are often a part of our job for in-house commercials and such, 'Join us on Sunday for...' It's recorded and TV puts it to a video. Just another part of the job!"

These men often host handicapping shows. They can be found emceeing in the paddock before the races. They introduce new fans to racing at breakfast shows like Daybreak at Del Mar or Breakfast at Arlington. When the races have ended, many announcers preside over the day's races for the television wrap-up. Some race callers, like Emerald Downs' Robert Geller, write and take part in weekly shows on the backside. Kurt Becker includes the Keeneland sales as part of his duties. And Terry Wallace works year-round as the media director.

Wages vary greatly, which is to be expected. Often track announcers are paid per diem. However, contracts may be drawn up for a lump sum per season or year-round employment that incorporates the announcing. Should the work involve networks other than the racetrack, special pay agreements may be added on or separately signed. Amounts vary widely depending upon location, experience of the announcer, and the budget. Salary can be anywhere from $100 per day to more than $1,000 per day.

I don't think that many track announcers go into this career planning to get rich. While the top pay suggests a prosperous income, one must remember that many men must move at least once a year, often to other states, to make a full-time living, and they incur significant expenses in doing so. Added to that, the meet might only last for 50 days, which translates into $50,000 per year with no benefits.

As of 2009 approximately 75 racetracks were still open and running in the United States, although several were on the auction block. The dwindling 75 include the county fairs which only run for a week or so each year. Racetracks have different racing calendars, and track announcers must find work at two or three tracks in order to earn a living. The circuit, in turn, creates seasonal work which often causes the announcer to move from one location to another. Robert Geller points out that, for many, the chance to call races for a living is more important than having job security. He says, "It takes a person with a certain personality."

In the end, the track announcer is unseen, alone in his booth on the roof of the grandstand. He imparts knowledge about the race and points out details that the average fan misses. He gives each horse a call on the backstretch. The track announcer times his delivery to coincide with the unfolding drama, getting more and more animated as the horses near the finish line. His rhythm and vocabulary are as much his tools as his state-of-the-art binoculars. And today's racing fans are well acquainted with the men who call the horses. Hearing a Midwestern voice shout, "Here they come into the stretch of the Apple Blossom," they know it has to be Terry Wallace, and the race can only be at Oaklawn.

CHAPTER 1

Tom Durkin

Tom Durkin: "The unconquerable, invincible, unbeatable Cigar!"

"Aaaaaaaand they're off!" announces Tom Durkin from his vantage point high above Saratoga's finish line. He is not only the official track announcer at Aqueduct, Belmont, and Saratoga in New York. He is the Voice of the Triple Crown races, and his 22 years calling Breeders' Cup races have guaranteed him a place in horse racing history books.

"There're so many race calls that he's had where people were just blown away. His ability to come up with the right words at the right time, and it's just a function of Tom Durkin being who he is: the best race caller in America," said Bill Nader, Tom's former boss at NYRA and now the executive director of racing for the Hong Kong Jockey Club. He went on to list preparation, enthusiasm, skill, and delivery as crucial to Tom Durkin's success as the premier track announcer in the United States.

Tom Dawson, a producer for ESPN, agreed: "The other trick to Durkin is the recall. It's one thing to study all that stuff, but to be able to recall the proper phrase and the proper situation at the right time within the call while not forgetting horses' names and keeping the excitement at fever pitch, now that's not something that everybody can do ... I have a lot of race caller friends out there, but I don't think anyone would be offended to know, and most of them do know, that I consider Durkin the best race caller around."

Tom Durkin was born on November 30, 1950, and grew up on the west side of Chicago. His mother, Betty, was a telephone operator, and his father, Jim, was an accountant. Tom, the youngest of three, chuckled and recalled, "I slept in my parents' bedroom until I was eleven years old. So we were not particularly prosperous."

Tom Durkin is proud of receiving the Good Guy Award from the New York Turf Writers in 1996. Credit: Adam Coglianese.

Beth Ann reminisced about her younger brother when he was five: "My grandfather took him everywhere with him. He owned the biggest horse shoeing business in America, but he also had a lot of real estate. My grandfather used to go and collect from his buildings. And there was a tavern in one of his buildings so when he would go and collect rent, as an act of good will, he would always say, 'Bartender, just give everyone a drink.' Tom went everywhere with him, and my grandfather used to go to Mass in the mornings, and he would take Tom with him. And you know back in the old days they had a communion rail, and my grandfather brought Tom up while he was getting Communion. And Tom raised his hand and said, 'Bartender, get everyone a drink!'"

"My father suffered from mental illness from time to time, and my mom had to go pick up, get a job in the 1950s so we could just eat. My dad tried his best and worked for the city of Chicago. They were very keen on education with me, and I went to Catholic schools, and at some hardship for them," Tom explained. There he received a classic education in Latin, literature, and philosophy. He made it through one year playing football at

Fenwick High School. Tom said, "I hated it! I just didn't like getting hit! I was a swimmer. We played a lot of baseball and basketball. I was the chief student goofball."

Tom's parents took him to the track when he was ten or 11. By 13 he and his buddies would sneak off to Arlington, Sportsman, or Hawthorne racetracks in Chicago. "Once I got over wanting to be a fireman or a candy vendor at Wrigley Field, track announcing is really the only thing I ever aspired to. I never really aspired to do anything else. So I didn't waste any time doing anything else," admitted Tom.

Kelly Collum, his college drama teacher, was the most influential person in Tom's career. "I was not a good student in college. I was very much the playboy," Tom recalled. When he finally did graduate, he quipped, "I graduated college in six terms: Nixon's, Ford's, Carter's, Reagan's, Bush's, and Clinton's." He tried out for a play in his junior year and got the title role. He said, "Kelly had a lot of confidence in me and taught me that energy is everything."

He continued to discover the importance of energy from Phil Georgeff, the revered Chicago track announcer for over 30 years. In his foreword to Georgeff's autobiography, *And They're Off,* Tom wrote, "When I grew up, I wanted to be Phil Georgeff." He noted, "Phil Georgeff just had tremendous energy and so that's what I took away from him more than anything else. And it seemed to me he was having fun at work. And he is the reason I am a race caller."

Tom admitted, "The hardest part was getting the first job ... cause I wasn't born into this. I had no contacts whatsoever. I'm happy to say I've done it on merit. 100 percent on merit. Without getting a recommendation from anybody. Other than my own work."

In the 1970s Tom's friend Jim Forrett was hitchhiking in Wisconsin. Marty Helmbrecht gave him a ride, and they got to talking about horses. Tom said, "Marty revealed that he ran these little county fairs in Wisconsin, and my friend Forrett told him that I was the assistant track announcer at Arlington Park which, of course, I wasn't. In fact, there was no such position. And I didn't realize that until I got introduced at the Fountain Head County Fair in May of '71 that I was the assistant track announcer because I had no credentials whatsoever. So this whole career of mine is based on a bold-faced lie."

Tom called Quarter Horse and Thoroughbred races for five summers beginning in 1971 at fair tracks in Wisconsin. In 1976 he worked for the *Daily Racing Form* as a call taker at Thistledown in Cleveland and Cahokia Downs in East St. Louis. Then in the late 1970s and early 1980s, he followed his passion to Florida Downs and Miles Park in Kentucky, where he announced Quarter Horse races, and to Quad City Downs, Cahokia, and Balmoral Park in Illinois where he called harness racing. A high point was being the track announcer at the magnificent Hialeah racetrack in Florida for the 1983–1990 meets. Its schedule allowed him to also call harness races at the Meadowlands from 1982 to 1990.

Tom Durkin and Dave Johnson are the only two announcers to call both the Kentucky Derby and the Hambletonian for a national audience. And in 1989 Tom called the first and last dead heat in the history of harness racing's most eminent race: "Neither of these brave trotters giving way. They are full-tilt down the stretch an eighth of a mile out. Park Avenue Joe digging in gamely. Probe pokes a head in front. Probe on the outside. Park Avenue Joe comes roaring back. A relentless drive to the wire. Park Avenue Joe! Probe! There's the finish. Too close to call!"

Tom won't ever forget that race and those two courageous horses: "Ahh-hhhh!!!!!! The Hambletonian, the one that really sticks out is the most unbelievably improbable. To say that two horses race against each other for a fourth time in the biggest race of a sport would wind up in a dead heat in a match race is just off the charts. It's infinitesimal. You can't come up with odds. It's beyond really the realm of explanation."

Tom Durkin is one of just a handful of top track announcers who has actual hands-on experience with racehorses. But it didn't last long. He recounted his experience in his keynote address at the 2006 induction ceremony at the National Museum of Racing and Hall of Fame:

> About twenty years ago I was working the Oaklawn Handicap, and a week later the Arkansas Derby for ESPN. So I figured instead of goofing off all week (another pursuit at which I'm in my element I might add), I decided to get an education. So I got a job as a hot-walker with Jack Van Berg. I arrived at the barn at four-thirty in the morning. Four-thirty in the morning! Do I really need to continue here? I am handed this leash with a twelve hundred pound animal on the other end with large teeth and two huge brown fierce eyes trained on me. Twelve hundred pounds of coiled sinew and muscle about to be unleashed on a shivering neophyte and at any moment capable of running off with me at forty miles per hour dragging me around the backstretch of Oaklawn Park.
>
> I am frozen in fear. Up walks this cute little exercise rider. She is one hundred pounds. She nuzzles up to this behemoth and says, "He's so cute!" And then she bounces away. I am still frozen in fear. I get my instructions: walk the horse ... keep turning left. It is very clear that I am the one that is on the leash.... At first I am merely petrified. But then before I'm able to make

my first left turn, I realize that I am not only petrified of horses, I am allergic to them!

It must have been quite a week for Tom, because there was a dangerous thunderstorm one race day in Hot Springs, Arkansas. ESPN's Tom Dawson remembered, "During rehearsal Tom did part of the show in host position, and then he went up and called the race. And during rehearsal, lightning hit nearby, and it zapped through the ground. And his hat fell off, and it was kind of a shaky experience. It got better, but during the show it was still kind of threatening. And Tom was on the roof to call the race and he said, 'Just what I want to be doing right now is standing here at the highest point of this building holding a metal microphone! If the call gets interrupted, you'll know why!'"

In 1990 the New York Racing Association hired Tom to be the track announcer at its prestigious tracks at Saratoga, Belmont, and Aqueduct. He has been there ever since, but included Gulfstream Park for six seasons beginning in 1995.

Tom Durkin's popularity and fame were cemented in two venues: the Triple Crown races and the Breeders' Cup races. He had the best seat in the house for his most memorable races. "Victory Gallop, Easy Goer–Sunday Silence, Ferdinand–Alysheba, Personal Ensign, even Smarty Jones. Just a lot of really magical moments. I don't know that one is more magical than the next," Tom remarked.

Tom Durkin's dramatic style is larger-than-life. The Voice of the New York Racing Association takes center stage and captivates his audience with breathtaking surges of energy that elevate the excitement of a finish to an indelible octave. Through his eyes, the racing world has traversed some of its greatest highs and heart-wrenching lows. His words have immortalized the roller-coaster storybook that is the Triple Crown. The power of the occasion is not lost on Tom, who remains fully present to the moment. He is well aware that in the theater of the Thoroughbred, fact is always stranger than fiction.

Bill Nader remembered the 1998 Belmont: "The Victory Gallop–Real Quiet race at Belmont was a great one. It was a very very tight finish. But Victory Gallop defeated Real Quiet by a nose. And it was a long long photo and Tom came up with, 'If a picture is worth a thousand words, this photo is worth $5 million.' It was the Visa Triple Crown bonus. It had to be the toughest defeat in the history of horse racing, because here was Real Quiet attempting to be the first Triple Crown winner since 1978. And it was so close! He had a four length lead with a furlong to go and just got beat on the wire. And I thought that was a great call."

Cigar was Tom's favorite stallion. And Personal Ensign was Tom's favorite filly. In his keynote address at the 2006 Hall of Fame induction ceremony, Tom remembered the only race of hers that he called.

Who saw the first undefeated champion in seventy years? Comes to Churchill Downs to face the winner of the Kentucky Derby that year, Winning Colors. The track comes up muddy. All the way around the track, it is apparent Personal Ensign is not taking to the track-going at Churchill that day. And while no other horse was able to beat Personal Ensign, it appeared that the forces of nature could. Well next door at the Hall of Fame, they have it on tape, the 1988 Breeders' Cup Distaff. Play it over and over and over, and you still can't believe that Personal Ensign wins. I described her final sixteenth of a mile as miraculous. And since her victory that day to retire the undefeated champion beating the Derby winner at Churchill Downs against Mother Nature herself, since that very moment, I have never been able to summon up enough cynicism to deny the existence of destiny. And that, friends, is the kind of inspiration that racing continues to give us today.

On July 13, 1996, Cigar (pictured) tied Citation's record of 16 consecutive wins. Credit: Tom Ferry.

Tom's awe of the champion mare was apparent in his stretch call that day: "Here comes Personal Ensign unleashing a furious run on the outside.... Personal Ensign, a dramatic finish and here is the wire and it is Personal Ensign and Winning Colors in a photo. Very close. At the sixteenth pole it looked like Personal Ensign was facing her first defeat but in those final 110 courageous yards she certainly proved herself a champion this afternoon!"

Tom Durkin has called races for over 35 years. He said, "The best part is the satisfaction I get from the job itself. I enjoy describing what horses and jockeys do. And frankly, I'm a little surprised that I still can find different ways to do it and still enjoy it very very much.

"The worst part is the stress. It's just part of the job. I mean I wish it did not exist. My subconscious tells me it's there, because I have dreams almost every night when I'm working," he chuckled, "about screwing up races. Yeah, I have performance anxiety dreams all the time. And it's just part of the job. Part of the deal so when I go off in the wintertime, I go to Italy. They disappear. In fact, I start dreaming in Italian."

When Tom started his long run in 1984 as the only Breeders' Cup announcer in its first 22 years, he was just three years from his stint at Cahokia Downs. It was quite a difference, and one that weighed on him heavily. He recalled:

> I was so nervous when I got the Breeders' Cup job, that I devised a contraption made to hold the binoculars in my hands and keep them from shaking.
>
> But the dreams are so constant. They tend to be more numerous and intense before the big races. Bizarre things: can't get to the track. The roof collapses. Totally off-the-wall things. Like last week I dreamt there was a cruise ship comin' down the stretch, and I couldn't see the horses; big cruise ship. I finally figured out that (and I'm a very big believer in the subconscious mind) it was my subconscious telling me "Hey, Moron. You can do this. You can actually do this. Until a cruise ship starts comin' down the stretch, you're probably going to be able to do it."
>
> Once I realized that, it's just a recent development, I don't get quite as apoplectic as I used to. One guy was interviewing me before I was doing the Derby and he goes, "What's it feel like to be one simple mistake away from being a national joke?" Thanks for that thought!

The 1987 Breeders' Cup had been so traumatizing that Tom vowed he would no longer be a race caller: "It was just too too intense and for some reason or other I got it into my mind that I was going to teach retarded children. Where that ever came from I have no idea. But I decided that as soon as I got this day over, if I can just get through it, maybe it was a promise to God: 'Just get me through this day, and I'll spend the rest of my life doing good for others.'"

Tom used the drug enderol for his nerves, but hypnosis was quite effective in calming him before Triple Crown or Breeders' Cup races. He said,

> I started getting hypnotized in the weeks leading up to the '88 Breeders' Cup. So one of the hypnotic images, kind of like a trigger, to relax, that when I saw the Twin Spires at Churchill Downs [where that year's Breeders' Cup races

were held] that I would relax, have confidence, breathe easy, see well, words would come up. And the hypnotist constantly drilled that into my mind for weeks. And so I get up Breeders' Cup morning, open up the window, and it's raining! This is the end. This is the end. Mud gets in the way, all the horses are full of mud, and it's really hard when they're full of mud, and Churchill's mud sticks to them, a lot of clay content and it just sticks. And I'm like, "Well, I'm screwed. I'm really screwed." So we're going up Fourth Street, and I turn on Central, and there are the Twin Spires, and immediately I just felt great.

Although Tom Durkin is one of the top track announcers in the country, there are still races he would like to have back. He admits, "Every race I'd like to change after calling because you have the benefit of the result. They're off and, boy oh boy, it looks like #4 is going to win by 4½ lengths. All of them can be improved upon. There's not a single race that I've ever done that I've ever thought couldn't be improved upon."

However, he has learned to control how he reacts to mistakes. Bill, the sound man for 20 years for NYRA, recalled that once Tom picked up his computer and smashed it against the wall when there was a horse making a big move on the far turn. "Omigod! I used to be terrible," Tom conceded.

He won't admit to being a perfectionist: "Well you know, it's a wide public forum, and I don't have an eraser. And if I make a mistake, that's it. And a lot of people are listening. So I think it was good that I used to be hard on myself when I made mistakes. It really cut down on it. Also I think one thing that cut down on the mistakes is that I worked for many many years through difficult circumstances calling those races from the back of a truck at county fairs. At Cahokia Downs the lights were so dim, you couldn't see the horses very well. Just working at a lot of places like that, I think cut it down."

In 2001 Tom called Monarchos' win in the Kentucky Derby as tying Secretariat's record time of 1:59⅖. He admits, "That was a pretty big faux pas. I wrote down on my program the fastest quarter in the history of the Derby, and I had that memorized because the track was playing very fast that day. But I always do that with all those races, and then I went to the charts of Secretariat's Derby, and that was the right record, went down there, looked at it, and looked right at the chart and wrote down one fifty-nine and four. And I didn't realize why I had written down 1:59⅘ until about six months later. I'm in Chicago, and I'm driving with my buddy. It's at night, and I said, 'I gotta get this windshield clean.' And he says, 'There's nothing wrong with the windshield.' I needed new reading glasses."

Tom Durkin is human and makes mistakes. However, listen to his friends and bosses and jockeys and trainers. They have nothing but praise and admiration for this man.

Gary Stevens is now retired from riding and working as a racing analyst for HRTV. The Hall of Fame jockey holds Tom in the highest esteem: "He's one of the greats of all times. I rate Tom one of the best of all time along with Trevor [Denman]. I could listen to his race calls all day long. Again a very distinctive voice and another guy who can paint a picture for you while the race is going on.... He's called so many big races throughout his career, and we've grown to be very close friends. We worked together on NBC, and he's another guy with just a great sense of humor and just a super person."

Hall of Fame trainer Bob Baffert was the trainer of Real Quiet who came within a nose of winning the Triple Crown in 1998. He acknowledged how hard it would be for him to be a track announcer: "Race announcing. I could never do it. It's a real talent.... Tom Durkin and Trevor Denman have seen the really good horses. There's a lot of pressure on them on those big days. They just have 'It.' You can tell Tom is very intelligent. Some of the words he throws in there, and he thinks about these things. Tom Durkin has historical calls ... I'll tell you what: Dave Johnson, Trevor Denman and Tom Durkin. Those are the three to me that if I had a horse in the Kentucky Derby, I'd want calling the race."

Tom's work ethic and preparation are legendary. Bill Nader explained,

> I don't think people have a real appreciation for the type of preparation that Tom will take on, especially for big races. He will watch video replays. He will take careful notes. And he will be ready when the moment presents itself to be able to deliver the right words at the right times. A hundred different things may happen during a race, different scenarios. This may happen or that may happen. There's no way to overestimate how many different things may happen. And yet he's always ready. That's just being really dedicated and really prepared and really skilled. Those horses are moving along at thirty-five to forty miles per hour. They're not going to stop and say, 'Ok, Tom. What do you think?' I mean there are so many race calls that he's had where people were just blown away. His ability to come up with the right words at the right time; it's just a function of Tom Durkin being who he is: the best race caller in America.

Bill Nader pointed to the 1994 Travers at Saratoga as an example: "He has a tremendous vocabulary. He is a great words-man. He knows the right words to string together. When I say the right words at the right time, I keep saying that, but it's true. And simple words like 'there's cause for concern' sound simple enough. But to be able to say it at the right moment if that

Holy Bull with jockey Mike Smith shows heart winning the 1994 Travers. He would finish the year as champion three-year-old colt and 1994 Horse of the Year. Mike Smith was inducted into the National Museum of Racing's Hall of Fame in 2003. Pictured coming in second is Jerry Bailey on Concern. Credit: Adam Coglianese.

scenario develops." And Durkin used the right words at the right moment in 1994: "And Mike Smith lets the bull roll. He's in front by five as they come to the quarter pole. But there is CAUSE FOR CONCERN!!!!! Concern comes on, second on the outside. Tobasco Cat is well behind in third. They're coming down to the final furlong. Mike Smith asking Holy Bull for everything he has. Concern is coming hard under Jerry Bailey. And still Holy Bull desperately trying to hold! Concern a final threat but it is Holy Bull as game as a racehorse can be coming down to the wire. Holy Bull wins!"

Hall of Fame jockey Mike Smith enjoyed that call and race better than one where he dropped his whip. He said, "I dropped my whip, and Tom announced it. So when I came back I didn't want no one to notice so I was kind of like just faking it? I came back and said, 'Durk! I was out there faking it, and then you called it that I dropped it! Don't do that!' We just laughed about it. It's no big deal. I wish he'd missed that one. He threw me under the bus!"

Mike continued, "Tom is brilliant. He's great! He makes it exciting, you know? And he's very accurate. He makes it flow ... and then he gets excited, uses big words." Mike laughed. "You gotta figure out what the words are."

The Mayor Daley is Tom's ring binder. It is huge because it's been added to and updated for years. It has 8,708 words in it that Tom can choose from to describe horse races. And it is well used as he tries to read a pertinent section every day. He explains, "I'll go through it with a specific.... Here in this situation there are no front runners in this race. They're all going to be over here so the pace is going to be 'slow, dawdling, plodding, precise, gallop, deliberately, troll, sedate, pedestrian, glacial, somnambulant.'"

Now who but Tom Durkin would throw "somnambulant" into a race call?! He has report cards for each race or, as he refers to it, a "plot." *A* denotes a front runner. Tom explains, "'B' is very close to the pace, pressing, in fact. 'C+' is close, very close. 'C' close, 'M' equals middle of the pack, 'T' equals trailer." He explains that *LL* stands for "likes the lead." And *W* shows that a horse weakens but *R* means it can be rated. It is time-consuming to grade each horse for each race each day.

Then there are the big days. Tom said, "For the Kentucky Derby I'll have an entire dossier. I'll have all sorts of notes on the Kentucky Derby. And get very very particular.... The Breeders' Cup is eight folders. And every horse gets a page. And then I'll actually put the colors of the jocks on flash cards and go through them at such a rapid fashion style I can't even switch the cards over fast enough to know the names. Just the colors ... so I can say those names faster than I can actually elocute them."

No wonder that, as Bill Nader says, "he is the play-by-play guy that the world loves to listen to when they're watching big time horse racing."

Bill added, "You have to be accurate. That's very important. And it's one thing to be able to put the words together but if you're not accurate, you're no good. He is very accurate. And he's able to pick up horses that are making moves that the average guy, even a good seasoned racing fan, may not anticipate; when a horse is really starting to gather momentum. But he senses that and when he says that, you can go to the bank. That horse is making a move. And that's a skill. He is a very knowledgeable racing fan and race caller."

Bill ended, "Tom knows how to have fun, and I think that's part of who he is too. He has fun with the crowd. He has fun with his job. And it comes across in the way he handles his responsibilities."

Tom Durkin is famous for his parties. Bill Nader described the person behind the parties: "He's a party person. After the Belmont Stakes he'll have a party at his home in Floral Park which is literally within walking distance of Belmont Park. A big party there, and it's a big celebration after the races. And then finally he'll throw everyone out and say, 'Hey! It's time to go. Tomorrow's a school day. I gotta go to work.'"

The first Breeders' Cup was held in 1984 at Hollywood Park. Tom was the announcer, and he went on to call those prestigious races for the next 22 years. Bill remembered, "He's famous for hosting the best parties in all of racing. In whatever city the Breeders' Cup is held, he will typically have a great party that he will host at a venue that he's selected. He gets everyone together and has a grand time. And I think it's his way of saying, 'Look. All of my preparation and all of the work that went into calling today's races is now officially over. So let the celebration begin!'"

And they knew how to celebrate. Bill reminisced about Tom and his college buddies: "They would actually dance in chairs. They sit in their chairs, and they dance to the music in the chair.... Those guys know how to have fun."

Tom's sister Beth Ann related it to loyalty and friendships that go back over four decades. She said, "He has a wonderful network of friends, kids that he's known since grade school.... They go there to support him on this big day. And they go in the name of friendship."

Tom went further, "We get together every year and do a very good job of imitating a bunch of eighteen-year-olds. You know, it's funny. We're still all just very very close. And we were goofballs. And these people have turned out as presidents of multi-national companies. The success level of this group of people is astonishing. Almost nobody got divorces. We're Godfathers of each others' kids. And it's a very strong circle of friends that is fifty, sixty, seventy strong.... But we're still goofballs."

"He's my brother, and he's also my dearest friend in the whole world," said Beth Ann. "Tom was so good to our mom. And on the anniversary of our mother's death, he came so that I wouldn't be alone ... wasn't that a kind thing to do. That just tells you what a kind good person deep down he really is. My father thought the world of him too. You couldn't not like Tom. He just has such a kind heart."

Tom has never married. He said, "I've just had a lot of girlfriends, very nice girlfriends." And he supposed that, at this point, he would remain a bachelor. A bachelor who hangs out with friends and does "guy things." A single man who could easily go to the opera every single night. A man who is a reader. A bachelor who spends two months in the winter at his villa in

Tuscany soaking up gelato, sunshine, and art. Tom admits, "But the job keeps me pretty busy. Very very busy."

In 2002 Breeders' Cup XIX was held for its only time at Arlington Park in Chicago. Beth Ann remembered, "They declared a Tom Durkin Day in Chicago [that October 26th]. That's huge!" In 2006 ESPN won the contract to broadcast the Breeders' Cup and chose to go with a new track announcer, Trevor Denman, to call the world renowned races. Bill Nader was philosophical: "A twenty-two-year run is a long time, in television years.... Tom now can rest comfortably on his Breeders' Cup laurels. And even though his twenty-two year run is up, those races are watched over and over again. And fifty years from now those race calls will still be appreciated by those in the audience."

Saratoga. It is a magical meeting place for six weeks each summer where well-known trainers bring their best horses to race in Grade I (highest-class races in the United States) contests. Top jockeys ride six days a week in 90 percent humidity, and they do it willingly. Standing in the tree-lined paddock are sheiks and Irishmen and Barbaro's owners Roy and Gretchen Jackson. Harvey Pack presides over handicapping sessions at nearby Siro's. (He retired in 2009 from those duties.) Michael Matz studies his horses during the morning workouts. Hall of Famer Edgar Prado smiles shyly at pretty girls as he mounts a prancing Thoroughbred. Todd Pletcher accepts yet another trophy in the winner's circle that stays true to custom and is drawn anew before each presentation.

And Tom Durkin calls the races from a tiny booth with a poor view of the track. And he couldn't be happier! Tom announced, "Post time for the first race is one o'clock. Enjoy your afternoon here at ... The Spaaaaaaaaaaaaa!"

For a passionate lover of the sport, it is history and opportunity and excitement all rolled into one. Talking about a two-year-old maiden race Tom noted, "These are million dollar babies. And one of these horses could jump up and be the next Secretariat. That happens here at Saratoga."

Besides the Grade I, II, and III flat races for Thoroughbreds, there are the steeplechase races held every Thursday. Tom said, "I do like Steeplechase. I don't like it when they fall ... God! I just hate it when they fall! But it's part of that sport. I do enjoy the spectacle of it."

Fourstardave was a fan favorite that ran at Saratoga and won at least one race during every meet for eight consecutive years. There is even a street named after him. Tom called the winner in all of those races. Tom recalled, "He was a very popular horse. I could play the crowd with him because he was an exciting performer, and people loved him. And I could just tweak the crowd. I could really work the crowd with him pretty good. And they got to know him over the years, and I always looked forward to his races because the crowd really got into it. And you can do that at Saratoga."

Tom referred to the standing ovation that the crowd gave him after his keynote address at the 2006 Hall of Fame induction ceremony as a high point in a career that has seen many pinnacles. He recalled, "That really was thrilling. That was quite an honor to do that, and I spent a lot of time preparing my speech. That stands way up there with the Good Guy Award from the New York Turf Writers in 1996, I think."

In his speech, Tom was quite positive about today's sport of horse-racing:

> If you are one of those sentimentalists who long for the Good Old Days, well welcome to them. Because for my money, these are the Good Old Days.... Stop wringing your hands, and maybe it'll free up your arms so you can embrace the exciting present that is Thoroughbred racing today.... These days the Triple Crown series is more popular than it ever was.... Real Quiet, a twenty year vacancy in the Triple Crown. He comes to the final furlong of the Belmont Stakes with a four length lead, and here comes Victory Gallop. And there's a seven minute agonizing photo finish, and he loses his place in immortality by a flared nostril. And who can forget Chris Antley cradling the leg of fallen hero Charismatic just a few yards past the finish line of Belmont? Or Afleet Alex, a plucky hero that literally fell at the top of the stretch, got up from his knees, and from there to our astonishment went on to win the Preakness in almost mythical nature. Or who could forget the roar of 120,000 throats as Smarty Jones entered the stretch at Belmont Park or the silence, with perhaps the exception of Nick Zito, of 120,000 broken hearts when he crossed the finish line. The Nine Muses in recent years have been working overtime in our springtime ritual, The Triple Crown. They have given us Smarty Jones and Funny Cide and Barbaro and Afleet Alex. All of them national heroes. They have captured the imagination of our country in their respective springs. And they are the Seabiscuits of our day!

Jack Knowlton was the spokesman for Sackatoga Stable who won the 2003 Kentucky Derby with the chestnut Funny Cide that Tom called "the gutsy gelding." Six years later on the day after the 2009 Derby, Jack was at the Hall of Champions in the Kentucky Horse Park visiting the popular resident Funny Cide. His favorite race call? He said, "Well I think that was really really easy. Uh, Funny Cide winning the Kentucky Derby. Every owner has a dream that that's the call they'll get, and we got it. Tom Durkin did a great job, and I revisit his call quite often."

Jack said that Tom is number one of his favorite track announcers. He explains, "He's a good friend, and I've known him for a long time.... Anybody who thinks they [track announcers] just step up a minute before the race and call the race, no! It takes a lot of preparation, particularly in a big race. I mean when you've got nineteen, twenty horses in the Derby, that's got to be extraordinarily challenging. Those guys do a great job, and they know what they're doing."

Neil Howard trained Mineshaft who was the 2003 Horse of the Year. And he conditioned Grasshopper, which in 2007 came in second in the Travers to Street Sense. He declared that he is friends with all of the track announcers but states that Tom is "the dean" of the race callers. Neil explains, "He's really really good. He's unbelievable. All Tom's calls are so good. And in the big races he puts in puns ... how he does it in a blink of an eye, I don't know. I couldn't think like that. I have a hard enough time telling my riders how far to breeze them.... One call I remember is when Mineshaft won the Woodward. As he was coming to the wire Tom said, 'And Mineshaft routinely brilliant.' He was so consistent. When an owner hears that, it makes them proud, makes them feel it's worthwhile with all the money and effort that they put into the business."

Michael Blowen founded Old Friends over seven years ago in Kentucky's horse country. Racehorse champions retire there to the good life. Two days after the 2009 Kentucky Derby, Michael stopped his golf cart at the farm long enough to echo Tom's energy and enthusiasm as he spoke about his favorite Durkin calls:

> I think my favorite race call ever involved a horse that we have here named Sunshine Forever. And it was in the Budweiser International in Baltimore, and Tom Durkin did the call. Tom Durkin I think is by far and away the best race caller we have. And he's a great guy and he helps these horses and does a lot of work for us but aside from that, just as an artist. I think he's a great artist. The horse that we have here named Sunshine Forever won the Eclipse Award that year, and we brought him home from Japan, and in that race he got passed. He had the lead in the stretch. He got passed by a horse on the inside and he got passed by a horse on the outside, and he came back and he won the race and Tom Durkin did a great job.
>
> And the other one that he did that was my favorite race call is another horse that we have here named Awad. When Awad broke the track record at Saratoga, Tom Durkin practically fell out of his seat. He started screaming, "And Awad demolished the track record! He demolished it! The old man demolished it!" He went nuts. It was fabulous. It's not like, "Well here comes the six and here comes the seven." Those are my favorite ones.

On September 28, 2008, the reigning Horse of the Year, Curlin, raced in the Jockey Club Gold Cup. If he won it, he would pass Cigar's all-time earnings. Cigar had won 19 races out of the 33 that he ran in a four-year career for $9,999,815. Who more appropriate than Tom Durkin to call the race? Tom announced, "Wanderin Boy, he is still in front, Merchant Marine makes a final move at him with three furlongs to go, and outside of them the daunting presence of Curlin as they make their way toward the top of the stretch. Mambo in Seattle is in an all-out drive, and he's still back in fourth and the field turns for home. And it's Wanderrrrrrin Boy in front ... and Curlin has taken the lead. It is Curlin now in front ... and here he is: Curlin under the wire beyond Cigar and into the records books. He is America's richest racehorse!"

Tom Durkin has met most of his goals in a long and successful career. In 2006 he answered the author's question, "What do you want to be doing ten years from now?" He responded, "Well, if I still enjoyed calling horse races, I'll call horse races. I would love to do it as long as I can. Ten years from now would be pretty reasonable, I would think."

He reflected,

> You know, I was saddled with this thing growing up; Irish in Chicago. And it's very important to be liked. If I was studying myself as a character to portray in a play, and Kelly [his drama coach] always taught us that you had to zero in on one thing that pushes a person through his life, I would think mine would be wanting to be liked. And so that's the one thing that still propels me. I want to be liked. And I think it's a very good way. I don't make any apologies for that. I think everybody should have a little bit of that. I think everybody's behavior would be much more civil. I think people would be more easy-going and entertaining. So I guess that would be my goal: to try to continue my life with that particular philosophy, not in and of itself, but I think that attitude makes you act in a certain way. You don't do things that would make people dislike you like lie and cheat and steal. [You do] little things like being courteous or bigger things like donating money to charity and doing charity work.

Tom concluded his thoughts about his life: "Today I like the general freedom of it. I like the fact that I don't really have any heavy cares like a lot of people. I'm very thankful, just very very blessed that a guy picks up some guy on a road in Wisconsin, and I wind up calling races at Saratoga."

CHAPTER 2

Kurt Becker

Kurt Becker: "Final furlong of the Toyota Bluegrass. General Quarters has the advantage. Hold Me Back is coming late. General Quarters and Eibar Coa spring the upset of the Toyota Bluegrass Stakes!"

"And they're off in the Shadwell Mile," announces Kurt Becker when the colts lunge from the gate for the Grade I Shadwell Turf Mile. He is the track announcer for both of the spring and fall meets at the immortal Keeneland Racetrack in Lexington, Kentucky.

Kurt Becker is a positive and deeply spiritual man whose character was shaped in America's heartland. He was born on St. Patrick's Day, 1969, in Altamont, Illinois, a farming community of about 2,200 people. In an Andy Griffith–Mayberry type of town, Kurt was raised to be polite and humble. He uses phrases like "Lord willing," and words like "fortunate" and "blessed." Very connected to his roots and the people there, Kurt still maintains a home in this town. His father, Carl, quit teaching to get into the horse business and announced many county and state fair harness races. Kurt's mother, Bonnie, supported Carl's decision and stayed home to raise Kurt and his older brother, Jon, and younger brother, Kris.

While his brothers showed no interest in horses, Kurt was always fascinated by them. His mom took him to his first horse race at the 1973 Effingham County Fair in his hometown. He recalled,

> My father was the track announcer, and my mother took me to the races on a hot August afternoon. She parked the car just as the first race was going to the starting gate, and it was a harness race. She carried me to the fence near the head of the stretch and held me aloft so I could see the horses, and I still remember the harness drivers yelling at each other as they came around the final turn. It made quite an impression on a four-year-old boy. Later that day,

my father's three-year-old pacing filly won the featured stakes race, and I again remember my mother hoisting me over the concrete wall in front of the grandstand and taking me trackside for the winner's circle photo. At the end of the afternoon she and my father took me to the stable area to see the filly, whose name was Byrd Talk. It made for quite a day.

Kurt still has the program from that day.

By the time Kurt was nine years old, he was going on the summer fair circuit with his dad on a regular basis. He attended grade school and high school in Altamont and in his free time, Kurt was happier to have a pen and notepad in his hand than a football.

Carl Becker noted, "I think when he was eight or nine years old, he contacted the Effingham Daily News ... and he was aggravated because they didn't carry the results of the demolition derby. So he sent them results of it that year, and they published it. And from that point on, he supplied the Effingham Paper with various bits of information which led him to a very good relationship with the sports editor.... Now Kurt does a lot of writing for the paper."

When Kurt was 16, opportunity knocked. After a rainout, his father had two county fairs to call at the same time and needed a sub. After phoning everyone he could think of, Carl was surprised when Kurt volunteered to call. Carl recalled, "There was an opening at the Coles County Fair, and he went up and filled it that day by himself and went from there. He would make a study of things he thought were good to use in a race call ... and he developed his own style from that. One thing that he was very very careful about as he developed was to make sure that any information he passed on was accurate and documented.... Probably the thing that sets Kurt apart from the rest of track announcers is the fact that he is such an unbelievable researcher."

Kurt began calling harness races but by the end of the summer, he went to a fair where there were both Standardbred and Thoroughbred races. Kurt chuckled as he said, "I can still remember the first Thoroughbred race I called because two horses bolted off the final turn and went running out to the barn area. That was a scary moment that makes for a memorable first race."

Kurt's father was his role model as an announcer. Kurt explains, "There's no track announcer in history that can do a stretch call like he can. His stretch calls were just incredible. He had what I would consider the perfect voice, the perfect delivery, and was such a genuine fan of harness racing that it came across."

More importantly, his father was his hero because of his honest, upstanding character. Kurt noted that his father did not complain when he was passed over in 1979 by NBC for the TV call of the Hambletonian Harness Classic. Although he had been the track caller at the DuQuoin State Fair in Illinois throughout the 1970s and his mentor Stan Birkstein had resigned, Carl Becker didn't let his disappointment keep him from giving a great on-track call.

Kurt said, "My father declined numerous opportunities to further his career as a Standardbred announcer, because he didn't want to uproot our family and adversely affect his wife or his three sons. He made things tougher on himself as a result, yet he always managed, by the grace of God, to make a good living. I have also never forgotten the way my mother supported his decisions, and how she helped him to succeed by the rock she was as a wife and mother."

Like his dad, Kurt turned negatives into positives. He graduated from Southern Illinois University at Carbondale with a degree in political science. Even though it took Kurt eight years to complete his degree, he didn't recall any bad experiences: "Everything that might have been a negative experience, actually taught me things about how to mature and get along with people."

Kurt was still in college when he met and married fellow student Kari. Needing a job, he happened to read in the *Chicago Tribune* that Hawthorne Race Course was looking for a replacement for track announcer Phil Georgeff. Nonchalantly thinking, "Why not?" Kurt auditioned in December 1992 and got the job. He said modestly, "I think that what worked to my advantage was the fact that I was young and didn't come in with a lot of demands."

February 1993 was officially Kurt's first day as a pari-mutuel Thoroughbred announcer. He stood in his booth that was the size of a broom closet at the Sportsman's Park in Chicago. Outside on the balcony hovered Chicago's media. They were there to photograph and videotape the brave man who was replacing popular Phil Georgeff who had been the track announcer for 35 years. One fan was asked what he thought of the new guy. He shrugged, "He ain't no Phil." Kurt had big shoes to fill.

The 1993 Beverly D. at Arlington Park was the most exciting race Kurt ever called. Charlie Whittingham's Flawlessly was entered in the Grade I filly and mare 1³⁄₁₆-mile race on the turf. Her competition was a filly from New Zealand named Let's Elope. The two battled each other down the homestretch. Kurt announced, "Let's Elope! Let's Elope TAKES IT by a nose over Flawlessly in the Beverly D!"

Fifteen years later Kurt looked back and said, "I seem to recall the thing which surprised at least a few folks, including myself, was the fact I committed to calling a winner despite the close finish. I'm a firm believer that the announcer should let the photo finish technician settle such matters, since calling the wrong horse in a tight photo is a terribly embarrassing situation. But the stretch run of that race was such that it seemed somehow incomplete not to declare a winner as the fillies passed under the wire."

Just at the finish line, Let's Elope slammed into Flawlessly before crossing the finish line first. The fans endured a 17-minute stewards' inquiry. When Kurt finally announced that Let's Elope was disqualified, the blunt Chicago fans booed loudly. "But that race," Kurt recalled, "had a driving finish. Earlie Fires was on Hero's Love, and she was right there at the wire with the others. There were three or four fillies separated by a half-length on the wire. And that race, to this day, still sticks in my mind as the most exciting that I've done."

Kurt recommends that an aspiring race caller would do well to begin on any track on the Chicago circuit whether it is harness or Thoroughbred. He feels that the knowledgeable Chicago fans are the greatest racing fans in the world. Their phone calls and letters helped Kurt to become a better announcer.

One who was quite opinionated was the Painter. This heckler wore white painter overalls and stood on the track apron at Arlington Park. With his loud booming voice, he would turn around and yell up at Kurt in a voice that carried through the entire grandstand. "His complaint was that I had a tendency back then to give a horse a big call off of the last turn. Well sometimes those horses would level off and not even hit the board," said Kurt. To his credit, Kurt learned to be careful and to give the horse recognition but not to go overboard. And he realized that he could learn more from the honest fans than from the overly complimentary ones.

However, after only two years, Kurt left the Chicago racetracks to work with NASCAR. He and Kari were struggling to keep their marriage alive, and she loved stock car racing. She traveled with him to the races, but the marriage couldn't be saved. However, Kurt continues today to work for NASCAR doing play-by-play for the radio broadcast. NASCAR has made it clear that it is happy to work around his horse racing, because horses are his first priority. Kurt admits, "It is a huge challenge. Never ever ever have I walked out of the racetrack at the end of the day and said, 'Boy, I really nailed it today.' There's always going to be at least one race every day that I wished I'd done differently."

NASCAR is about man and machine. Kurt reflected, "With horse racing, you've got man and animal, and that is the difference to me. The two living breathing things where not only does the jockey have his or her own personality but so does that colt or filly. Wow! To watch those jocks work with those horses to try to get to the finish line first! It's an amazing thing to see."

In the summer of 1996, Kurt learned that Keeneland was going to put in a public address system. The beautiful racetrack is one of a kind with its gigantic Rolex clocks by the walking ring, wallpaper in the bathrooms, and extremely knowledgeable fans. It was breaking a long-held tradition of having no announcer. For years, horsemen who went to the races at this track in Lexington, Kentucky, felt they did not need someone to explain what was happening on the track.

What other racetrack would showcase the magnificent Rolex clocks but Keeneland? Credit: Tom Ferry.

Kurt had missed horse racing. With his usual luck and fate working for him, he got the job at Keeneland as well as at Churchill. He recalled, "I had originally just applied for the Keeneland position, and then Churchill Downs came into the equation. They were looking to do some restructuring, and so when that position became available, I thought, 'Shoot! The more the merrier. It would be a real privilege to call at Churchill.'"

From the beginning, Kurt loved everything about Keeneland: the elegant entrance on Versailles Road, the winding drive past the renowned Keeneland Library, and the immaculate grounds of the facility. From his announcer's booth, he'd look out across the backstretch at the gently rolling hills. He didn't feel a lot of pressure being the first announcer because he had not grown up in Lexington. However, he was surprised that it was not the old-timers who minded having a track announcer. It was the university

Keeneland's spring and fall meets are three weeks each of top-quality racing. Credit: Tom Ferry.

students. But in time they got used to hearing Kurt's race calls, and he didn't detract from the races by talking too much.

Kurt's call of the 1998 Commonwealth Breeders' Cup was quite precise and unemotional: "El Amante is closing some ground and takes second. But he's running out of time to catch Distorted Humor. El Amante is not going to get to him. Distorted Humor takes the Commonwealth Breeders' Cup."

But in the 2000 Blue Grass Stakes his enthusiasm was apparent: "And in the final furlong of the Toyota Blue Grass High Yield is dead game on the inside. More Than Ready is right there with him. These two to the line. High Yield takes the Toyota Blue Grass."

He very seldom editorialized during a race. He let the race happen and called it that way. In the fall of 2005, however, on Opening Day there was a nine-year-old named Rochester. For the third time he won the Grade III Sycamore Breeders' Cup. And Kurt called: "And here comes Rochester ... the grand, nine-year-old gelding is turning in a run on the outside ... how about Rochester?! He is kicking on with a five-length lead."

Kurt said, "He had that look that day when Gary Stevens moved him out to the center of the course. You could just tell at the head of the stretch, he was going to win."

Kurt has called over 3,000 races at Keeneland, and some sound as smooth as a lawyer's closing argument while others not so much. Kurt said, "I can recall announcing a race at Keeneland in April of 1997 in which the jockeys simultaneously rose from the saddle before reaching the finish line. I was still calling the stretch run, and I was desperately searching the track for a sign as to why everyone had simply stopped riding in the final furlong. Suddenly, it dawned on me ... Keeneland uses alternate finish lines, depending on the length of the race, and I was calling a race which had already ended. There is nothing more embarrassing as the track announcer than to be the last guy in the house to realize what has happened."

Kurt pointed out, "As for dealing with one's mistakes in the course of a race call, the key is to maintain confidence in one's tone of voice. Typically, it's when an announcer begins to sound distracted or uncertain that it becomes clear to everyone present that something has gone terribly wrong. Thus, it's okay to feel a sense of panic or embarrassment, so long as one never lets the public hear it in his voice. As difficult as it can be, one must learn to take a deep breath at such moments, to measure his words, and to pace his delivery so that he still sounds as though he is in complete control ... even if he isn't."

Kurt's most memorable race was the 2004 Darley Alcibiades. Eli Gold, a NASCAR colleague, was in town and called to see if he could watch Kurt announce a race. It was a typically chaotic Opening Day, but Kurt graciously arranged for him to be guided to the booth on top of the Keeneland grandstand. Eli arrived right in time for the feature race. Kurt was trying to concentrate on the horses while, at the same time, a radio anchorman was talking for the Keeneland network. Eli began chatting with the radio broadcaster as the horses were going into the starting gate. Kurt explains,

> And now it's just me calling the race. Thankfully, the call is going well. It's settled into a routine, and they're turning for home. In The Gold and Sharp Lisa are slugging it out. They are side by side coming down the stretch, and I'm giving what I think is going to be a great race call. And all of a sudden way out on the grandstand side comes a filly charging from way off the pace and, I'm telling you, I have no idea who she is. And since she has come from off the pace, the jockey is covered with dirt and mud. I'm tap dancing and stalling for time for all I'm worth. The only thing that saved me was right before the wire, the jockey Rafael Bejarano, turned his arm so that I could see the number eight on his sleeve. I quickly looked back in the program to find out who in the hell #8 was and I mean right when she hit the wire was when winning Runway Model finally got a call.

He did not want to leave the booth that day. And while he hated doing that to the owner and trainer, Kurt also felt bad for the horse: "People probably think I'm crazy, but horses may be able to communicate with each other. What if this poor filly came back to the barn that day and said, 'I won!' and the other horses said that they never heard her get a call?" After that experience, he knew that he had to buckle down and work harder. And he hoped that the Darley Alcibiades race that Runway Model won would remain his most memorable race.

Earlier in the year, he relished calling the 2004 Blue Grass Stakes: "The Cliff's Edge trying to track down Lion Heart who's still there with the lead. The Cliff's Edge from DEEP in the pack draws alongside of Lion Heart. Lion Heart very game. The Cliff's Edge is going to get him. The Cliff's Edge to take the 80th running of the Toyota Blue Grass Stakes."

That was the year of the popular Smarty Jones that dominated an incredibly strong three-year-old crop. Kurt said, "Many a Toyota Blue Grass Day, I've left the track in complete awe of the three-year-olds on the Triple Crown trail, and it's abundantly clear to me how fortunate I've been to call that caliber of horse."

For two years Kurt was also the track announcer at Churchill Downs in Louisville, Kentucky. He said, "I will say this unequivocally. Churchill Downs has the greatest sporting event on the globe. That Kentucky Derby; there's *nothing* that compares to it!"

He was adamant about Derby ghosts. After both of the 1997 and 1998 derbies, Kurt hung out in the booth until nine in the evening. He watched the sun set and reflected on the day. Walking to his car right outside the first turn, he could feel the presence of the great horses from the past. He said, "I'm telling you that their ghosts are there. You think about Native Dancer suffering his one loss. You can almost swear you can see him out there in the dark."

Kurt got along well with the management at Churchill. But there was friction with some of his coworkers. Like most people, he hated conflict and controversy. He wasn't going to tattle to his boss. Therefore, after two years, Kurt resigned as Churchill's track announcer. He was 29 years old, and some people felt he had snubbed the historic track. To this day, Kurt regrets that perception. It wasn't true, but he took the high road and kept his mouth shut.

Back in 1979 Kurt had listened to the famous track announcer Dave Johnson call the Affirmed and Alydar Triple Crown races. Dave knew the Becker family well: "Kurt's father was the harness announcer at several fairs in southern Illinois where I was working, so I knew Carl and his wife early on in the '60s. I even substituted for Carl.... Kurt Becker is just a super broadcaster. But he took himself out of Churchill. He did it himself.... He gets his kindness from his parents. They're the salt of the earth. They're wonderful."

Kurt returned to Keeneland, a track that has managed to attract a younger crowd than many of its fellow racetracks in the 21st century. Kurt said,

At Keeneland you see a lot of young people. It's a college town, and they'll cut class to come to the races. The biggest hurdle is getting them to come to the track, and then they'll be hooked.... Let the world see that we have fun. That's going to win fans every time.

Loosen up and have fun. People are going to see that and want to tune in or come to the races. And, hopefully, maybe want to own a racehorse. And that's another thing I see happening. I see more and more people putting together partnership packages. That I believe is a great way to get new owners in the sport because this sport can be intimidating. It really can. And if you have a chance to get involved in a partnership, you can invest for a nominal fee and go to the races with a big group of people and have fun. That's what it's all about.

We had that here Opening Day in the [2005] Alcibiades. When the filly that won the Alcibiades, She Says It Best, they apparently have twenty or twenty-five partners on this filly because they had a throng of people in the winner's circle. What a great thing that was! People of all ages, and they were laughing and smiling. There's a promotion for racing.

Dallas Stewart, a prominent trainer, said that Kurt is just as good as you can get: "He does a great job of announcing. He's very articulate in his own way and can pick up things in a race. These guys can just pick up things in a race, and it separates them from different announcers. It's very enjoyable to hear them when they pick up something in a race about a horse or a rider, something great has happened in a race. They can articulate different scenarios and make you say, 'Wow!'"

Kurt became involved in the annual sales. Whether it was the yearling sale in September or the Breeding Stock sale in November, Kurt worked with John Henderson announcing the horses' pedigrees. He was there in September 2005 when the yearling was auctioned for $9.7 million. And two months later, he got to see the beautiful filly Ashado sold for nine million dollars. In life's continuing cycle, Kurt met some horses as weanlings on the auction stand. Next he got to call them as they raced around the track. Often he saw the Thoroughbreds one more time as they were sold in the breeding stock sale. For someone whose passion was horses, Kurt got to play an intimate part of their lives. And he was part of the Keeneland family too.

But, in the end, Kurt was connected by his heartstrings to his home

$1,500,000

Kurt (not shown) enjoys working at Keeneland's four prestigious horse auctions held in January, April, September, and November. Credit: Tom Ferry.

state of Illinois: "I love Chicago. It's the greatest city in the world." While Arlington is a beautiful track, Kurt says that blue-collar Hawthorne has its history as well. One of his favorite jockeys is Earlie Fires from Chicago. Kurt explains, "He's sixty years old and still riding, and riding well.... He seems like a fella that found his niche years ago. He knows what he's supposed to do with his life, and he just genuinely seems to be so pleased to be involved with the sport." (Earlie would retire after the Arlington summer meet in 2008.)

Trainer Dale Baird was from a nearby town and had won over 9,000 races before he was killed in an accident in December 2007. When he won the Special Eclipse Award in 2004, he brought it home to share with his neighbors, and Kurt said, "Having grown up on the county circuit myself, it was so much fun to see how much they admired Dale Baird."

Kurt's favorite male racehorse is Recoup the Cash from Illinois: "He ranks as my all-time favorite male racehorse because he always gave such an honest effort. While I was in Chicago, from 1993 to 1994, he won eleven of his eighteen starts. For a young, inexperienced race announcer, it was not

Kurt Becker's idyllic view from the best seat in the house.

only a pleasure but a luxury to have him in the lineup, because one generally knew what to expect from him. In other words, one could give him a big call and feel confident that he would be prominent at the finish. When he came to Keeneland years later in 1998, it was like seeing an old friend when he came onto the racetrack for the post parade."

Retired and well-respected track announcer Phil Georgeff called races for years in Illinois. Kurt said, "I have talked to so many people who grew up in Chicago that said they became fans of the sport because of the way Phil called races and made them so exciting."

Kurt's father and mother still live in Altamont. So does a brother and his family. And so does Kurt. He explains,

> There are always things that draw me back to my hometown and ultimately, it's the people. I like being close to my niece and nephew.
> The best part of my job is being able to take a craft taught to me by my father many years ago and to make a living with it. In my hometown of Altamont there are lots of folks who have learned trades and crafts which have been handed down from generation to generation, and I enjoy being able to share in that heritage.

The worst part of my job is the travel schedule — and keep in mind that this included Thoroughbred auctions and NASCAR radio duties — and the adverse impact it has on my ability to be involved in my hometown community.

Kurt listed three necessities for being a top-class announcer: "Number one is making sure that at least twenty-four hours in advance I've gone through all of the names on the program: names of horses, trainers, jockeys, and owners." Keeneland features many of the most prominent stables in the world. Kurt explains, "If I'm uncertain about the pronunciation, I will stumble over the name every time, and it will throw the whole call off."

The second necessity is being left alone during the ten minutes that the horses are on the track before they go into the starting gate. It can wreck the entire race call if he hasn't had time to focus on the small details of each horse and rider. Kurt uses that time to study the horses and to visualize their shadow rolls or jockeys' caps so that he would know them even if they were covered in mud. Kurt insists that "the booth is essentially the race announcer's office, and the presence of anyone else in that environment can only serve as a distraction."

Kurt noted the third necessity: "Absolutely the third thing is to have the proper tools of the trade, and I think for a track announcer, having the right binoculars, is just paramount to doing the job correctly." It is easy to get nervous in Grade I races and Kurt's hands shook sometimes as the horses turned for home. Canon invented binoculars that use a stabilizer technology. As the horses loaded into the gate, Kurt hit a button on the binoculars and they locked into what he was seeing and kept the image from shaking. He admitted that he fretted for an entire week about the cost of the expensive binoculars. Then he went ahead and bought them. He drove up to Cincinnati to buy the new pair and on his way he listened to Pat Day being interviewed on the radio by a woman named Francine. He proudly christened his new binoculars "Francine." They are state of the art, and he credited them with the Opening Weekend going so smoothly.

At a racetrack that features elegant Rolex clocks, the announcer needs to dress accordingly. Kurt said, "I am a firm believer that the race announcer should always look his best. Thus, I tend to wear dress clothes virtually every day on the job. Keeneland management has made it clear that they prefer I attire myself in this fashion, but I maintain the same policy on the occasions when I substitute for other announcers at other facilities. [In 2008 he subbed for Tom Durkin at Belmont during the weeks of the Derby and Preakness.] As my NASCAR colleague Eli Gold once said, 'You never know who you will meet, and you don't want to look like some kid trying to bum a ride to Woodstock.'"

Kurt has been a part of many of racing's privileged moments: "I remain grateful for having been involved with the celebration of Pat Day's career which took place during a fall race meeting at Keeneland in 2005. It was my privilege, along with Keeneland Director of Communications Jim Williams, to interview Pat in the paddock prior to the races that morning, and it was tremendous to see how the fans responded to him.... I noticed that Keeneland had posted a large photo of Pat on the video board on the back of the grandstand, and it was a picture of him aboard High Yield after the latter's victory in the 2000 Toyota Blue Grass Stakes. It really hit me at that moment how fortunate I had been, as an announcer, to call a number of Pat's races, including some of his Grade I victories."

Over the years one's style of announcing is bound to change. Kurt confided, "I've learned to relax, pace myself, and enunciate more clearly. This is something which came with gaining more experience as a race caller, which, in turn, helped my level of confidence."

If he had it all to do over, he would still choose to call races: "There is nothing I would do differently. In fact, the trying and difficult times were probably where I learned most of my lessons through the years."

Today Kurt Becker is a content man. He looks forward to going to work. In fact he enjoys it so much that he doesn't consider it work. However, he feels strongly about knowing when it's time to retire: "You owe it to the dignity of the sport, to the people involved, and to the horses to know when the time has come to bow out gracefully."

Kurt was emotional about how he would like to be remembered. He got tears in his eyes as he said softly, "I would like to be remembered as someone that fulfilled the Lord's plan for his life. That more than anything is how I want to be remembered. I want people to be able to look and say, 'This guy did what the Lord put him here to do.'"

CHAPTER 3

Dave Rodman

Dave Rodman: "OHHHHH it's close. Could be Silver Charm in between Free House, Captain Bodgit in a Preakness we will remember!"

"Ichabad Crane looking for the line ... Ichabad Crane wins it by half a head." Dave Rodman calls this race for three-year-olds at Pimlico, and a month later Ichabad Crane will come in third to Big Brown in the 2008 Preakness Stakes, the second leg of the Triple Crown.

When MTV debuted in August 1981, the music channel chose the bubblegum hit by the British new wave group, the Buggles, for its launch. Top of the UK charts two years prior, "Video Killed the Radio Star" seemed the perfect choice. The catchy lyrics about the golden days of radio captured the moment with the passing of the torch to a new medium. Its nostalgic message may have been lost on the general public, drowned out by its hypnotic tune, but for radio buffs themselves, the resonance was all too familiar.

For budding deejays trying to break into the field at the time, there was a sense of great uncertainty. Radio was facing new challenges, in flux with format changes and downsizing that would ultimately lead to increased syndication. Dave Rodman was one such music buff who had had his heart set on being in radio from a tender age.

Dave recalled, "I wanted to be in radio first. During my high school years, I was running public service tapes on Sunday mornings at a local radio station. There would be like an hour and a half show taped. Each Sunday morning, very early, when maybe ten people would be listening, I got about an hour and a half on the air playing music so it was my first job in radio.

I bugged enough people and found enough people in the business that would be willing to give me a full-time radio gig, so I moved to Mississippi, to Pascagoula/Moss Point and worked in an AM radio station there, WKKY-AM. It was appealing to me that the move wasn't far from my hometown of New Orleans, only about an hour plus away."

His parents, Hyman and Mary, settled in Jefferson Parish, New Orleans, but divorced when Dave was still in grade school. Despite some disruption that followed, the address changes kept him in close proximity to the greater New Orleans area, living on Dumaine Street before the move to the suburbs of Metairie, Louisiana, for his high school years. Dave went to private school pretty much the whole way through, Walters Middle School then later Walters Prep High School.

Despite being one of a handful of no more than a dozen in his graduating class, college was never in the cards since Dave kept his sights firmly on radio. Putting their differences with each other to the side, both parents, as they had always done, lent their support, encouraging their son to pursue his dreams.

Dave explains "In about eighth or ninth grade, I was into this big weather thing for a while. They bought me everything I needed   the board a weather map. I changed it every day. Whenever any member of my family had an extra five minutes, I'd do a mini-weathercast for them. I wanted to be like a meteorologist. They were supportive about it, but that all changed when I began listening to local radio stations and AM radio powerhouses like WLS from Chicago at night."

That sort of get-up-and-go had him up at the crack of dawn, happy to pay his dues in small-town America in order to get a shot at the bigger leagues. (In the 1970s you could still get a radio job in a small market, then work your way up to the next market.) Dave recalled, "I got up at 5 A.M. and signed on the transmitter. It was just a local, real small AM radio station that played the Top 40 music in a real small town. From there I went to WTIX in New Orleans which was a big, big move up. I mean major league move up from a small town to the station I grew up listening to. WTIX was one of the great Top 40 stations of all-time."

Radio not only put Dave behind the microphone but it also put him in touch with gregarious, outgoing types who began to bring him out of his shell. Dave said, "I was pretty quiet and independent, a pretty shy child."

Although Dave has two half brothers, Tommy and Ronnie, from his mother's first marriage, they had already moved away from home when he found the radio bug. Dave, born December 3, 1958, was only nine when Tommy served in Vietnam. Dave recalled, "He was hurt pretty badly in Vietnam. A howitzer cannon-shell backed out, exploded, basically blew out most of his stomach. When he came back, he was about ninety pounds. Miraculously, he's still alive."

Nevertheless, Dave was like an only child and hung out with the kids on his block. The Dumaine Street neighborhood Dave grew up in was not far from the Fair Grounds. Dave's high school years, lived in Metairie, were just a stone's throw away from the old Jefferson Downs, destroyed by Hurricane Betsy in 1965, some seven years later. It is now Lafreniere Park, a local recreational park.

Dave noted, "My father used to take me to the Jefferson Downs. He would leave me in the car, park near the fence, and tell me to 'watch the clowns on the horses.' He'd go and make the bets and then come back. He said 'clowns' because of the funny silks.... I remember when my dad used to take me to the Fair Grounds, on the weekends. I remember the distinct smell of the corned beef at the Fair Grounds in the clubhouse. One of my great memories is you walk up to the Fair Grounds, you walk in the door, and you take a whiff of the corned beef. We would have lunch and play the horses — well, he'd play the horses for me."

Dave regrets that his father did not live to see him call races: "I think he would have really dug that a lot. He introduced me to racing and loved it. He loved to gamble. I still recall a little system he had on how to bet winners. It was a very simple kind of system. He taught me to enjoy the gambling part of the game. Enjoy it and not go over your head. He used to keep track of every bet he made on the back of the program."

A Russian immigrant who found his way to the United States where he met his wife Mary, Hyman was a gambler in more ways than one. Dave said, "My father's family, and my father, like so many Americans, were Ellis Island immigrants, but I've heard stories of him being smuggled out of Russia in a hay truck. He was very young. I don't think there is a birth certificate for him so I don't know his true age at death. He passed away in 1980."

His mother, Mary, has also since died, in 2006. Both sides of the family instilled Dave with solid values. "Honesty, and a good old-fashioned work ethic," according to Dave. His mother was an executive secretary for several years at Amoco, a petroleum company. Dave said, "She was very organized, unlike me."

His father was always able to eke out a decent living. Dave explains, "He managed movie theatres in the Depression, later moving to the dismantling business. He would bid on government jobs. At the time they were bidding to dismantle WWII barracks at many bases in the region so he with his partner would bid, 'I can tear this down for $40,000.' but salvage $20,000 worth of usable materials. He would salvage the lumber from these jobs and resell it. Resalable items — faucets, copper, lumber, anything. So he was very good with numbers and looking at a building and saying, 'We can get x-number of cubic feet of salvage material.' He did that for a long long time."

No surprise then that Hyman was drawn to the betting side of horse racing and that Dave's introduction to the sport was as a budding handicapper. The interplay between his radio gigs and his deep-rooted interest in the track would set the tone of what was to come.

By 1976 Dave was out there playing that funky music, a real Top 40 deejay. He recalled,

I was in radio basically from 1974 doing the Sunday morning thing through 1981. The station I worked for didn't change formats, but they changed from playing more Rock and Soul to a more middle of the road approach. And I'm young. I'm a rock-n-roller. I don't want any part of that. So they turned to more of an adult contemporary stance, and I just got fed up with it

Even during the radio years, the racetrack was still part of the fabric of growing up in New Orleans. I knew some people that were involved with Jefferson Downs, some jockeys and trainers that I'd met. Eventually, I got a job on the backstretch, just walking horses, being around horses a little bit. I'm not an official hot-walker, but I know people and trainers and I'm mucking out a few stalls, just doing stuff. I heard that Jefferson Downs' Rick Mocklin was going to leave to train horses.

He had a lucrative job offer. This was in 1981. He found an owner, Wilton Helveston from New Iberia, Louisiana, who was willing to put him in the business and give him horses to train and claim, and would fund the whole operation. So he says, "This is for me. I want to do this." And he decided he was going to leave, summer of 1981.

So somehow, I talked to him, "I'd like to try." So he put me on the roof at Jefferson Downs with a tape recorder and a pair of binoculars. I sat outside where the booth was. There wasn't much of a floor there either. It was 2×4's, 2×8's, pigeon poop all over the place. It was really ratty. So I sat up there and just kind of practiced. I'd say, "They're off," call for about a furlong or two [eight furlongs make up a mile], and that was the end of that. They're off and they'd get in the first turn and I'd stop 'cause I was too busy rooting the horses I was betting on.

After a while I let him listen to a couple of my calls. He critiqued my calls and after a period of time he said, "I think you're ready to call a race." It was a Thursday night, the slowest night of the week. He put me in to call the last race of the evening. I think the field scratched down to eight, and I called the wrong horse on top. I called the second horse as the winner but got them all the way around. I guess they liked my voice or whatever, or the fact that I was clear and they needed an announcer for next season and weren't paying a lot of money. Perfect for a kid eager to jump into the booth.

The situation Dave found himself in was akin to a trainer with a talented barn whose second-string runner turns out to be the stable star. Even though radio had provided Dave with more than a handy start, he was starting to realize that his real trump card had been on the back burner all along. Dave explains, "Without the radio foundation, without working on the air, being unafraid to talk into a mike or in front of people, going to high schools and handing out albums, playing deejay at different clubs and representing the station, without that I would not have been able to talk into a microphone and do race calling."

The next summer, Dave took up the job as Jefferson Downs track announcer, making the switch from being on-air in the studio to being on-air at a racetrack. Since the Fair Grounds in winter was the premier meet in New Orleans, Jefferson Downs was seen as the working man's track, described by Dave as "the bread-and-butter track."

His own bread-and-butter it had become, slightly enhanced by receiving a little added income as a clocker in the mornings. Dave had passed up a potential career in the radio industry for the racing game, only to find that the uncertainty he had hoped to escape from one industry seemed just as prevalent in the other.

True, he had a steady summer gig, but the question of what to do the rest of the time remained unanswered. Winters started out rather spartan with no security blanket to fall back on. Soon into Dave's first season at Jefferson Downs, the idea of being a trainer struck him. Dave said, "During the winter, you've got to remember, money was scarce. So I walked a few horses at the Fair Grounds for Frank Brothers, Jack Van Berg, and others. The next summer at Jefferson Downs, I went in 'halvesies' on a horse with a trainer I was working for no money, but I had no training bills. Lorenzo 'Ricky' Diaz. I heard he was a real gregarious type of person, hard-drinking type of guy. I was working in the mornings, sometimes taking care of the horse, working off some training bills."

Dave's trainer aspirations received a shot in the arm when his horse, Hammer Down, won. Dave explains,

> I got to call my own horse winning. That was pretty neat. Robert Kelly rode him. He's now a jockey agent. It was a nine or seven horse field. The favorite broke down, and another fell over that horse, and we stumbled in, in 1:24 flat

for 6½ furlongs, for probably the slowest clocking in Jefferson Downs history. So we won the race, and then I leased a couple of other horses in the meantime.

I'll never forget walking horses at Frankie Brothers' barn on the far turn at the Fair Grounds and every time you come around the barn with a hot horse, and there are some horses working on the Fair Grounds track, they hear that and they go "YEAH!!!" And they take off with you in the shedrow. I didn't like any part of that. My very unreliable car broke down so I didn't really work for any of these trainers for any length of time, and visions of becoming a trainer waned.

Dave was grateful for all the experience but knew in his heart this was not for him. Perhaps it was the Russian blood in his veins as Dave was always a realist. He lived within his means, drawing unemployment in the winter, living back at home so that even when he wasn't earning extra dollars on the side, he still managed to get to do what he loved best, playing the horses. Horse players tend to be real characters, and Dave delighted in them all. When the chance arose he would hit the road with Jefferson Downs horse-player J.D. Fox and anyone else that wanted to make a road trip for a gambling jaunt.

Dave recalled, "J.D. Fox was a cigar chomping horse player, not a big gambler and not a great handicapper but loved to bet, a two dollar player. He never really had a lot of money. Our gambling forays back in the day were before off-track betting. We'd have to drive from New Orleans to Lafayette to Evangeline Downs to play which we would do once a month on our day off. Anytime J.D. would lose money, which was quite often, he would start singing 'Old Man River' (off key) in the back of the car for much of the two-hour drive back to New Orleans."

Dave found no shortage of racing characters in the winter. He became part of a regular posse of six to eight race trackers who would hang out to the far right of the old Fair Grounds grandstand that they called "Coffin Corner."

Dave said, "I think my horse playing friend Skippy nicknamed it the Coffin Corner, because everything we played put the nail in the coffin. At that time there were New Orleans celebrities at the track, even on a weekday. Our group was full of characters. We had one guy, Daryl, who worked for Delta Airlines. My buddy Skippy, whom I'm still friends with today, works on the river-front in New Orleans. Freddie 'One Bite' cuz he could always eat a hot dog in one bite. Boss Ruler. Big Cy. Every character had a nickname. Harold and The Commander."

It was inevitable that Dave would get to meet Fair Grounds track announcer at the time, Tony Bentley. The Fair Grounds ran in owners' silks unlike Jefferson Downs that used house colors, and Dave was keen to experience the difference. Tony was more than happy to accommodate his request to practice. Dave explains,

> He let me come up on the roof at my leisure. A lot of times I would go in the radio booth and practice if it was cold or I'd go up top, the very highest part of the grandstand above the booth. A lot of times I'd practice until a race I was betting on, and then I'd put down the binoculars, abandon the call, and start rooting for my horse.
>
> So finally one day, Claude Williams who worked with the *Racing Form* at the time said, "Let him call a race." Sometimes Tony would have to leave early for his other interests away from the track: acting, opera, or just to cook a gourmet dinner for friends. He had a reputation as a great cook. He's a renaissance man. I would maybe just do the last race of the day. I forget how many times I did a full card, but usually it was just one or two. And it was much more difficult than Jefferson Downs.

When summer came around and Tony headed to Louisiana Downs in Shreveport, Dave continued to fill in for him whenever he could. He made sure to send on a couple of tapes to Louisiana Downs general manager, the late Tom Sweeney, whom he credits for giving him his breakthrough job. The old-school type, Tom had started off as a program seller at Naragansett, eventually working his way to the top. With no pari-mutuel betting in Texas and the lottery yet to take hold, people would drive two to three hours to Bossier City, rent a hotel for the weekend, and head to the track. Crowds of 18,000–20,000 were not uncommon on a Saturday afternoon.

In Dave, Tom saw more than just a track announcer. For the upcoming summer season of 1984, he wanted to make a change. Tom's decision was a major league step up for Dave.

Dave's winter unemployment dilemma was quickly put to rest since Louisiana Downs turned into a full-time job. He said, "During the off-season, I'd work in the press box, and I'd help work on the media guide and continue to author a tip sheet for the track from 1984 to 1991, enough to keep me busy. That's as close to a nine to five job I've ever had in my life."

But once live racing was in full swing, Dave did not have a minute to spare. From a weekend morning workout show to hosting a nightly TV replay show, handicapping for a track-produced tip sheet, and, oh, yes, announcing the races, Dave did it all.

Dave explains, "Each Saturday morning, I would co-host 'A.M. Trackside.' We'd serve coffee and doughnuts, have a guest trainer, jockey, or handicapper and watch the morning workouts. Even as early as 8 A.M., it could get pretty hot in Louisiana. The temperature is usually in the 80s, with high humidity there, so for us, at the time, being that young, it was sweating out the tequila from the night before, and you'd just run on adrenaline the rest of the day."

On occasion, Dave would cohost the morning show with friend Gary West, a journalist for the former *Star Telegram* and for the *Dallas Morning News*. He had plenty of support from Kent Lowe, the media relations manager, and Randy Moss, who worked for a local paper and put out a tip sheet. The depth of racing talent was such that fans were ensured a steady stream of named guests each Saturday morning.

Dave recalled, "The Roster of trainers included Gene Norman. Frankie Brothers was kingpin. Larry Snyder was the leading rider. Ronald Ardoin was one of the big jockeys. 'Cracker' Walker was the big claiming trainer. There were a lot of good names there. There was a real thirst for racing in the town. That's why thousands from Dallas-Fort Worth made a weekend of it."

A further boost to quench that thirst came with the inception, in 1980, of the Super Derby. Dave was in full stride at Louisiana Downs, versed in all aspects of the racing industry. His comfort level continued to grow as did his respect for the man who had given him his biggest break: "I liked working for Tom Sweeney. I loved the people there."

So it was with some trepidation that the thought of moving on crossed his mind. Word was out that there was an opening in Maryland. In contrast to the long-standing careers of track announcer Dick Woolley and his predecessor, Ray Haight, who died in the booth, the state was struggling when it came to a change.

Delaware Park announcer John Curran was filling in at Laurel Park, after Jehan Mahlerbe's attempts to call at Laurel Racecourse lost out to visa issues. And South African sensation, Trevor Denman, had been called in at the expense of Milo Perrins simply to cover the Preakness Stakes weekend.

Dave threw his hat into the ring by submitting a tape. With not a single word back after repeated calls to the management, he had no inkling that he was the number-one choice. Finally, he got the call, and the Top 40 hit "Wind of Change" could have been Dave's theme song.

Maryland racing would flip-flop back and forth between both Pimlico and Laurel racecourses year-round. The offer was not merely for full-time employment, it was full-time announcing that brought with it the chance of a lifetime: to call the middle leg of the Triple Crown, the Preakness Stakes.

Dave said, "So I told Mr. Sweeney, 'I have an offer and this is it.' His

last words to me were 'Teach them the de Bartolo Way.' De Bartolo owned
Louisiana Downs. I guess that meant there was no counter offer coming."
Tom had given Dave his blessing, and he felt free to go. Dave explained, "I
think he knew it was a positive career move."

Louisiana had been more than his training ground. Dave had built on
a solid foundation, emerging as an accomplished announcer that people
could trust. His style, patterned in the more traditional mode of U.S.
announcers, was to run through the field clearly and thoroughly. Dave
explained,

> I was taught to call races by Tony Bentley who learned from Dave Johnson. I
> remember sending a tape to Dave Johnson early in my career, and he was kind
> enough to write back, and he didn't criticize anything I did even though I was
> really bad. It might have been Jefferson Downs or pre–Jefferson Downs on the
> roof. But I do remember he said, "You're not placing the horses appropriately
> in the race. You're just calling horses' names and you're not saying fourth or
> fifth." He told me to pace my call a bit more.
>
> And, of course, Trevor [Denman] came along in the '80s and changed the
> long-accepted American style. That allowed American announcers to become
> more and more descriptive. I'll listen to an old tape from Louisiana Downs,
> God forbid I found one day. Thankfully the VHS format is a thing of the past,
> and I just found one, stuck it in, and I had to turn it off around the far turn.
> It's the truth that over time you change. I have changed my style dramatically.

As Dave's clear and accurate style evolved, the emotional undercurrents
he had previously harbored seemed to bubble to the surface in his calls.
There was no better vehicle for this than the Preakness Stakes, where the
waves of excitement often engulfed the moment, allowing the true racing
fan in him to impact a finish with genuine excitement.

The irony was that in the 1991 Preakness Stakes, his first ever, the trainer
of the winner hailed from his home state. Dave said, "I came all the way
from Louisiana to here to watch Frankie Brothers win a Preakness, with
Hansel. Brothers was the top trainer at Louisiana Downs, my old track."

In a sense, the hometown connection represented the bridge between
the two circuits. The Maryland circuit that Dave inherited in March 1991
was not the same as it is today. Dave explains, "At the time, it was Maryland year round, and now it's not. Colonial Downs in Virginia completes
the circuit now. They'd go back and forth between Pimlico and Laurel. Laurel would shut down, and open here [Pimlico] two days later. It was year
round though."

Colonial Downs opened in 1997 and, at the time, was under the management of the Maryland Jockey Club. Even though they still share com-

mon employees, such as the gate crew and valets, Pimlico and Laurel officially ended their association with Colonial Downs in 2006.

A predominantly grass track with a European-style layout, Colonial Downs runs in 2010 from late May through mid–July. Dave said, "I live in a hotel there, come back and forth every two weeks to check on my home in Maryland. It makes a nice circuit."

There is something refreshingly pragmatic about Dave that echoes through both his professional and domestic life with an acceptance of the nature of the business. Married in the early 1980s, he and his wife, Lisa, went their separate ways after a couple of years.

Dave noted, "One marriage. Divorce. No kids. When you work every weekend, you work every holiday except Christmas, it's tough sledding."

Dave even fits in the eight-day meet at Timonium as part of his duties. His heart will always feel a pull to Louisiana, but it is Maryland with which his voice has become synonymous.

And with winter racing at Laurel, Dave quickly stretched his ability to announce under duress. He explains, "A day after a snow at Laurel Park where we've had six inches and the sun comes out and all you can see is white and glare, that's one of the things I dislike about winter racing."

Add in multiple finish lines, two on the main track and two on the turf, and the level of concentration rises exponentially. Dave said, "So you're trying to remember to try to think of them and the pacing of a call because I'm not at the line. There is only one announcer's booth here so my position is static. I am at the regular finish line so the angles can be deceptive. If it's a close photo, I can't tell from there. I have to look at the TV, and it's very distracting."

Yet that is not the only curve ball that Laurel has thrown his way. Without turf racing the winter meet tends to see a cheaper quality of horse on the lower end of the spring and fall. Dave explains, "The cheaper the race is, the tougher it is to spot flow because horses will make false moves. The better the quality of the race, the more reliable is the horse. If a horse is perched off a three-way duel and the rider is sitting motionless and he turns him loose at the 5/16ths and he opens up four, I've seen them falter and finish third. That's only something I've gotten better at since moving to Maryland."

If there is one race call that marks Dave's coming of age, it is the 1997 Preakness Stakes won by Silver Charm, a call that caught the watchful eye of speed-figures guru and ace-handicapper Andy Beyer, who backed up his admiration the next day with a glowing column in the *Washington Post*. Dave truly captured the excitement of the thrilling stretch battle as the same three place-getters from the Kentucky Derby renewed their rivalry. He called, "They're in very close quarters. Shoulder to shoulder, head to head, nose to nose, Free House, Silver Charm, Captain Bodgit. OHHHHH it's close. Could be Silver Charm in between Free House, Captain Bodgit in a Preakness we will remember!"

Whether it be color coding his program as he was taught by his mentors or noting catchphrases, Dave strikes a healthy balance between preparation and staying open to the moment, not held hostage to a preconceived notion of a race. He noted, "You prepare a lot of things. I'll jot down phrases, situations, think about them. Write them down on a yellow legal pad. Throw them away. Put them in the back of your mind. I don't really have a book of phrases or a spreadsheet. For awhile, I was keeping a file or folder, but in between races, you have plenty of time to think up something fresh to say."

Nonetheless, there are some occurrences that nobody could be expected to be prepared for, and Dave, it seems, has had more than his fair share. Oddly enough, the two strangest moments both struck on Preakness Stakes Day.

On Preakness Stakes Day in 1998, the temperatures continued to soar into triple digits. The infield at Pimlico could accommodate 100,000 people, but the grandstands themselves were literally, beginning to feel the heat. The track's worst nightmare happened — the power went out.

Dave recalled, "It was real unfortunate because it cost the track millions in handle [money bet] and more the comfort to people. People of all ages were packed into a crowded building. No elevator was working, no escalator. Some people on the third and

Fifteen-year-old Real Quiet is the sire of two-time Breeders' Cup Sprint champion Midnight Lute. Credit: Tom Ferry.

fourth floors had to take the stairwell down because it just got unbearably hot. It was an extremely, unusually hot day there."

And, no, the power did not come back in time for the Preakness Stakes.

Dave continued, "There were certain areas that had power — the infield and that pavilion out there, the track kitchen, but most of the building was dark. I believe they started a generator up here on the roof, to power up whatever was left of the PA or get any kind of sound to the TV trailer."

Perhaps it was an omen for eventual winner Real Quiet. The national audience was oblivious to the local drama, and Dave soldiered on like a trooper under deflating circumstances.

He said, "The power's been out for hours. It's 100 degrees plus in the booth, and here's the Preakness, and they're coming down the stretch, and you're trying not to be miserable, but it was hot. Of course, people don't know how you feel." Hot and sticky Dave called the race: "RRRRRRRRRreal Quiet for a wide sweep comes up to the front. Victory Gallop is right there. The one two finishers in the derby HIT the quarter pole at Pimlico one two again. And it's Real Quiet and Victory Gallop ... Real Quiet has the lead from Victory Gallop. Desormeaux going to the stick. Real Quiet right on that rail past the sixteenth pole. Keep — hope — alive for another Triple Crown winner! Real Quiet from Victory Gallop!"

That incident however, seemed to pale in comparison to what Dave saw coming down the stretch two years later. Admittedly it wasn't the Preakness Stakes itself, but it was on the undercard, during the running of the Maryland Breeders' Cup Handicap (G3) as the field turned for home.

Hot off of track record-breaking wins on the New York circuit, Artax was aiming to consolidate his claims for the autumn Breeders' Cup Sprint when the unexpected happened during the race. Artax was travelling third into the stretch when a crazed fan barged onto the track from the infield in a fistlike pose. His attempt to land a punch square on the horse's white blaze missed as rider Jorge Chavez swerved at the last second, taking the brunt of the blow on his leg. If ever there was a case of needing to have eyes at the back of your head, this was it.

Dave recalled, "A lot of people said, 'Well, how come you didn't see that guy on the track well before the horses got to him?' Well you have to understand where I am and my perspective of looking. I'm not looking ahead of the horses. I'm looking down on them, and I'm not panning out seven, eight, nine lengths ahead. I'm looking at the action of what's going on behind. I think I just said, 'There's a person on the track.' I don't remember to be honest with you. If it ever happens again, I have the line planned for it: 'There's a LUNATIC on the track!'"

Lee Chang Ferrell, the fan who pulled the stunt, was immediately arrested and subsequently handed "a three year suspended sentence and five years probation, ordered to continue psychological counseling and enroll in a vocational skills program" (*Baltimore Sun*). All monies on Artax were refunded, and his fifth place finish proved inconsequential as he did fulfill all expectations by capturing the Breeders' Cup Sprint in October.

Dave noted, "Preakness, the rowdy fans, some intoxicated, are in that infield area. That's where everybody just drinks beer and parties. They don't even know the horse race is going on. They're running a race from the turf course and aside from all the crowd and obstructions, just as they go into the turn a couple of times, I will have seen beer cans flying through my binocular field of view. And even though you're this high up, it's very difficult to keep your concentration in the far turn on the turf."

Despite all the crowd antics, the show would go on. The win by Charismatic in the 1999 Preakness Stakes marked the third successive year that Triple Crown hopes remained alive with a lull of two years before the drama built back up again. The Voice of Maryland was now rapidly building memorable archives, and the fans were truly getting their money's worth.

War Emblem's triumph in the 2002 Preakness Stakes kick-started another three-year run of false hope for that elusive Triple Crown winner as Funny Cide and Smarty Jones sailed through Pimlico unscathed. But alas, even Smarty Jones, who Dave believed was the most likely to break the Triple Crown jinx, fell short of the mark, albeit narrowly in the Belmont Stakes.

At Pimlico, Dave had really found his sweet spot, both figuratively and literally. With the added height of his vantage point from the booth, the view into the lane is more head-on than most other tracks. A stickler with his binocular set up and for marking the right spot, Dave, who by now had come to expect the unexpected on Preakness Stakes Day, would again be asked to draw on all his experience the following year.

"This is the spot. Mark it and don't move," he chuckled, "until they come down the stretch to the 16th pole, because if you place the binoculars in the wrong spot, you don't get the ultimate, unobstructed view."

As heads came for home in the 130th Preakness Stakes, it was not Dave who would take an awkward step, but race favorite Afleet Alex. Like millions of watchful eyes, Dave felt glued to the spot as leader Scrappy T bore out drastically into the path of the rapidly closing Afleet Alex. Stopped in his tracks, the favorite stumbled to his knees, inches away from falling.

Dave recalled, "I couldn't believe what I was seeing. I remember pressing down hard on the monopod, [to hold the binoculars steady] like, don't freak out and then trying to maintain composure on the call. But what was more than the point of where he was almost wiped out for good was his comeback which I thought was the most impressive run I've seen, a great athleticism on Jeremy Rose's part and also on Afleet Alex's part too."

The same could be said for Dave himself who offered up another riveting call: "Afleet Alex has room to rrrrrrrooooooolllllll!!!!!! At the quarter pole. Afleet Alex is coming after Scrappy T ... oh, Scrappy T! Taking out Afleet Alex who almost went down ... Afleet Alex, boy does he have some heart! Look at him come back, a furlong to go. And down the final furlong in the Preakness. Afleet Alex! Scrappy T! How much the best is he?! Afleet Alex strolling home in the Preakness to win by three ... Afleet Alex, AWESOME!!!!!!!!!!"

The worst, you could say, was yet to come. Fast-forward 12 months. It was inconceivable at the time, but for 2006 Kentucky Derby winner Barbaro, the Preakness Stakes would be his last race, pulled up by jockey Edgar Prado within seconds of leaving the gate after difficulty in loading. Dave explains,

> When I've said, "They're in the gate" and you hear it echo and the crowd roars and you go, "Whoa!" So it makes you wonder how noise and atmosphere and barometric pressure and everything else combined affect human nature and the nature of the animal too. So I don't know. I don't think anybody would know. I can't blame it on any particular thing but yeah it was sad. The Preakness start is at the 3/16ths. They race right into the shadows of the grandstand at that time of day, and because it was the Derby winner, I kept my eye on him and boom! I saw it happen.
>
> I was comparing, just listening at the calls. I wanted to make sure that I caught it at the same time Tom [Durkin] had caught it, and I think we both did at the same time. But we each kind of handled it differently and handled the entire race differently I think as well. In other words, he's calling for a national TV audience and I just basically said, "Barbaro has pulled up" and I know in his call I think he elaborated more on it. I think in Dave Johnson's call on the radio, because it was radio and there's no visual race going on, he paid a lot of attention to what was happening and "jockey Edgar Prado is off and cradling."
>
> Anyway, after Barbaro pulled up, there is a race to call and it was very easy to get shaken up. It really wasn't until midway up the back stretch that you kind of regain your composure, because I know the horses are going into the far turn. There are lots of people over there and obstructions and who knows what and that's really the point you have to concentrate on the call as they round the far turn, midway on the turn, and at the top of the lane, Bernardini

made his move winning big. You have to call the race and give the winner his due. So that's the most difficult part about it. Part of you wants to put the binoculars down and take a look at Barbaro who at the time now was almost out of my sight because he was on the inner rail. The race unfolds like a novel, like a story, and you want to keep everything in perspective.

Dave focused on the race and announced: "Bernardini's firing and he's firing big ... in the stretch of the 131st Preakness and here comes Bernardini and he's roaring and pouring it on. Bernardini, and Javier Castellano goes to the lefthanded stick, but he's well clear from Sweetnorthernsaint and all the others... Bernardini! In the Preakness going going away by five!"

The Barbaro story would dominate racing news and bring into light many questions from the shadow that his breakdown had cast. Dave explained, "It really changed the mindset of the industry. Some of my friends, not necessarily racing fans, called me the next day asking about the incident. So, it impacted more than just the racing industry and people involved in racing. I think it's had a lot to do with the synthetic track movement too. I mean I've been in racing a long time, and I've seen horses take bad steps all the time and break down once in awhile. Years down the road there may be more written about it and we may find out more."

With so many twists and turns to the Preakness Stakes, it is easy to forget that Dave has been witness to many true champions. The best, he claimed, was yet to come. When Curlin snatched victory from Kentucky Derby winner Street Sense in the 2007 Preakness Stakes, the winner went to the top of his list. In a brilliant stretch call he nailed the tight photo, and the horse he dubbed "Courageous Curlin" would go on to further greatness.

Dave said, "Even though it was only two horses to the line, I thought he was probably one of the more courageous winners that I've seen. As far as talent, calling, seeing, I would say at this point, he's probably the most talented horse I've seen. Of course, the Breeders' Cup [2007] confirmed that and then Dubai, for him to keep going at such a level. He's tough. A lot of horses will do great things once or twice or a memorable moment or a stretch drive. Curlin, right now, is my favorite horse."

That is high praise, given that his most memorable champion as a fan was 1973 Triple Crown winner Secretariat. Dave noted, "I was in high school when Secretariat did his thing."

Almost four decades later, Dave relishes his job and claims there's no stress or politics: "I basically come up here and do my job. Nobody ever sits you down and says, 'Let's listen to that fourth race today. That horse was in

Dave says, "A pinnacle of my career is being able to do something that very few people can do and get paid for it. Calling a Triple Crown race." Credit: Jim McCue.

front by three, not six.' Or 'How come you didn't call the fourth horse in the superfecta?' The only people that do that are fans. There's no stress. You make it as easy or tough as you want it."

He is extremely modest but will admit that his race calling has changed over the years, for the better: "The things I bring are clarity, accuracy, and being able to spot the flow of the race pretty well. I'll keep an eye on the favorite and tell the people what they're doing. You know, the top two, three, four choices in the race, because those are the ones with the most money bet on. But at the same time I should be able to call the entire field, at least a couple of times, to give the $2 bettors a chance to know what's happening with their horses."

The two-dollar bettors got to relive the Seabiscuit–War Admiral match race of 1938 when Pimlico reenacted it on May 16, 2003. Dave recreated the radio call of well-known Clem McCarthy: "I researched it on the Internet a little bit and found an audio tape of his call and transcribed it; I wrote down everything he said word for word, and I said, 'Let me try to do it in his voice or in an old-timey way.' And it probably turned out a little bit hokey, but people seemed to enjoy it. And it was probably a tribute to his call and his style and that era. It was a fun thing to do."

Dave reiterated, "Expect the unexpected. That's why I like racing so much. There's something changing every 20–25 minutes. You're not going to get bored." Along that line he noted, "Just a couple of weeks ago, we had a goose on the turf track at Laurel, and he was just there with his little flock down in the field lake there but he was literally on the track, and the horses came into the first turn. And he scattered. Luckily he got out of the way. That could have been a disaster in the making.... We've seen small rodents run across the park. There are plenty of deer in the wetland area of the backstretch run at Laurel. Once in a blue moon I've seen them delay a race."

Horse racing in Maryland has struggled in the last decade as neighboring states have gotten revenue from their slot machines and been able to get big fields with the lure of big purses. Top conditioner Michael Dickinson retired from training in 2007 to promote his Tapeta Footings, the synthetic track that he invented. He said, "Yes, I know Dave very well. Nice man. I know him, obviously because he's from Maryland. He's a good caller. He's had a difficult job the last couple of years because Maryland racing has been on the decline. Don't have slots. They haven't had as many runners. The quality of racing has gone down a little bit. Yet Dave Rodman has kept his enthusiasm up the whole time. He has kept trying to keep the Maryland racing ship afloat... Dave calls the races for someone who is playing the race. He caters to the $2 bettor and the simulcasting fans. He always has the $2 player in his mind. He is very good at picking up trouble and happenings in the first half mile of the race which, of course, becomes very relevant at the end of the race."

Michael's favorite race that Dave called was the 2003 Grade I De Francis Memorial Dash. Michael recalled, "A Huevo had been off for four years, and he came back to win a Grade I. That was my horse. Dave called him two out. He called him a winner. And when he won the race, just before, he said, 'This is another Michael Dickinson Miracle.'"

Josh Pons, a Maryland native, has chronicled horse racing's struggles in *Country Life Diary* and *Merryland*. He said, "Dave has the trick that all great race callers have. He understands that the horse in that race is the most important one to the guy that owns it. Even if it's a claiming race, he gives it a full-hearted call ... I think he's a treasure for Maryland. He's one of the strong points and the positive things about Maryland racing. He's a great caller."

Another great call by Dave came in the 134th running of the Preakness

Rachel Alexandra exudes class! Credit: Tom Ferry.

on May 16, 2009: "And it is Rachel Alexandra looking to make Preakness history and she says, 'If you want to beat me, you'd better come get me and get me right now.'... The Derby winner Mine That Bird closing a length back, but it is Rachel Alexandra. She's simply ABOVE AND BEYOND them! A filly has won the Preakness! Mine That Bird was second. Musket Man was third. Followed in fourth position there by Flying Private. And the time was 1:55. We've seen history, a dazzling display by Rachel Alexandra, the first filly to win the Preakness in 85 years!"

Dave's enthusiasm was apparent as he continued to add to the race even after the finish.

He reflected, "It was another one of those great Preakness moments. Rachel is awesome ! I may never see another filly win the race in my life-time. At the end of the day, I got to congratulate Calvin Borel in person. I've known his agent, Jerry Hissam, since Louisiana Downs days. He is a first-class person, and a perfect match with Calvin."

Dave is convinced that despite Maryland's racing decline, the Preak-ness will always be held at Pimlico. He explained, "The reason is where else in the nation are you going to get 100,000 people in the *infield*? A lot of people say, 'You can run the Preakness at Laurel.' No, you can't. The grand-stand won't fit that many people. The press box can't fit that many people. The Laurel infield is low ground and a lake ... Preakness Day is the one day that makes the whole meet at Pimlico go."

Dave would miss the general atmosphere if he no longer called races. He said, "When the horses come out, and they're warming up. The people. The characters. I don't know if I would miss the gambling part of it. But I think once I retired I would probably be a casual player again."

However, he feels that that is the biggest misconception about him. He noted, "Probably that some people believe that I bet the races I call. Which I really don't. Some announcers play, and some don't ... that I'm sitting up here betting like a fiend which is not true. Now after the live card is done, I certainly enjoy playing a few simulcast races."

Dave has his own idea of how to help racetracks: "I'd love to see a race-track have a little paddock area. Sponsor three or four retired horses, fan favorites. Let them roam around.... Nice field for retired horses to run around in. Kids come out and pet them. They [the track] would feed them and help them. Pay the vet bill and show them a little good will. In Maryland it is very common to see kids gather around the ponies [outrider ponies and lead ponies] and pet them. I think it'd be a great family attraction. And promote greater awareness and importance of giving retired Thoroughbreds a proper home."

He feels that the pinnacle of his career has been calling a Triple Crown race: "Just being able to do something that very few people can do and get paid for it." And he would like to be remembered as "an accurate compe-tent race caller who likes the sport."

Dave loves the horses and the racing. And he stated, "Unscientifically speaking, each day you spend at the track, should add ten minutes to your life."

CHAPTER 4

Michael Wrona

Michael Wrona: "The crowd rises to a champion ... sixteen in succession as Cigar assumes the crown of immortality!"

"Racing!" growls Michael Wrona as the gates spring open. For over 100 days each year, Australian native Michael Wrona calls races at Golden Gate Fields and considers himself one of the lucky people inhabiting the earth who loves his job.

Michael was born February 3, 1966, in a suburb of Brisbane, Australia. Even though his parents, Edward and Carol, divorced when he was seven, Michael enjoyed a happy childhood. Carol was a stay-at-home mother. Michael said that she "had the happiest disposition of anyone I've ever known and was the epitome of unconditional love." She wholeheartedly supported both Michael and his younger brother, Wayne, when they each followed their rather uncommon passions. Michael's was race calling and Wayne's involved cinematography.

At Aspley High School Michael played tennis and squash, and outside of school he participated in club soccer. He was bitten by the racing bug when he was in his early teens. As he became a fan, he listened avidly to the track announcers on the radio. He recalled, "I found myself marveling at the race callers I heard from around the country. Mimicking them and wanting to emulate them quickly became the facet of racing that I was most attracted to."

Michael's teachers told Carol that Michael had listed race caller at the top of his list when asked to put down his desired profession. Carol said, "It's something that has just been inside Michael. It has always been there."

When Michael was about 13, his maternal grandfather gave him a horse racing board game which involved plastic horses that moved to the roll of the dice. Michael said, "I found I gained the most enjoyment from abandoning the regular rules and just pushing them along to the roll of the dice and calling out their names. And I can still remember most of their names."

Now one of the top track announcers in the United States, Michael Wrona got his start sitting on his bedroom floor with brown paper bags full of hundreds of little pieces of paper colored with the silks of the horses of that era. They were divided into various classes of races.

Michael recalled, "I'd decide I wanted to call a Sydney staying race so I delved into the appropriate brown paper bag, grabbed a fistful of those pieces of paper, lined them up, started pushing them about, and taped the race calls. I probably drove the neighbors crazy, but I was absolutely hooked on race calling and knew it was what I wanted to do."

Wayne, three years younger, remembered those phantom race calls: "Michael's paper race calling mostly annoyed me! He was loud and constant." Carol said that he even called races in the shower!

Michael realized that he didn't want to still be on that bedroom floor pushing those pieces of paper when he was 30. Carol related,

> When Michael was in high school they had Sports Days, but Michael used to go to the racetrack. He would have his little recorder. And he would record his calling of the races just standing near the fence. At that stage the main race caller was a gentleman by the name of Vince Curry. He was the top caller. This particular day, and it would have taken a lot of courage for Michael, he decided that he would climb up the ladder to the calling box and introduce himself to Vince Curry. Mr. Curry said to Michael, "Ok, I want you to play back the race," and Michael played it back. And he was very very impressed with Michael, and he told him, "I can see potential in you. Try to get to the track as often as possible, because it's definitely in you to be a race caller."

Vince Curry took Michael under his wing and offered him chances to practice in a spare booth. He critiqued his calls and eventually Michael got a part-time job at the radio station in Brisbane that covered racing.

He had graduated from high school and had a secure job at the Bank of Queensland. But he gave that up for a foot in the door at the radio station after taking a year-long course called Air TV that taught him quite a bit about radio and broadcasting. Michael started out part-time behind the scenes. He got to do a bit of everything: run errands, work in the control room and production, operate the studio's controls for the late-night religious program, and even help the main race caller on weekends out at the track. He also gained experience with race calling by announcing greyhound and harness races.

And away from the radio station, Michael went to country tracks outside Brisbane to call both Quarter Horse and Thoroughbred races. His very first call on a PA system came in April 1983 at Kilcoy. The main announcer, Paul Dolan, had helped Michael and decided that he was ready. The race call went well, and Michael got to call two races that day.

Two months later he substituted at Brunette Downs, which was a huge cattle station in the outback where ranchers came from hundreds of miles for the two-day race meet. Michael remembered, "The hired announcer pulled out at late notice, and Paul Dolan was contacted in Brisbane but was scared of flying in a small aircraft. That's how it got palmed off on me! The final leg of the journey involved a two-hour flight in a three-seat plane. It was piloted by a gentleman with the confidence-inspiring name of 'Tex Battle.'"

There he got to call his first full card. Michael said, "This was my first job where I was The Man (or The Kid). I did two days of race calling in Brunette Downs, an absolute dust bowl. No outside rail. One horse didn't take the turn in a race, and they had to hold the next race back ten minutes while they went to round him up. You just basically saw the leader followed by a cloud of dust. Very, very basic." Seventeen-year-old Michael was literally a happy camper under the stars each night.

Beaudesert, another bush track, was where Michael called his first Thoroughbred race for radio. He would like very much to have that call back. He explained, "A horse was left behind the gate. He wouldn't load and was kind of over behind the trees and difficult to see. I was nervously ad-libbing on air, running out of things to say, and I glanced around to update some tote figures and remind people of what the favorite was. There was no communication between the starter and the stewards, or certainly not to the announcer's booth, and I never got any phone calls that they were scratching the steed. Then the resident announcer rushed into the booth and turned me around to face the field which had gone fully a furlong.... I just looked at them, and the first word out of my mouth was 'Racing!'"

The next seven years in Australia Michael lived his passion for race calling. One could almost feel the merino sheep wool in his voice. His words were succinct, his delivery direct, and his commitment unflinching. His favorite racehorse, Kingston Town, had burst upon Australia in the late 1970s and continued to race through the early 1980s.

Michael said, "I would say that he was a catalyst in my becoming as crazed about horse racing as I was and still am. He was a jet-black gelding. He actually ran stone motherless last in his first start, and they gelded him.

Michael (right), at age 24, with his idol John Tapp outside the Hollywood Park booth in May 1990. By permission of Michael Wrona.

He came back off of a layoff and just proceeded to take all before him. He'd break 1:10 for six furlongs and could also win at two miles. He had sizzling acceleration, and he was just breathtaking. He was based in Sydney which is where John Tapp was calling. He was my idol. He was the man I wanted most to emulate as I became involved in the sport. The combination of Tappy calling Kingston Town pretty much sealed my fate."

It was John Tapp who was offered the job of track announcer at Hollywood Park in 1990. Today he is retired from race calling, but Michael considers his friendship with his mentor as one of the pinnacles in his entire career. He explained, "Having been selected by John Tapp to accompany him to Hollywood Park and to have worked with him, he certainly aided in the transition. It would have been a lot tougher coming in cold without him there. And knowing his opinion of me, and the chance to befriend him; just the way that the whole American opportunity arose makes me want to pinch myself."

In fact, Tapp recommended Michael for the prestigious job announcing at Hollywood Park. Michael said, "I had always aspired to be a full-time

Thoroughbred announcer. Never imagined it would happen with Hollywood Park. Things had just kind of evolved, gaining more experience as I went along across the mid to late eighties. And then I came here [California] in 1990. Hollywood Park. I'd been living with my mother in Brisbane which is the third biggest city in Australia behind Melbourne and Sydney. But still, straight to Los Angeles: hell of a culture shock!"

And he was only 24 years old. On top of that, one of his most memorable races occurred just six weeks after he began calling at the historic Hollywood Park track in Inglewood. It was the million-dollar Hollywood Gold Cup. In those days the announcer was discouraged from calling photo finishes. Michael convinced his lady boss Marje Everett to let him call them and, of course, the race came down to a nose between Sunday Silence and Criminal Type. Luckily, Michael correctly proclaimed Criminal Type the winner: "Criminal Type, Sunday Silence locked together.... Past the eighth pole Criminal Type, Sunday Silence. It's a soul-stirring duel. There's nothing in it. Criminal Type the inside and Sunday Silence. One head up and one down. Sunday Silence, Criminal Type hit the line. Criminal Type! Criminal Type on the rail has won the Gold Cup by a nose to Sunday Silence."

In that very first Hollywood Gold Cup Michael adopted the practice of retiring his one-of-a-kind phrases. He said, "I was able to use a phrase that belonged to the number one race caller in Brisbane as I was growing up, a gentleman called Vince Curry. One phrase that he liked to use was 'soul-stirring duel.' Here I've since come to realize that dueling is more associated with horses in the first half: the speed duel. But in the context of Vince Curry's use of the phrase it was more 'intense battle' in the closing stages which is what unfolded with Criminal Type and Sunday Silence. And I found myself saying, 'It's a soul-stirring duel' and I was really pleased to have injected that into the race call, and I've never used it since. I retired it immediately."

Another "Wrona-ism" that Michael will always be remembered for appeared in his call later that year of the Hollywood Turf Cup. Itsallgreektome was "clearly the horse to beat on class, but he had never gone a mile and a half before," Michael explained. "That was the only query. Would he get the distance? As he was coming home clear of his rivals I said in the race call rhetorically: 'Can he stay the distance? He stays like a mother-in-law.'"

Michael is a perfectionist. He stresses over the reality that there is no "take two" in race calling. He said that his short-term memory enabled him to "wipe clean the mental slate and start afresh for the next race." He continued, "I don't know whether I had a strong short-term memory, and that

Two Aussie expats getting together in Lexington: Michael with Strawberry Road, 1993. By permission of Michael Wrona.

helped me in becoming a race caller, or whether becoming a race caller has kind of fine-tuned my short-term memory. But I can tell you my long-term memory sucks!"

Added to his ability to memorize the fields is his excellent vocabulary. His precise delivery makes it easy to understand his Aussie accent. English had been his favorite subject in high school, and the first thing he did each day was to "fix" the horses' names in the program. He would quickly correct names that had been strung together or needed apostrophes. Michael admits, "I'm a stickler for grammar and spelling which is why so many horse names are abhorrent to me. But ultimately I commit each set of colors to memory. In the case of similar colors within the one race, I'll look to distinguishing equipment such as different colored blinkers. Shadow rolls can help a lot. Obviously it's nice to see a grey.... The program is there if you need a sneaky look. But the ideal for me is to do it by memory."

Of course, even an elite announcer has times when he finds himself in a tight spot. That's when Michael prefers to take responsibility for his blunder: "Part of the art of race calling is to sound like you know what you're talking about when you don't have a bloody clue. And there are plenty of times when you're either on the verge of being in trouble, or you actually are in trouble. And you have to size up in an instant whether you think you can gloss over it and work around it, or whether you have to own up to it, and actually make a correction. When it's pretty obvious, I think you're better off to correct it because people are not stupid. You can't just pretend that no one is going to notice something, a glitch of that nature. And I prefer owning up to it.... It's an imperfect art form, and you have to keep the flow going. The show must go on."

He is quick to admit that he is his own worst critic: "People would be amazed at how rarely I'm walking across the parking lot at the end of the day giving myself a pat on the back. The vast majority of the time I'm trudging across the parking lot kicking myself up the ass knowing what I either could have said differently or what I could have added. There are so many ways that a race call would have been better." He laughed. "It's a terrible thing! The irony of it is that I'm doing what I've always wanted to do, and what I feel so passionate about. And when I think I've nailed it, it is a great feeling. But few and far between are the races when I actually experience that. More often than not, it's frustration, knowing it could have been better. So I'm a sick puppy!" And he added, "One phrase that I read somewhere many years ago in Australia that's always stuck with me, that I try to remind myself of now and again is 'Only the mediocre are always at their best.' I love that! But I still have a lot of trouble convincing myself of it."

Michael's brother Wayne remembered the trip of a lifetime: "After the first year in America, Michael gave the family an amazing Christmas present. He paid for a six-week trip to America for myself, our Mum, Grandparents, and Aunty. It truly was an incredible gift. He was eager to show us his new home, share some of his experiences ... that wonderful six weeks together will remain with me for all of my days."

After announcing at Hollywood Park in 1990, Michael ran into visa problems and went up to Golden Gate Fields and Bay Meadows (in northern California) where he called races for the next several years. At least, that was the official reason given. Eighteen years later Michael Wrona would like to set the record straight: "Visa problems was the publicized reason, but the *real* reason was the takeover that forced Marje Everett out. During her reign, relations had been very strained between Hollywood Park and the other southern California tracks. The reason Marje looked toward Australia was because Santa Anita had refused to allow Trevor Denman to work for her.

When R.D. Hubbard took over there was a 'honeymoon' period, part of which was his ability to hire Trevor. Quite simply, I was turfed out less than a year after moving my life halfway around the world. However, I certainly hold no ill-feeling towards Trevor. Indeed, his popularity is the sole reason that John Tapp and I were sought. I've always admired how Trevor has been the trailblazer."

In 1995 Michael called the inaugural season at Retama Park in San Antonio. He hoped it would give him the opportunity to be the announcer at Lone Star Park as well, but it didn't open until later. By then Retama had declared bankruptcy right after its first season.

Michael moved to Arlington Park in Chicago in time to call Cigar in his 16th win in a row. It was to be one of his most memorable calls: "And now Jerry Bailey sets Cigar alight ... Cigar and Dramatic Gold making runs together ... Cigar comes to the eighth pole taking over by half a length ... Dramatic Gold is running a mighty race on the inside ... but Cigar seems to have his measure.... He's starting to stretch away now! Cigar is an unstoppable dynamo! The crowd rises to a champion ... sixteen in succession as Cigar assumes the crown of immortality!"

Michael remembered, "Cigar's race probably took on even more significance when he was beaten in his next start. So it was actually the last one in the sequence when he tied Citation's record. It was covered live by CBS nationwide ... literally the whole world of racing was zeroed in on that. And the atmosphere was absolutely amazing at Arlington. It was a track where I had to work with the window open to accommodate my binocular stand, and so I always fed off the crowd more at Arlington than elsewhere. On this occasion, it was bananas."

Michael called two full seasons at Arlington. Ironically, he had been offered the job of announcing at Lone Star when it opened in 1997. But he turned it down to show his loyalty to Arlington. This backfired when Arlington closed for economic reasons and did not race for two years. Michael recalled, "Again I was left out in the cold. I could easily suggest that I'd still be at Arlington if they didn't close the doors as they did. But they were out of operation for '98 and '99, and that's when I did Turf Paradise in conjunction with Hollywood Park in 1999 and 2000. There was the satisfaction I derived from being rehired at Hollywood Park [and Bay Meadows at the end of 2005], two tracks I had lost in the early 1990s. It gave me a great sense of closure, particularly with the same management in place all those years later. Arlington reopened in 2000 and approached me to resume, but I declined to show loyalty to Hollywood Park." Michael admitted, "It's been a rollercoaster ride. It does wear you down. A lot of uncertainty hanging over me and a lot of packing up and moving about between meets. Just no feeling of groundedness."

Back at Hollywood Park for the 1999 Hollywood Gold Cup, Michael did what he does best: he painted a picture of another great horse race: "And Real Quiet has to wait. He's in behind a wall of horses at the top of the stretch ... Real Quiet's getting up along the inside. Budroyale, Real Quiet flying through on the fence. Real Quiet takes the lead. He's won the roses. Now he's got the gold!"

And Michael was once again fortunate to be in the booth at the racetrack where another big race was about to take place. For days Laffit Pincay Jr. had flirted with breaking Bill Shoemaker's all-time number of most wins. Michael explained,

> He was on fire, and it became apparent that it was probably going to happen at Hollywood, and so it generated a lot of attention.... I had to be very cognizant of what Pincay was doing in every race and had to be actually referring to him by name more than you would typically in a race call. It was hard. I felt like I was overdoing it a little bit, but it was what management wanted. With a feature race like Cigar or any stakes race, you know when the race is happening. But with this you didn't know exactly in which race it was actually going to happen. You had to be ready time and time again. And so I found it stressful in that sense. There was just this prolonged anticipation. And sometimes he might go close to winning, and then you realize in the last hundred yards that it's not this race. So then you've got to regroup. It was a very fun time and great to be a part of.

Finally, on December 10, 1999, Laffit Pincay Jr. became racing's all-time win leader riding Irish Nip for his 8,834th victory. And Michael called from the booth: "Pincay gets a whiff of immortality as Irish Nip is finding plenty on the lead. Responding to the Pincay Power, it's Irish Nip surging clear and it's history at Hollywood Park, as Laffit Pincay Jr. becomes the world's all-time winningest jockey!"

The longtime bachelor married Julie, an aspiring actress, in 2000, and Michael wanted more job security from Hollywood Park. When management dragged its heels, he moved to Lone Star. He said, "Lone Star offered me a really nice package and security. Plus it's halfway to New York City where Julie was. It's in the middle of the country, and so I went there in 2000 and did five seasons for them."

Lone Star had Thoroughbred racing in the spring for about three and a half months. Then there was a Quarter Horse meet in the fall. Michael preferred calling Thoroughbreds because there was time to paint a picture and be more descriptive than in the short Quarter Horse races.

By 2000 Michael was gaining more exposure. In May he called the Preakness to a national radio audience when he substituted for Tom Durkin.

A year or two later he had the opportunity to be the racetrack announcer at Fair Grounds in nearby New Orleans. That fit in well between the two meets at Lone Star and created an enviable circuit. Michael noted, "I was very happy with that setup. And I had a good solid run of a few years with them. Then I lost both jobs in a two-month span." It was in October, about six weeks before Fair Grounds was to open, that Michael was told he would no longer be the track announcer there.

In 2004 the Breeders' Cup was held for the first time at Lone Star. Michael recalled, "It wasn't an enjoyable day for me. The resident announcer at Triple Crown tracks still calls those races on the PA system and through the simulcast network, and I've always believed that the same should apply with the Breeders' Cup ... you call there year round and then the big day comes and you have to stand aside. And then after the Breeders' Cup meet,

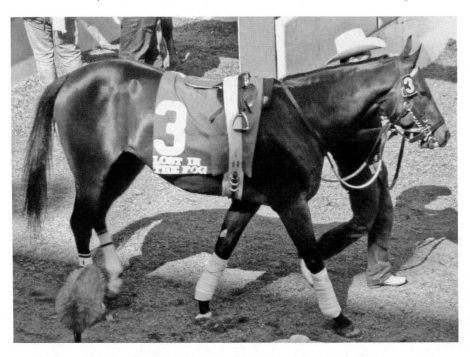

When four-year-old Lost in the Fog ran on April 22, 2006, Golden Gate Fields gave away bobbleheads of the popular horse.

the wheels fell off at Lone Star. I got that phone call three days before Christmas. And so my entire livelihood had evaporated in the span of about two months."

This was the first time that Michael lost a job due to money. Lone Star had not gotten slots like its neighboring states. There were budget cuts in all of the departments as well as layoffs. He said, "It was an exciting place because they really had a lot of enthusiasm, and marketing savvy. They were successful for a new track" until things bottomed out after the Breeders' Cup like the stock market in 2008.

Michael has been as frustrated about his many career moves as a person trying to win the Pick Six. He admits, "I've worked at so many tracks, I could understand people thinking that I lack loyalty and/or am purely money-driven. Neither is the case, as virtually all of my moves have been circumstantial, through either track closures or new management/ownership wanting to implement a change."

Michael spent an uncomfortable, shivering few months in New York at the beginning of 2005, in one of the many sublets that Julie had occupied. He hoped to be able to announce on the East Coast where Julie was trying to break into acting. However, that didn't work out. He coped with disappointment and, as he had always done, rode it out. He never worked in the United States at any other job. Track announcing was it for him.

And he knew that he wanted to remain in the United States. Michael declared, "I proudly took my oath of citizenship in New York, in September 2005. I remain an Australian citizen, thus enjoying the best of both worlds!"

Ron Charles, the Magna executive in California, was responsible for "singlehandedly resurrecting" Michael's career. He brought him back to Golden Gate Fields near San Francisco. And there awaited Lost in the Fog, the brilliant sprinter who had won ten races in a row and an Eclipse Award in 2005. Michael noted the tremendous popularity of owner Harry Aleo's bay superstar: "Lost in the Fog has helped Golden Gate Fields a lot! The people love coming out to see him. And we get big crowds which are hard to draw these days, and it's because of him."

Foggy so outclassed his opponents that Michael struggled to call his races. "When a race is not competitive at any point, it's difficult to not miss a beat or two and start wondering how I can keep this interesting," he explained. "You've got a three horse field with the odds-on favorite straight to the lead by a couple of lengths, and that's the closest they get to him. Then it's actually not a very fun seventy seconds!"

Michael continued, "The thing that I admire most about Lost in the Fog is how many different tracks that he won at. It is rare to see a horse travel as far and wide and successfully as Lost in the Fog. In that sense he reminded me of Cigar. He was masterfully handled and beautifully placed in his races."

Michael called the colt's first race back after Lost in the Fog had enjoyed a well-deserved break. It was in the 2006 Golden Gate Fields Sprint, and no one yet realized that Lost in the Fog was fighting not only the other horses in the race, but the tumors in his body. Michael announced: "Carthage has slipped away from Lost in the Fog. Carthage at the 3/16ths by 2½ lengths. Lost in the Fog under a left-handed whip is laboring. Elegant Ice a length and a half away. But it's Carthage coming to the sixteenth pole by four lengths. Lost in the Fog unable to match him coming back off the layoff. Certainly there are bigger fish to fry down the road."

Tragically, the four-year-old champion was euthanized on September 17, 2006, after courageously battling cancer. His classy conditioner, Greg Gilchrist, respects Michael's race calling:

> I just know that Michael's a very capable race caller. And when you look at it from my side of the street, very seldom do you get an incorrect call out of Michael. If you were blindfolded, you could picture the race in your mind. It would be just like it is coming out of Michael's mouth. He's very knowledge-able about when horses are starting to pick it up or making their run or if they're in trouble or the other way, you know, if they're shortening stride, backing up in the race. I know he covers all his bases. There've been two or three times that he's called me about horses' names that he wants to pronounce correctly. So you know he's going over everything and doing his homework. Longevity is always a sign of success, in my mind. He's certainly been doing this a long time so I respect the guy a whole lot for the job he does. He's another guy who is not going to go away. Michael will always have a job some-where.

Without Lost in the Fog, Golden Gate Fields doesn't have many crowds now. It also doesn't have big fields. Michael says that that is his biggest frus-tration: "I feel like slapping people who say, 'Oh you have it easy today; a six horse field.' Nothing could be further from the truth. I like variation in my delivery and to mix things up, keep it interesting. It becomes all the more difficult when you're saying the same five horses over and over, especially in two turn races.... The order doesn't change, and it's a procession the whole way."

Russell Baze was the jockey of Lost in the Fog. And in December 2006 he broke Laffit Pincay Jr.'s record of most races won. Astonishingly, the same track announcer who had called Laffit's race seven years earlier, called this one at Bay Meadows: "But this is the race! Russell Baze on Butterfly Belle winning 2½ lengths and a sterling career becomes gilt-edged!"

A great race caller makes it look easy. But it is anything but! Michael explains, "When Pincay was chasing The Shoe, and then Baze was chasing Pincay, there is an amazing buildup. And you're aware of the growing interest and focus. You know the jockey is the cynosure of all eyes. And it's hard to prepare for that kind of thing because you don't actually know when it's going to be. And you don't know whether you'll have time to say anything, depending on how close the finish is."

That was the case when Russell won his 10,000th race on February 2, 2008, at Golden Gate Fields. Michael said, "He got that 10,000th victory by the skinniest possible margin. In fact, it was a very deceptive photo finish that most people didn't think he'd won. And there was no time to do anything with it." Michael had to settle for recognizing the victory in the winner's circle.

Like a teacher on the first day of school, Michael works hard to keep it all fun and fresh. He said, "I try to incorporate as many different phrases or adjectives as possible. I hate being repetitious. And anything that I might read or hear somewhere, I'll be wondering how it might be applied to a race call. It's particularly difficult with small fields. That's when I'm most conscious of repetition and predictability, and I abhor it. I abhor predictability!"

Trainer Neil Howard has been the leading trainer at Churchill and Keeneland and conditioned the 2003 Horse of the Year, Mineshaft. He said, "Michael gives a whole new meaning to the term 'ad-lib.'"

Englishman Michael Dickinson travels around the world selling Tapeta, a synthetic track surface that he created. But before this fairly recent venture, he was a champion amateur steeplechase rider who, according to NTRA's bio stats, rode professionally for ten years. As a winning trainer, Dickinson coaxed two nonconsecutive Breeders' Cup Mile victories from Da Hoss. He credited Michael Wrona with having "perhaps the clearest pronunciation of any race caller. He is a horseman. He has experience, passion, and a great sense of humor."

And Michael loves Dickinson's Tapeta surface, which was installed in time for the 2007–2008 fall and winter meet at Golden Gate Fields: "It's been fantastic. I believe the Tapeta surface has seen a boost in field sizes. The racing is more competitive. There's no kickback. Horses can split the field from last on a wet track, and the jockey is in the winner's circle spotless.... And it wasn't as speed biased as a lot of dirt tracks can be in California particularly. So I am a huge fan of Tapeta!"

The dry-witted track announcer loves his microbrewed beer and says it is an excellent stress reliever. Hiking and chess fuel his interest. His obsession for European soccer caused him to rise very early the morning of the 2008 El Camino Real Derby. And Michael has remained connected to Australia, where horse racing is more popular than in the States. He said, "Australia races horses longer — in distance and career — and more often. It's exclusively turf racing so it is easier on horses physically. The Australian race course is bigger in circumference, and they have greater variation in their layout and design whereas American tracks are your standard oval. They just don't vary. That's why I get a kick out of that downhill turf course at Santa Anita. It's just so unique."

He points out that the huge network of off-track betting shops in Australia is everywhere: strip malls, pubs, and clubs. He explained, "Racing is more accessible in Australia. Here [in the United States] you seem to have to go out of your way to be a follower of horse racing.

"These days I'd say Australian racing is my biggest hobby because I follow it closely. I stay in touch with it through the Internet. I actually do a weekly report for a Sydney radio station on U.S. racing." And he incorporates phrases from down under, like "Hoo Roo." He said it's "an old, casual farewell in Australia, equivalent to 'see ya'" that he signs off with each day after the final race.

Julie believed that Michael is a great track announcer for many reasons. She said, "I would have to say his accuracy, his humor, but above all else, his ability to paint a picture. You can actually close your eyes and see the race in front of you ... and I know that that absolutely has to do with his upbringing in Australia. Because in Australia, back when he was a kid, there was no televised horse racing. So the only way a person would know what was going on in a race was the radio. And the only way you would know was with the race caller being as descriptive as humanly possible, and that's where he learned to do that. He listened to Bill Collins and Vince Curry, John Russell, and Johnny Tapp who is his absolute hero."

Julie continued, "At any point you know where your horse is. He calls every one. He tries to get through the field two, three, five times if he can depending on how many are in it. He just knows that there are some people that are really truly listening, and he calls for those people. That's why he calls every horse going through to the finish line."

However, after 14 years of calling the full order of finish, Michael brought it to a halt: "I always felt as though there was validity in calling every horse at the finish because if the last you hear of your horse is when he's running eleventh at the 5/16ths, and the horse happens to finish fifth passing half the field in the last furlong and maybe it's galloping out strongly, to me from a future form standpoint, that has some value. And while some people liked it, just as many didn't and thought it was unnecessary. I finally decided to disarm the critics who thought first and only of that when discussing my style."

The gypsy life of a track announcer is desperately hard on relationships. In the summer of 2007, Michael and Julie separated. Michael emphasized both the pros and cons of his race calling career:

I followed the dream through and persisted. I never wanted to leave myself wondering "what if," and I never wanted Julie to wonder the same thing about her dreams. We supported each other unconditionally but, ultimately, we each would have been better off with someone who didn't have such a geographically-specific career.

I'm working within an industry that I love and enjoy. It's not a particularly long work day. But, at the same time, once it's underway I don't get a lunch break, and it's fairly intense. There's not much time to get out and about between races.

Michael called the last Winter/Spring Meet at Bay Meadows in 2008.

But that's a minor thing. The hardships would be more along the line of the work being seasonal and sporadic. And it's very difficult to secure a circuit in the same geographical area. It really wears away over the years. Even when I had a pretty good pairing of tracks at Lone Star and Fair Grounds, I was still counting the number of days per year that I was losing in my life just by virtue of packing up and moving and getting set up again. In and out of temporary accommodations all the time, never really feeling grounded, storage units dotted about the countryside.

On one hand it's an adventure to see so many places. I've seen more of the United States than my own country as it's turned out. And I've had the chance to live in a lot of different places; Chicago to New Orleans is quite a contrast. I've seen a great variety of the American lifestyle, but there's just this feeling of being unsettled. It's a nomadic lifestyle, and it might be fine for awhile but eventually it just starts to wear you down. It's not a profession conducive to married life. And kids? I don't think it's fair to a woman to be married to a track announcer let alone kids.

In the spring of 2008 it appeared that Bay Meadows' days were numbered. The historic track where Charles Howard's beloved Seabiscuit raced was scheduled to be demolished. Michael was quite philosophical about the demise of the northern California track: "It's more of the same for me. I've had the rug pulled from under my feet so often. It's not definite, but most nails are in the coffin. I've already called the last race at Arlington as I was there when they closed for a couple of years. But obviously there would be much greater finality to it than with Arlington. If anybody has to call the final race ever I would be privileged to." He put a lot of thought into that last day of race calling and said, "I have some ideas of what I'm going to do on that day. I'm thinking of inserting the names of past great horses who have raced here into the race calls. Just throw them in once randomly across the day's races."

And that is just what he did. On May 11, 2008, Bay Meadows closed its final Thoroughbred meet with nine races. Throughout the day Michael combined professionalism with sentimentality as he smoothly inserted famous horses into the fields. Majestic Prince, Citation, Cavonnier, Snow Chief, and Ole Bob Bowers each got a call from him. Race three saw "Brown Bess coming into it strongly." Race four had "Seabiscuit splitting horses." And in Race five, "Lost in the Fog begins brilliantly." Finally it was time for the last race of the final Bay Meadows meet, a seven-and-a-half furlong claiming race and Michael announced: "The crowd cheers! Racing ... John Henry mounting a mighty challenge as they swing for home ... as they thunder down the Longden Turf Course homestretch ... an historic finish line is beckoning."

For all intents and purposes, Bay Meadows was finished. But in August came the ten-day San Mateo County Fair meet where the final race was named the Last Dance Stakes. Michael, once again, was forced to call a final race and on August 17, 2008, he did it eloquently: "Dancing. And the big crowd gives the grand old lady a fond farewell cheer.... They're in the backstretch and it's a surreal scene as three quarters of a century's tradition is evaporating before our eyes.... The final field to grace this hallowed ground heads for home.... And You Lift Me Up showing the way home in the Last Dance."

The Australian in Michael Wrona is as robust as the first day he stepped foot on American soil. So is his repertoire of animated phrases that he has successfully imported from a culture that regards horse racing as a national treasure. So quick-witted, Michael is like a verbal hymnist, turning a call on a dime with just the right word at just the right time.

Michael said, "The best part of my job would be the satisfaction I feel on the rare occasions that I actually do allow myself to acknowledge a race call as that's pretty much as good as I or anyone could do. There's just select moments of the race, maybe if the field bunches, there are horses trapped out wide, and maybe the complexion of the race that you're in control of it. And not reaching for anything. That's a special feeling."

There are certain talents that a top-class announcer must possess. Michael explains, "A race is constantly evolving, and I think a top-class announcer should be able to have the call evolve to match the race. That might sound pretty obvious, but a lot of announcers are very regimented in their procedure of going through the field.... As you're saying something in a race call, the situation might actually be changing. I mean literally as the words are coming out of your mouth, a move might begin, positions can change. I try to let myself go with the flow of the race as it unfolds. The ability to just be willing to make split second adjustments, even midstream in what you're saying."

Along with that comes the all-important binoculars: "The Comfort Zone for me really is my binocular stand. I cannot call races by holding the binoculars. I can't keep them steady enough, and as the intensity builds, and the horses come near the top of the stretch, every little quiver of my hands is like an earthquake! For my Comfort Zone I actually have a stand to which the binoculars attach. It has an arm rest. It pivots. It swirls. And that's when I'm locked in."

Ten years from now Michael would like to still be calling races. He said, "I'd like to be more entrenched ... carving a niche for myself. And that's been a bit of a frustration. I think it's been detrimental to people identifying with me. They can't keep track of me, and I can't keep track of me either. And I would like to have become more engrained at a particular circuit or a particular track where there is more of an identity. It has seemed very elusive for me."

"Hoo roo!" is Michael Wrona's signature wrap-up at the end of the race day at Golden Gate Fields. His brother Wayne reflected on his brother's passion: "Michael's career really is amazing. He really did start at the bottom and work his way up.... In doing so, he has never forgotten where he came from, and he understands the rewards of hard work. But unfortunately, Michael has suffered both mentally and financially over the years spent in America as his calling position has changed along with the management and owners of tracks. This has seen Michael out of work, sometimes for lengths of time. It's a great pity that the work and demand for such a talented and refined caller has been inconsistent and intermittent. But race calling is Michael's life. There simply isn't anything else out there in the world for him."

Michael Wrona agrees: "For all the setbacks and disappointments I've had, I know that these days there's no such thing as job security for anybody. So why not be doing what you love?"

CHAPTER 5

Terry Wallace

Terry Wallace: "Here they come into the stretch of the Arkansas Derby, and it is Smarty Jones who takes command and draws clear by three lengths.... It is Smarty Jones one step for the Kentucky and one giant step to five million dollars!"

"They're in the gate. And they're off in the 71st Arkansas Derby!" exclaims Terry Wallace as ten three-year-old colts erupt from the gates at Oaklawn. It is April 14, 2007, and this is the signature race at the Midwestern track that opened in 1904.

Terry Wallace has the distinction of calling the most consecutive races of any announcer at the same racetrack. The racetrack is Oaklawn Park in Hot Springs, Arkansas, and he's been doing it every year since 1975.

Terry said, "This is a job worth guarding. You don't want to let anybody get a foot in the door." He lucked out one winter when he got sick and couldn't get to work; the races were cancelled that day due to a snowstorm. Because of his longevity, Terry Wallace is known as "The Most Recognizable Voice in Arkansas."

"I didn't start out to set this record, but it got that way, and I am so used to coming to work and being a part of everything, and that's just the way it is," remarked Terry. "There are generations of kids who have only heard my voice, and now are raising their own kids."

Terry credits his work ethic to the strict upbringing that he received from his parents. He was born on June 21, 1944, and grew up in Cleveland, Ohio. His father, Ed, put in long hours in the Dan-Dee Company, a regional snack-food company. His mother, Millie, worked hard as a stay-at-home housewife.

Terry's childhood was a traditional one that he shared with his sister,

On April 9, 2010, Terry called Zenyatta's 16th consecutive win. "It is Mike Smith and Zenyatta in a triumphant return to Oaklawn."

Judy, who is five years older. Because of their age difference, they didn't hang out together, but he could be a pest. When Judy's husband was courting her, Terry liked to join them in the living room and blare away on his trumpet. Judy's future husband paid Terry a dollar to get outta there!

Judy recalled, "Being that he was younger than I am, sometimes he got in my way.... We were the typical brother and sister. We came from a loving home.... We weren't what you'd call a wealthy family, but when we wanted something, our parents usually gave it to us. Like at Christmastime if the finances were there."

Terry played ball with the neighbor kids and attended Catholic schools. When he didn't make the sports teams at St. Ignatius High School due to being short and chubby, he exercised his writing talent and wrote for the school paper. He ended up being the sports editor.

Sports always played an important role in his life. And growing up in a suburb of Cleveland, it was natural to be a fan of the Cleveland Browns. Terry said, "I loved sports right from the beginning. So the only clash I ever had was between sports and education, and I chose sports. Could have gone either way. Would have had a good deal of success, but it looked to me that there was a chance to make a better living with sports."

As often happens, he gained more insight from one very miserable job that he had than from all of the good ones. His father had a hand in his getting work in a tool and die making plant in the summer of 1963. Terry did not enjoy the tedium of drilling holes in copper tubing. The added chance of losing a finger didn't inspire him either. He was frustrated when he couldn't finish a pan full of pieces needing to be drilled before a new pan was placed before him. He said, "You don't even have the pleasure of looking at the completed pan.... But that taught me a lesson about what I wanted to do in life. That made me sure I wanted to get an education and get a job that was more challenging for me and more fulfilling."

Terry enrolled in Xavier University in Cincinnati, Ohio, and majored in modern languages. He took off one year and spent it at a seminary, but he quickly realized that he didn't want to become a Roman Catholic priest. After he got his BA degree, Terry spent a glorious year at the Sorbonne in Paris, France. He never lost his love of the City of Light and has returned several times. On two occasions he traveled with a group that was put together by the late Lee Tomlinson, who created popular pedigree research for the *Daily Racing Form*. Those travels included the Prix de l'Arc de Triomphe at Longchamp Racecourse. Terry called them joyful trips and said, "It is always fun to go back to Paris." He was especially excited to witness the great Dylan Thomas win in 2007.

Terry's career in racing began as a summer job while he was going to college. Cincinnati's racetrack was, and still is, River Downs. Terry was a press box runner. He met a lot of people while he earned money getting food and drinks for the guys in the press box and placing their bets. It turned out to be a great place to watch the races, and Terry got interested in the Sport of Kings.

Fast forward through college graduation, his year in Paris, and returning to Cincinnati to teach high school kids to speak French. In the summer of 1967 Terry returned to River Downs' press box. Jim Hines was the announcer, and he overheard Terry pretending to call a race in French. He encouraged him to call a few races in English and gave him suggestions.

Later that year fate stepped in. Jim Hines was calling races at the Great Barrington Fair in Massachusetts which, in those days, handled a million dollars through its pari-mutuel windows as well as another million through the bookmakers. John Battaglia, the manager of Latonia (now Turfway Park), called to see if Jim could fill in for Chic Anderson. Chic was the regular announcer, but his schedule overlapped with Arlington's by ten days. Jim couldn't, but he suggested that John contact Terry. John declined, because he wanted a more experienced person.

Two days before the Latonia meet, the replacement was seriously injured in a traffic accident in Lexington, Kentucky. That's when Terry received the life-altering call from John Battaglia. He immediately accepted the last-minute assignment. He had the energy and enthusiasm of youth; he taught school during the day and announced races at night. And after ten days, it got even better. He met Chic Anderson.

Terry recalled, "That was pretty cool because Chic was a great announcer. As great an announcer as we've ever had. And I met him. I was filling in for Chic Anderson. And it went ok. I was like any new kid. I studied the horses every minute they were on the racetrack. It was a big deal for me. Night racing is harder. It's harder on the eyes. It's a tough schedule. But for me, I was rolling!"

Terry continued to teach, but he filled in for Chic at Churchill Downs, Latonia, Miles Park, and Ellis Park. And he continued working at River Downs in the summers. And the more he enjoyed racing life, the more he considered doing it full time. At one point, when he was coaching track, field, and cross country, he interviewed at Moeller High School for a job with Jerry Faust, the same Jerry Faust who went on to become head football coach at Notre Dame. Terry, however, felt that there was a chance for him to work full time in racing through the *Daily Racing Form*. It was the summer of 1971, and he combined writing for the *Form* with announcing at the track where it had all started: River Downs. Terry also announced at the winter meet at Florida Downs (now Tampa Bay Downs), continuing to add to his resume.

Terry talked to people who had been in the racing business for 40 years who were still learning new things. He said, "This is pretty interesting stuff. And the other thing that occurred to me is that there are not that many people into it at [the announcing end.] The competition may not be as tough. You may have a better chance of making it to the top in the racing industry than you might in some others because you might be able to get there on your merit rather than having to know somebody."

Terry witnessed history being made in 1973 on the first Saturday in May. He was Chic Anderson's back-up man and was standing behind him right there in the announcer's booth at Churchill Downs when Secretariat shattered the Kentucky Derby record for one and a quarter miles. More than

34 years later, Big Red's world-record time of 1:59⅖ still stands. Terry declared, "Secretariat fed my initial enthusiasm."

In 1974 Terry had been a racetrack gypsy long enough, and he was ready to settle down. He was still heavily involved with writing for the *Daily Racing Form*, and he reached an agreement with them to move to Fair Grounds Race Course in New Orleans. He arrived there on Thanksgiving weekend.

Three weeks into the meet, Terry got a call from the general manager at Oaklawn Park. His announcer was leaving and was Terry interested? Terry decided to go for it: "I hated calling the *Racing Form* people after we had just agreed on this thing." But the rest, as they say, is history. Terry Wallace has been at Oaklawn Park ever since.

Terry had married Susan whom he met at Xavier University. Their first child was born in October, but he died two months later from a liver problem. Soon after, Susan became pregnant with another son, but when she was seven months into the pregnancy, she had a stroke. She was hospitalized, and Ernie was born two months later. But the stress of her illness and Terry's constant moving around took its toll. The marriage did not last.

Since Oaklawn did not open full time until 1995, Terry spent 20 years working at the Hot Springs track part-time. Therefore, he was able to announce for 14 years at Omaha's Ak-Sar-Ben racetrack during the summer. And in the fall and winter he worked as a jockey agent for Eddie King at the Hawthorne meet in Chicago. "Everything has been built upon racing for me. Racing has been my closest companion for thirty-five years," Terry reflected.

Bill Peters ran Mariah's Storm at Ak-Sar-Ben. She was the mare who inspired the popular 2006 movie *Dreamer*. He said, "It was a big stakes race, and that was right after she got hurt. Nobody thought she had a shot, but she won and set a track record." Bill has known Terry over 35 years at both the Nebraska track and the Arkansas track. He declared, "I like Terry. Terry's a nice man, and he's been good down here [at Oaklawn.] Good to the people down here and good for the track.... I've never seen Terry have a lot of bull about him. He's pretty down to earth. And we don't need that bull around the racetrack. We get enough of it anyhow."

It was at Ak-Sar-Ben where Terry's race calling of Who Doctor Who captured the public's attention. Terry's enthusiastic shouts of "WHO DOCTOR WHO?!" shined the spotlight on the two-year-old bay Thoroughbred. It didn't hurt that the horse was fast. He was the favorite of the locals at the Nebraska track, and he raced until he was nine. And he always drew a crowd.

His popularity was evident in the July 23, 1988, match race between the gelding Who Doctor Who and the filly Explosive Girl. After the fan favorite surged ahead to win, many ecstatic fans left the grounds. Amazingly, they departed before the Cornhusker Handicap that future Hall of Famers Bill Mott's horse won and jockey Julie Krone rode.

In July 2007 Terry Wallace was inducted into the Nebraska Racing Hall of Fame. He had been forever linked with the well-loved horse that was euthanized at 24 because of laminitis. "I hated to see the departure of a horse with whom I was so identified," said Terry. "I'm sure it is my calls of Who Doctor Who, more than anything else, that put me there [in the Nebraska Racing Hall of Fame]."

But it was at Oaklawn that Terry found his niche. And it wasn't just in race calling. Besides being the track announcer, Terry became the director of media relations in 1984 and has held the position ever since. And now he is a member of the Oaklawn Senior Management Team. During the racing season, he handicaps a half-hour show on race days, and during the rest of the year, he is the simulcast host.

Terry said, "When you're the spokesperson for the track, you get to steer the course a good part of the time. When I was a younger guy, the idea that I could not just work at the racetrack but have some influence in the directions that we took, that would have been the ultimate end.... I'm so much different than the majority of race announcers because I'm so involved in so many things."

In 1985 Hall of Fame jockey Gary Stevens won the Arkansas Derby on Tank's Prospect. The now-retired Gary said, "He has his own distinct style. You hear him. He's got a distinct voice. And when you hear him, there's no mistaking it's him."

Terry has a mouse pad with the champion mare Azeri and Take Charge Lady who are in exact rhythm as they fight to the end in the 2003 Apple Blossom. And in 2004 the gallant six-year-old mare won that prestigious race for her third straight victory. Terry announced, "Here they come into the stretch of the Apple Blossom, with Azeri the leader. Wild Spirit moving up on the rail to challenge. Island Fashion to the outside.... There's a furlong to go. Azeri with the lead. Wild Spirit can't get to her! Azeri opens two lengths. It is the great champion Azeri trying to pull off another one at Oaklawn. Azeri in front a length and a half. She has done the impossible!"

John Servis trained Smarty Jones, the very popular dual classic winner in 2004. His take on Terry: "Well the one thing about Terry, he wears a lot of hats. You know, he's the announcer. He's the handicapper. He's the head

Terry called all three of champion Azeri's Apple Blossom wins. Credit: Tom Ferry.

of publicity. He does a lot. He works very hard. You know, when you think of Oaklawn Park, you think of Terry."

It was Smarty Jones's spring campaign that put Oaklawn on the map for most people. The chestnut horse won the Southwest Stakes, the Rebel, and the Arkansas Derby, and all of those races took place at Oaklawn. When the son of Elusive Quality entered the 2004 Kentucky Derby, he went into it having never lost a race. What made it all even more exciting was that Oaklawn's owner Charles Cella had offered a five-million-dollar "centennial bonus" if Smarty won the Kentucky Derby. The Smarty Jones team of owners Roy and Pat Chapman, John Servis, jockey Stewart Elliott, and the courageous colt prevailed and won the Run for the Roses on May 1, 2004.

John Servis reflected, "You know, having Terry on board and through the whole Smarty Thing was great. Really was, and I think he's kind of Mr. Cella's left-hand man.... When Mr. Cella came up and gave us the bonus, Terry was there. He came up with Mr. Cella, flew up in his jet. He covered everything with Smarty.... When all the press really started heating up, he always ironed everything out, made sure it was comfortable for me, and he was a big asset to me through that whole thing. And he's a good track announcer."

Unlike many announcers, Terry often visited the barn area. The old barns all have names of famous horses that raced at Oaklawn: Alydar, Count Fleet, Susan's Girl, Lady's Secret, Snow Chief, Elocutionist, and Kelso! John Servis operated out of Vanlandingham. He recalled, "Terry was always here for me. That was even before everybody knew Smarty was as good as he was. And the fact that it was our first year here, and he came back a few times, made sure we were comfortable, everything was going well, if we needed anything. So like I say, he's a whole lot more than just a track announcer."

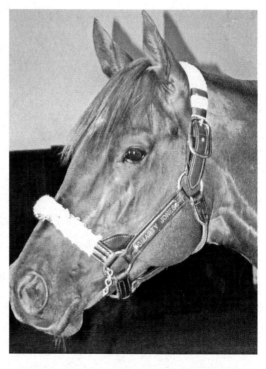

Smarty Jones, standing at Three Chimneys Farm in Midway, Kentucky, needs his own secretary to answer his many fan letters. Credit: Tom Ferry.

Afleet Alex arrived at Oaklawn in the spring of 2005 and attempted to follow Smarty Jones's formula for success. But he passed up the Southwest Stakes and instead won the Mountain Valley handily. Then a lung infection hurt Alex in the Rebel. However, he showed his class in the Arkansas Derby when he won by eight lengths. Terry called the race: "Here they come into the stretch of the 69th Arkansas Derby with Afleet Alex showing the way.... But Afleet Alex has kicked it into gear! One of the most impressive Arkansas Derby wins ever! Afleet Alex blowing the field away! He'll win this one by up to eight lengths!"

His trainer Tim Ritchey returned to Oaklawn the following year. He shared his impressions of Terry Wallace: "He has a very distinctive voice. He's very knowledgeable which also helps. He's been a great asset obviously to Oaklawn Park because he does a lot more than just announce the races. I've done a few interviews with him, and he asks the right questions. When it was with my horse, Afleet Alex, he asked the pertinent questions at the right time. What was my training routine between the Derby and the Preak-

Popular trainer John Servis and his son, John Tyler, visit multiple graded-stakes winner Rockport Harbor. The four-year-old son of Unbridled's Song was retired due to an injury on March 20, 2006, the day this picture was taken.

ness, because we never breezed him. We just galloped him. What were the thoughts behind training him twice a day some days?" Tim appreciated that Terry found positive points to tell the fans about the horses.

Tim had four track announcers that he liked best: "Terry Wallace actually is very good. Tom Durkin I think is very good. Dave Johnson is good. Trevor Denman is outstanding in California. Those are the four that I think bring something special to the game because they have distinctive ways of calling races, and they go through the whole field, and they do it in a professional way. So if I was going to pick them, I'd pick those four as the top ones."

In 2006 Oaklawn Park maintained its reputation for attracting top three-year-olds when the spectacular Lawyer Ron won all three stakes races there in the spring. His 73-year-old trainer, Bob Holthus, is the winningest trainer ever at the Spa. Bob said, "Terry is a workaholic. He's at the track long before daylight every morning working all day long.... He loves the sport and does an excellent job of calling the races."

Terry reflected on his race calling skills: "I'm just a brute memory guy. I tried doing the crayons and then I found myself relying too much on the program. I'm better off relying on my brain power.... People are sometimes surprised that announcers don't have spotters, but there's no way in racing that you can have a spotter."

There are always races that track announcers would like to have back to call. Even the best announcers. Terry admits,

> I've called the wrong horses along the way. Fortunately that never happened in a major race. Every time you open your mouth, something stupid is likely to come out.
>
> My first live TV race was the Arkansas Derby in 1986. It was an awful day. Stormy. Tom Durkin was a commentator for ESPN and was down in the infield. He even got struck by lightning. Full field of fourteen. We haven't had fourteen since then. So there were fourteen in that awful slop and in that awful condition. There were four horses in red silks, and Rampage happened to be one of them. When they were on the final turn, and because of the storm you had a crowd of 60,000 people or so jammed into this grandstand so the sound waves from the crescendo were building up anyhow. And you were holding your glasses steady, and the whole building was shaking. And this field was kind of all coming together. And I had to try to figure out who that horse was who was sneaking through on the inside. And the only thing I could find was a little spot of red because the horses were all mud covered. I saw a little spot of red and took a stab that it was Rampage. He did get through and ended up winning the race, and I called the right horse!

On March 31, 1995, Terry hit the Pick Six. The timing was great because he had been offered the full-time job at Oaklawn and was able to put a down payment on a house. Before taxes, it was $77,000. "Three days later I finally got to sleep," he said.

Oaklawn earned its nickname, the Spa, due to being located in Hot Springs. The quaint town in central Arkansas first attracted visitors to its medicinal bathhouses. Not only did Terry feel right at home at Oaklawn Park, but he was also ready to put down roots in the town. He explained, "Nobody likes what they do better than I do, and the beauty about this is when I'm done with the races every day, I'm still in Hot Springs, Arkansas which is just wonderful. A lot of other guys might be at a track with a bigger name, but they have to deal with a lot of things that I don't have to deal with."

One thing that Terry did have to deal with was the end of his second marriage to Kayleen. He had met her when he was announcing at Ak-Sar-Ben. She was a native of Iowa and had just graduated from college. They had two children, Jake and Sarah, but the lifestyle of so much time on the road took its toll.

Eight years later Terry found happiness with Marty. By then he was settled in Hot Springs, and his girlfriend didn't have to deal with the on-the-road living.

Marty Walker grew up in Hot Springs, where she went to school with future president Bill Clinton. After her father and his sister died of cancer during her senior year of high school, she left her hometown. When her 28-year marriage ended in divorce, she returned to her roots and found work at the convention center. One day during lunch with Bill, a track worker, she told him, "You can find me a man ... a nice man, that's all that I require." She added that he should speak English and have teeth.

Bill called her 30 minutes later with Terry's name and number. Marty remembered, "I called him not that day but the next day, and then it took him several calls before he finally asked me out ... we've been together ever since."

Marty is now the business manager for the Miss Arkansas office. She enjoys running her office and schedule. But, she said, Terry's passion for his job is on a totally higher level: "To be honest, I've never seen anybody just love their job like he does, and he wants to make it so good for everyone else. He loves making it exciting. He loves people so it's fun for him to do. This is the honest truth. He just sees the good in everybody. He's a very positive person. I sometimes tend to get a little down or nitpicky. He won't let me. He's amazing with his attitude and his stamina too. He puts in so many long hours ... I have been able to adjust to his schedule. And I know how important his job is to him. So I don't fuss. Now sometimes I get a little tired of having to sometimes play second fiddle, but that's ok. He does a good job, and people in this state just love him."

Terry found another passion: helping to fight cancer. He became heavily involved with the American Cancer Society and Relay for Life. His father died of lung cancer, and his sister, Judy, is a 20-year survivor of cancer. Judy noted that Terry was the one who got her involved in the Relay for Life. She said, "He came up and walked with me along with my husband."

Marty credits Terry with saving her life. She was having a few symptoms, but wasn't due for another colonoscopy yet. After Terry hounded her daily, she decided to shut him up and went ahead with the exam. She said, "He saved my life because it was there, and I was at a stage 2½, not quite a

3. They caught it early ... I was shocked. I was not expecting that call at all. But I was so fortunate. It was just a blessing, and it was all because of him."

Marty emphasized that Terry enjoys meeting people in the community through his cancer work. She explained, "Because of who he is and because of the kind of person that he is, people really react to him and will respond to his asking them for something. Since he started Relay for Life, they have raised over two million dollars, in ten years. Hot Springs isn't that large of a community. We are the #1 Relay for Life in the state, and 99 percent of it is because of his dedication and leadership."

Terry knows that he will continue to volunteer in the health field: "I will always be devoted to the cause of getting rid of cancer. Helping folks will be how I will spend my retiring years."

However, Terry Wallace is having way too much fun at the racetrack to retire yet. And Oaklawn is a fun-loving track. There are cartoons by PEB everywhere that reflect the sense of humor that exists at this Midwestern track. Terry admits, "We are silly around here sometimes, and we don't mind being silly to make it fun for the people who come here. And that's why people keep coming in the door." This attitude was evident on St. Patrick's Day when the "guest speaker" called the entire race with an Irish brogue.

Unlike many of today's tracks, Oaklawn Park attracts young fans as well as the older handicappers. It helps that Oaklawn is the venue of the only professional sport in the state. And it has been around for over 100 years. Terry said, "It's a fun place to gather. Attitude has a lot to do with it. Maybe it's just the people here too. Arkansans have a little chip on their shoulders about everybody else in the world who talk about the greatest of everything. So as a result, our people do have a regional feeling about the racetrack.... Everybody in New York doesn't go to Aqueduct, but everybody in Arkansas goes to Oaklawn."

Just like Terry Wallace, Oaklawn Park is going strong. It is the only racetrack in the United States to receive the prestigious Eclipse Award for Lifetime Achievement and Service. In early 2005 after the previous spring of Smarty Jones, Terry attended the ceremony with track owner Charles Cella. Terry quipped, "There's nothing like an overnight at the Wilshire/ Hilton in Beverly Hills to brighten up one's life. It's the same hotel used for *Pretty Woman*. Julia Roberts failed to show up at the bar that night. The only downer of the trip."

The addition of electronic gaming, Instant Racing, at Oaklawn produces many more dollars than are wagered and continues to guarantee that there will be big purses. Those purses, in turn, attract the big horses. In the spring of 2007 Curlin showed up. The future two-time Horse of the Year won both the Rebel Stakes and the Arkansas Derby. Terry called the Arkansas Derby: "And here they come into the stretch of the Arkansas Derby with Curlin taking the lead.... It is Curlin leading the way. On the inside Storm in May. Flying First Class is there with Deadly Dealer. They're driving for the wire. But Curlin is on his way. He's got an engagement for the Triple Crown races. Curlin is going to decimate this field winning the Arkansas Derby by nine lengths."

And on April 5, 2008, Terry called the great filly Zenyatta who would end the year with nine victories in nine starts and compete for Horse of the Year honors against Curlin who was still racing as a four-year-old. She won with her ears pricked. Terry announced, "And here comes Zenyatta under a full head of steam on the extreme outside. Four of them across the track and it is Zenyatta to the outside with Brownie Points. Ginger Punch can't keep up. It's Zenyatta and Brownie Points as they drive for the wire but Zenyatta under Mike Smith is going to pull away and Zenyatta goes to four in a row with a flawless performance winning the Apple Blossom by four."

Super filly Rachel Alexandra raced at Oaklawn two times in the spring of 2009. On February 15 she won the mile-long Martha Washington Stakes easily. Terry called, "Rachel Alexandra and Calvin Borel just opening up at will with a sixteenth to go. It's a hand ride for Calvin and Rachel Alexandra, a great start to her three year old campaign. She wins it by about seven."

Lucky Terry got to call her again on April 5 when she returned to conquer the Fantasy Stakes: "Here they come into the stretch of the Fantasy! Rachel Alexandra the leader.... But it is Rachel Alexandra and Calvin Borel sitting just chilly as can be. Rachel Alexandra, one of the greatest fillies ever to race at Oaklawn is giving us a spectacular performance in the Fantasy as she draws clear by seven lengths. Rachel Alexandra, a great filly, winning the Fantasy by eight lengths!"

Terry declared without hesitation that announcing at Oaklawn Park has been the pinnacle of his career: "Oaklawn is great for me. And with the Oaklawn experience, the Eclipse Award, and the centennial year with Smarty Jones, all of that happening in one stretch of time, that was really a heady experience."

Everyone agrees that Terry Wallace is a workaholic. And he loves it. He declared, "I love the sport. That's number one. I love to entertain the folks ... I'm emotional. There's no telling what I'm going to say when I'm calling the race. They tell me I've surpassed 19,000 races called here at Oaklawn without a miss. I'd like to get to 20,000, Good Lord willing." On March 25, 2010, he did.

CHAPTER 6

Larry Collmus

Larry Collmus: "Any Given Saturday has taken the lead, and he's moving away!"

"They're off in the Sunshine Millions Classic!" announces Larry Collmus. He called his first Sunshine Millions Classic on January 27, 2007, as a full field of 12 older horses charge out of the gate at Gulfstream. Thirty-four to one long shot McCann's Mojave wins the one-million-dollar race.

Larry Collmus will never forget the 1996 Massachusetts Handicap (MassCap). And neither will anyone who hears him describe it: "It was Cigar's second MassCap. Jim Moseley wanted to start the track [Suffolk Downs] back up, and he was a local horse owner and businessman who said, 'One day the best horses in America are going to run here.' And everybody said, 'Yeah, yeah, yeah, whatever.'"

Larry continued,

So that day came, and the people came out, and Suffolk Downs which on a good day gets 4000–5000 people, had 23,000 people jammed into the place. And you would have had to be there to really appreciate it, but I'll give you a good idea. The stable area at Suffolk is at the top of the stretch. And all the barns are on the far turn, so the MassCap had wall-to-wall people on the outside on the apron, and from the eighth pole up are all the backstretch workers. [The eighth pole is positioned one-eighth of a mile from the finish line. The quarter pole is a quarter of a mile from the finish.] Grooms, and hot walkers, and other trainers and all that. And they lined up at the rail too. So Cigar: they started doing The Walk, you know, like the Kentucky Derby. The horses start making their way over. And as soon as he came out of the barn area, you could distantly hear as he came up the stretch, you could hear this [Larry clapped.] and as he got closer, it got louder, louder, louder, and literally the grandstand was shaking.

One gets goose bumps listening to Larry recount the incredible day. He continued, "And he [Cigar] got a standing ovation for just being there. There was this guy with his daughter on his shoulders holding up a sign, 'We love you, Mr. Cigar.' See, to me, this is what it's all about. But the other thing was: I was like, 'Omigod! I have to call this race!' And I remember I had to put down my head and start to try to relax myself. And, of course, he's in the paddock. The paddock is right here, and the people are just cheering as he's walking around. So then we have to announce the post parade, and you mention his name..."

Larry admits he was really nervous: "The one saving grace I had that kept me together was there was a horse in the race named Hogan's Goat who had this silly name, and he was the last horse to go into the gate, and he just ran in little allowance races all the time. And so I said, 'The last horse to go in is Hogan's Goat' and in my head it was like, 'Ok, Hogan's Goat is in here. We're good. It's just like another race.'"

But it wasn't just another race. It would be Cigar's 15th win in a row before he won again tying Citation's record. Larry described it: "They went by the half-mile pole. Jerry Bailey just didn't want to let him go. He's sitting third [in the 1⅛ mile race], and he just lets him go, and round that half-mile pole, and that horse just shroo! Takes off! And as he makes his move I didn't plan on this, but the words that came out were, 'There goes the legend.' And it had nothing to do with what I said because probably no one could hear me, but just as I had said that, there was just this deafening roar because people had watched him sweep to the lead. And then it was just an exhibition from then."

Larry was up to the call: "The Peerless Cigar putting on a spectacular show. Fifteen for fifteen. Citation's record is next. Cigar wins the MassCap!"

And Hogan's Goat? Larry answered, "He was up the track. But he ended up becoming a claimer, and he ended up here at Monmouth winning five races, and people always laughed because I give him these big calls." Larry was so attached to the horse that he asked for and got the Goat's shoes when he was reshod. When asked if he wanted Formal Gold's shoes, he declined, getting a laugh from the trainer, Bill Perry. Larry chuckled, "Why would I want those? The Goat was *my* horse."

Larry Collmus was born in Baltimore, Maryland, on October 13, 1966. He grew up in nearby Ellicott City and was the youngest of three children. Sally, who was 13 years older, described their childhood: "We had a great childhood, very happy. Things were wonderful until my mom got real sick, and she passed away in her fifties.... I always felt sad that Larry lost his mom at such a young age because my dad was gone so much that he kind of took care of himself as he hit the teenage years."

Larry liked school a lot. He remembered, "A couple friends and I would go to the track after school. I was a pretty good student but not great. I was more interested in other things like racing, but I enjoyed school. I had a lot of good friends, and we had a good time ... I think I still act like a teenager half the time. When I was a kid in high school between classes we'd be in the cafeteria reading the [*Daily*] *Racing Form*. I'd be pretending to call races."

His brother Bob, eight years older than Larry, had a different memory of growing up in the Collmus family: "We were provided for well, and I think we had a comfortable childhood from that standpoint. It wasn't a real loving type of scenario ... Larry had a tough childhood, I would say. Certainly my heart goes out to him. I think about the things he missed out on. He probably saw a lot more of the world than I think he should have had to because he was there alone, and Dad worked at night ... Larry grew up quicker than the rest of us. Dad was a good provider but not a loving type of person."

Larry was 14 and a freshman at the Catholic Mt. St. Joseph High School when his mom, Mary Jane, died after a long battle with breast cancer. She had been a stay-at-home mother who helped run his dad's business. His father, Bob, was a sound engineer for several places in Baltimore. One was the Baltimore Symphony. And another just happened to be the Timonium racetrack.

Larry said, "He was the guy that put in the sound system at the track. My job was to help him out if anything went wrong. He was over at the fairgrounds because it was the Maryland State Fair. He put me at the racetrack because basically I was mechanically incompetent. So if anything went wrong with the sound I would call him, and he would come fix it. So it turned out that I'd be hanging out with the announcer in the press box where I totally fell in love with horse racing, got to know all the people involved, and from there just got the bug to want to do the race calling stuff myself. And it all worked out."

That is an understatement. Brother Bob had worked at Timonium before Larry. To him, it was just a job. To Larry it was a passion. Bob explained, "It was very clear from the very start that when Larry was at the racetrack, he was in his element. I can remember in his early childhood when he started working at the track, there was an elderly gentleman WW Sullivan.... And here's my brother all of fourteen years old, and they would just sit there and commiserate about who was going to win, and I don't know that they even bet on it.... He engaged with all those people who had the love for the track where to me, it was just a place to be, and a job. But for Larry it was home in a lot of ways."

Larry said, "My first real job was working for my father, but I wasn't really doing anything. But the fellow who ran the press box in Maryland was a guy named Eddie McMullen. Eddie kind of let me hang out and got me a job as sort of a gofor and let me have a room where I could hang out and practice my race calls. I worked for him when I was sixteen-seventeen years old, running errands, whatever they needed."

Larry practiced calling races in the room at Pimlico that had previously been used for the photo finishes. He had a tape recorder and diligently called races into it. When his brother came home for visits, Larry played them for him. Bob said, "And then one day Chick Lang heard him up there doing that and said, 'Larry, you know, you're pretty good.' And I guess Larry is sixteen or so, and he said, 'Look, I can't pay you because you're not old enough, and you need to be an official of the track. You can't be paid, but would you be interested in doing this, one race a day?'"

Larry eagerly agreed and became the youngest announcer in the country. He called his very first race when he was only 10 years old at Bowie Racetrack. He left Loyola College of Baltimore after just one semester when Chick Lang, the general manager at Pimlico, offered him the job of backup announcer in Maryland. That lasted for two years.

Larry's sister, Sally, discussed his ability to memorize the field: "The fact that he memorizes like he does is totally phenomenal. He'll be talking away, having a conversation about something totally unrelated and then he'll say, 'Excuse me a second.' He'll turn his back for like thirty seconds to a minute and repeat the color of the silks and what their names are ... and then he turns back to you, has a conversation, and two seconds later he can call that race."

Larry admitted that it came down to a lot of practice: "You've done it so many times that it's sort of second nature. To me, it's just what I've always done, and I've never done anything else.... Try to memorize all the horses, make sure I know who they are before the race, and then basically just call what I'm seeing."

However, recently he did take a voice and speech class. His teacher was another Maryland native, and together they worked on getting rid of his local accent. He wanted to strengthen his voice, but realized that his best asset was his clarity.

Larry credited certain track announcers for influencing his style. Dick

Woolley was at Maryland, and Larry grew up listening to his race calls. Dave "And down the stretch they come!" Johnson was hitting his best stride nationally. Other role models for Larry include Trevor Denman, Marshall Cassidy, and Tom Durkin.

When Larry was only 22 years old, his father died. That was in 1988, and he was the track announcer at Golden Gate Fields in Berkeley, California. He remained at the West Coast track for three years. From 1990 to 1993 he called at some of the fairs too: Santa Rosa, Vallejo, and the Bay Meadows Fair. And Larry filled in at Bay Meadows when needed.

Larry believes that everything happens for a reason:

> When I was out in California at Golden Gate Fields, I thought that that is where I'd be, never even imagined coming back East. My path came quick right to northern California ... and then one day they decided they wanted to change announcers out there. What happened was I had to start looking around, and I found Boston very quick, and I consider myself a New Englander now. And I never imagined ever being in Boston. And that led to Monmouth, and that led to Gulfstream. But there were so many bumps along the way. [Larry was runner-up four different times for jobs at Churchill Downs, Hollywood Park, and Gulfstream Park.] You'd think, 'Now why did this happen, and I thought sure I'd get this job.' And you get all disappointed and they say, 'Well, you know everything happens for a reason.' And it's so true.... It seems like every place I've been, I never imagined being there, and every place, I've felt like I belonged there.

Along the way Larry learned the art of getting out of a tight spot: "I think that that's something that again is an experience factor. After calling so many races, you just get better at that. Instead of a pregnant pause, you come up with some sort of seamless segue. You just go right back to the front and hope that 99 percent of the people have no idea that you're an idiot, and you don't know who that horse was. You just go on with it. But if you have a pregnant pause of a few seconds, chances are more people would say, 'Well this guy doesn't know what's going on.' Just go back to the front and let things sort themselves out. We all have better days than others."

Larry's most embarrassing race was the 2001 Molly Pitcher at Monmouth Park. It was also one of his saddest races because the six-year-old mare License Fee broke down. Larry recalled,

> They've changed the infield here, but there was this huge bunch of trees on the backstretch. And she was right up with the leaders. I went back to call the horses in the back, and when I came back to the front, she was gone! Couldn't find her, and she was the heavy favorite in the race, and I said in the call, "License Fee must have fallen."

Now if you're watching the race on TV, you see it. But I didn't because I was calling the horses in the back of the pack, and by the time I got to the front, she had fallen. Pat Day [her Hall of Fame jockey] was under the rail so I couldn't see him. She was behind a tree so I couldn't see her. And I didn't know what happened to them. I literally had no clue. As soon as the race was over, I ran into the stewards and I said, "What happened?"

And then they showed them down on the track. Unfortunately, she had broken down so that was pretty sad. But, at the same time, for me it was very embarrassing, because I didn't see it happen. You hate for that to happen.... A lot of times it's a lot of you're in the right place at the right time. It really is.

Larry was able to help Travis Stone land his announcer's job at Louisiana Downs. He had good advice for aspiring track announcers: "Go to a racetrack and get a tape recorder, a pair of binoculars, and just start practicing more and more, listening to yourself, just honing your craft. I think I called 500–600 races into a tape recorder before I ever called a real race on a mike. I think that's what you have to do. You really need to practice a bunch of times cause you'll get better, and there's nothing like a live race in person. Totally different thing trying to call it off the TV."

He added, "The other thing I would teach them is patience because it's not easy to get a job in this business. There are so few openings. A guy like Travis was able to get a track like Louisiana Downs. It's a great place to get started. A lot of guys have to work as a backup announcer at a small track or start a full-time job at a very small track. It's not easy. Then once you get in there and once you get the job you want to do, the main thing is treat people right. Be nice to people, especially the people you work with. Because, I think, that's how you're going to be judged. Other than your skills as an announcer, if you're not a good person and don't treat your co-workers right, you'll be frowned on."

Larry lives by that philosophy both on the racetrack and off. In his personal life he never married, but he is a good uncle to his six nieces and nephews. And his sister listed loyal and caring among his qualities. She said that he had a Lhasa apso when he was young. Boomer got hit by a car and killed soon after his mom died. She said, "I couldn't believe that that could happen to that kid."

Sally wanted to do something special for Larry's 40th birthday. She succeeded by surprising him with a party made up of his family and landlords and racetrack friends. It was the weekend before his actual birthday, and he was at a sports bar in Boston with a friend watching a Patriots game. Sally said, "I walked up first and kind of tapped him on the shoulder and said,

Future two-time Horse of the Year Curlin schooling in the Monmouth Park paddock.

'Happy birthday!' And literally he stood up so fast that he knocked his barstool over."

Larry remembered, "In walks my brother, his wife, my sister, her husband. What the hell is going on?! My sister plotted this whole surprise 40th birthday party for me. It was really cool."

Larry called races at Suffolk Downs in Boston beginning in 1992. He continues to call races there when his schedule allows him to, because he loves the people whom he works with there. And he loves Boston. Larry noted, "I just got the Lou Smith Award, and it's for contributions to New England racing 2006 ... I was proud of that cause I've got so many friends in New England. It meant a lot."

He became the track announcer at Monmouth Park in 1994 and remains at the Jersey Shores racetrack, host of the first two-day Breeders' Cup in 2007. This easy-to-get-around track has a friendly paddock judge named

Like many track announcers, Larry (right) handicaps the races and gives the daily scratches, here at Monmouth Park.

Cookie. And there's Joe, a valet, who exercised the great Kelso when he was a two-year-old. Fans know their racehorses, and they are not turned off by the suffocating August humidity. The green-and-white stripes and picnic tables remind one of Saratoga (only there the stripes are red and white), and it has to compete during its summer meet with its more prestigious neighbor 200 miles to the north. However, on Haskell Day, Saratoga looks deserted when the top trainers and jockeys head to Monmouth Park.

In 2007 there was one of the best fields ever invited to compete in the one-million-dollar Grade I race for three-year-olds. That season's colts had been compared to the 1957 greats: Bold Ruler, Gallant Man, and Round Table. Runner-up in the Derby, Hard Spun was entered with his fun-loving trainer, Larry Jones, and his jockey, Mario Pino, who had regained the mount after losing it for the Belmont. Trainer Steve Asmussen and jockey Robby Albarado had complete confidence in Preakness winner Curlin who had been schooling all week in the paddock. Cable Boy with local trainer Patrick McBurney and local jockey Jose Velez Jr. was the favorite for the hometown crowd who had never seen him lose in his three races there. Todd Pletcher

From the best seat in the house Larry calls the horses coming out of the gate.

had won the Haskell Invitational Handicap in 2006 with Bluegrass Cat. This time he brought Any Given Saturday who was coming off of a Grade II win, and the talented Garrett Gomez would be riding him. Rounding out the field were Imawildandcrazyguy, Xchanger, and Reata's Shadow. The only horse missing for the showdown was Kentucky Derby–winner Street Sense.

More than 43,000 fans watched the thrilling race, and Larry's call matched the exciting stretch run: "They're turning for home in the Haskell. And Hard Spun has taken the lead. Any Given Saturday. Cable Boy gives way. Curlin's coming. They're into the final furlong. Any Given Saturday has taken the lead, and he's moving away! He's opening up the lead. He's in front by three from Hard Spun and Curlin who will battle for second behind a powerful performance by Any Given Saturday in the Haskell!"

Curlin lost that day, but he would go on to be Horse of the Year in 2007 and again in 2008. Larry was one of many who thought he would win the 1¼ mile race that August 5th. He had been quite impressed with him when he called his maiden race on February 3rd at Gulfstream: "Curlin! Wow! He's fourteen lengths in front!... Look at Curlin. Curlin romped!"

Gulfstream hired Larry for the 2007 meeting, and Larry saw it as the pinnacle of his career. He said, "I just loved the atmosphere! I had fun with the people I worked with. They're a great crew to hang around. And you get to call all of these horses! The first thing when I got the job, just whipping though the stakes schedule, 'Who's gonna run in this race? Invasor!' We have all these three-year-olds we haven't even seen yet. And you're just like, 'This is gonna be great!' And it was! It was that good! It lived up to everything that I was hoping it would live up to. It was terrific."

On February 3, 2007, Larry also got to call 2006 Horse of the Year Invasor in Gulfstream's Grade I Donn Handicap: "How good is Invasor! He was stopped, and he wins the Donn in hand! A triumphant return for Invasor. Number one. Invasor was first!"

Dave Johnson ranks Larry Collmus in the second tier of present-day announcers: "Larry is a pro. He's really a good announcer too. And he's a funny person too. He does his imitations too."

Not so much anymore. Larry explains, "The only time I ever do that [impressions of other track announcers] is when it might be a dead day at Suffolk Downs, and I'm just in the mood for it. Somebody says, 'Oh why don't you do it?' Then it might happen. But otherwise it's something that a couple of other people do, I let them do it, and I sort of grew myself out of it, I guess. Some people like it, but I prefer not to."

The XXIV Breeders' Cup was held on two of the worst racing days in the history of the championship, weather-wise. Larry recalled, "We just got deluged with rain which was a shame. And I happened to be upstairs and working with Trevor Denman ... Monmouth Park is so much better when the windows are open, and you can see. Well, on Friday, the wind was blowing straight in on us, and Trevor was actually experimenting every race: windows open, windows closed, one window open, one window closed, and he was getting rained on. Just trying to be able to see."

Luckily conditions improved by Saturday when seven Breeders' Cup races were held. Larry noted, "Even though it rained, the wind direction changed. And when the wind direction went away from us, it didn't bother us at all. Our windows were open, and we were good to go. So that made things very good for us, and that was the big day anyway. I just wish that we'd had better weather. It would have been nice to see just the whole place packed outside all day long, and that wasn't the case because people had to keep running inside to not get drenched. But just to be part of the Breeders' Cup was a lot of fun."

However, he did not watch the races from his announcer's booth. It was a first for Larry to have someone come in and take over his booth. But that's how it's done. The Breeders' Cup, in conjunction with ESPN, brings in its own announcer. That didn't upset Mr. Positive who, in August, discussed the logistics: "It'll be fun because I'll call the undercard, the non–Breeders' Cup races. I don't know where I'll be watching from, but I'll have one of the best seats in the house."

Larry ended up watching from the room next to the announcer's booth. He recalled,

The whole day passed, and these have been great races, and then we see Curlin hit the finish line. And I'm standing there in the press box, and I just look back, and I went, 'Oh, no! We made it the whole day, and there's George Washington. You gotta be kidding me!' [The four-year-old European star injured his right front leg in the homestretch and had to be euthanized on the track.] I was amazed at the speed in which people came over and put up the screens around so that people didn't see. I don't think most people that were there that day had any idea what had happened. That part was very sad. We had made it all the way through. There wasn't a single horse in the two days despite the sloppy and bleak conditions and the soft turf, and the whole thing, everybody made it around, and then the last race. This horse with such a huge reputation in Europe. That has to happen. It was a shame. And because he was the only one, that pretty much tells you, you can't blame it on Monmouth Park.... No, I don't think it was [the track.] It was the track in that he wasn't used to conditions like that so it was a shame that it happened, but I don't think the track was unsafe.

Larry says, "Ten years from now, I'd love to be doing exactly what I'm doing. I have a great circuit between Monmouth and Gulfstream."

And Curlin? In January 2008 Larry looked back: "Curlin was fantastic! He's obviously the best horse in the country, and there's no doubt about it. I've always had a little bit of a soft spot for him because he broke his maiden here [at Gulfstream Park], and I got to call the race.... You knew he was going to be something special, but nine months later, that he'd be the winner of the Breeders' Cup Classic after just breaking his maiden here at Gulfstream! I would love to see him come back."

Another impressive three-year-old colt appeared at Gulfstream on March 29, 2008, and won going away in the Florida Derby. Larry called Big Brown's third race: "As they come to the top of the stretch in the Florida Derby and Kent Desormeaux and Big Brown have the lead. They're in front by four lengths at the eighth pole, and they're widening here from Smooth Air who's been left behind. And Big Brown has done it! Big Brown undefeated on his way to Louisville as he wins the Florida Derby!"

Big Brown went on to triumph impressively in the Kentucky Derby, only the second horse to ever win from gate 20. After his romp in the

Preakness, hardened race trackers and eager fans alike pinned their hopes on the son of Boundary to finally capture the 12th Triple Crown. It was not to be; Big Brown was pulled up by Hall of Fame jockey Kent Desormeaux at the top of the homestretch at Belmont. What happened to the classic colt would remain a mystery, but Larry was in the announcer's booth at Monmouth on September 13th when "Brownie" ran the last race of his career. It was the 1⅛ mile Monmouth Stakes, a turf race that had been created for him. Once again Larry gave the brave colt a terrific call: "And Big Brown to catch. PROUDINSKY! On the outside alongside and then comes Silver Tree and Shakis. Big Brown digs back for all he's got here. Proudinsky cannot get by him and Big Brown wins!!!!!!!! He has won the Monmouth Stakes. He was great on the green."

In 2007 Larry began calling at the Meadowlands' fall meet. It was mostly weekends while he continued to announce at Suffolk Downs early in the week. Larry said it involved "lots of driving back and forth in the fall." And on September 20, 2008, trainer Nick Zito brought his seven-year-old gelding Commentator to run in the historic MassCap. Larry called the race: "There he goes! There's Commentator! And he takes the lead right at the three furlong pole! And Commentator's in charge now. And he's in hand with a two length lead.... And he's into the stretch ... and he's got an eight length lead.... Passing the 16th pole, A tour de force for Commentator in the MassCap."

Bob Collmus talked about what makes Larry one of the top track announcers in the country: "I've seen him in action enough to know that he takes his job very seriously. Accuracy is a very important aspect of his job.... He doesn't try to be overly flashy.... He wants to let the race speak for itself ... I think he works very hard to make sure that accuracy is first and foremost, and that he doesn't take away from what's going on on the racetrack."

In October 2008, Larry was once again at the Breeders' Cup. This time the world-renowned races were being held at the Oak Tree Meet in Santa Anita, and Larry enjoyed every minute of it. He recalled, "I had a great time at the Breeders' Cup. Santa Anita is a terrific place, and it was a thrill to make all of the announcements and actually get to call a couple of races. [non–Breeders' Cup] ... Frankie Dettori may be the single best ambassador for racing. Not only is he a terrific jockey, but he's a flamboyant character who brings life to the sport by just being himself. I'm a huge Frankie fan."

It is obvious that Larry thrives on race calling, and everything that goes with it. He explains, "The best part of my job is everything! I think it is the fact that every race is different. Gives you a chance to use your vocabulary and kind of express yourself in a different way. The other really good part is I get to work with people that I really like. I've got so many friends in racing that I've met over the years.... A lot of these guys will come here, and they'll eat lunch, right here in the announcer's booth with me. And I enjoy doing that because I get a chance to see all the racing guys. We like to hang out. I know a lot of announcer's booths are small. There's just the announcer. But I'm, 'Come on in.' I think that is a great part of the job. I've met all these people that I've had the chance to meet."

Larry plays golf. He religiously watches the Boston Red Sox. He loves football and the New England Patriots. He likes to go to the gym and exercise. But his passion is horse racing. For him, the worst part of his job is the last day of the meet, saying good-bye to his friends who are also his coworkers.

Larry knows he's lucky: "You know what they say: if you love your job, you're very lucky because most people have to actually work for a living. I don't. I love racing. I love calling races. I've always wanted to do it. And I can actually make a living doing it. There are days when you have a bad day, or you have a big day where you have to do a little additional work and get more prepared. But that's not stress. That's a good thing. That means that that day matters. So that's how I feel. I'm a lucky guy. Real lucky."

CHAPTER 7

John Dooley

*John Dooley: "To her long list of laurels you can add the Beldame....
Here she is.... Go for Wand a decisive winner of the Beldame."*

*"Away and running at Arlington," proclaims John Dooley in the 29th
Running of The Black Tie Affair Handicap on June 21, 2008. Eight
horses race down the homestretch at Arlington Park, and Gentleman
Chester beats the favorite Fort Prado to the wire.*

"You know, you're not going to believe this, but I'm your announcer
today. I'm John Dooley, your announcer, but I need to rent the best pair of
binoculars you have."

It was October 7, 1990, at Belmont. Regular announcer Tom Durkin
had flown to Paris to call the Prix de l'Arc de Triomphe. His backup, Frank
Dwyer, had just fallen off his horse in a celebrity ride-a-thon. That left the
backup to the backup, John Dooley.

John explained, "Frank had asked me the day before, 'Would you mind
coming in and doing the program changes?' Anytime you have a chance to
be in the Belmont announcer's booth, I don't care to clean it or call in it, I'd
go up! Windex or binoculars, I don't care!"

Shortly after John had done the changes, publicity director Glen Mathis
came up and asked him, "How do you feel about calling today's card?" Being
a practical joker himself, John figured his boss was kidding. When he realized he wasn't, John charged down to his locker like El Toro in Madrid's
corrida. He grabbed his binoculars, but in his haste, he dropped them on
the floor.

Frantically John ran back up to the booth and peered through the
glasses. Immediately he realized that they were completely out of alignment.

He had approximately 23 minutes before the first race. John said, "I pan-
icked. I went down to the press box, approached Dave Litman, approached
a few people in the press box, 'Can I borrow your binoculars?' But none of
them seemed to have the magnification of what I wanted. So that's when I
actually wound up going down to the binocular rental stand in the clubhouse. Actually waited in line. Maybe it's my polite nature. I was so polite
that I still waited in line looking as time was ticking away until the opener."

John was 24 the day he called Go for Wand winning the Beldame. He
recalled, "Calling a couple of Grade I's that weekend. It was just an incredibly fun experience!"

John Gerard Dooley was born December 21, 1965. His mother, Mary
Ann, promised the patron saint of baby boys, Saint Gerard, that if she had
a healthy child, she would name the boy after him. She insisted, "We're Pol-
ish. 'Dooley' sounds Irish. They refer to him as 'the Irish kid from Staten
Island.' And my husband, John Charles, was Slavic."

Mary Ann worked for the United States Lines when the luxury liner
Queen Mary was the popular way to travel across the Atlantic Ocean. After
her only child was born, she quit and embraced her stay-at-home job like a
child with a new puppy. John Charles worked for United Postal Service, and
John was extremely close to his father. He said, "He was a dedicated worker.
And he was dedicated to his family and was always there for me. He is the
reason I'm so dedicated to my job."

John made the most of each day. His mother remembered, "From the
time he was a little boy John never let a minute go by. He tried to be active
twenty-four hours a day, if possible. It was like every day was precious to
him."

John remembers his parents' unconditional love and support: "Great
parents. I was always very happy because I had a great family." His memories are of a mother who taught him manners, understood his shyness, and
dressed him in shirts and ties for Catholic school at Our Lady of Good
Council. His father worked nights but found time for football, tennis, basketball, and trips to Yankee Stadium and Belmont Park. And there was always
sports: hockey with his friends in the streets, Little League, and Babe Ruth.
But even as John was playing, he "still had that broadcasting itch." John
explained, "As much as I liked being the goalie, or wide receiver, as I was
catching the ball, I'd imagine, 'That was a great catch!' Almost like I'm
broadcasting."

In 1979 John informed his mother that he wanted to be a lawyer when he grew up. Knowing that he loved history, she was not surprised. But in 1981 the family took a trip that would change everything.

That was the summer when John told his parents he wanted to go to a dude ranch for their annual vacation. For a city kid, John thought that "upstate New York" meant Yankee Stadium: "To me there was nothing north of George Washington Bridge." However, his mother found a resort in upstate New York. Hidden Valley Ranch was located on Lake Lucerne, near a town called Saratoga. And it was August. But that first year, fate only set the stage as John and his parents played tennis, rode horses, and swam. They also met Louie Capposella, who was related to the legendary caller Fred Capposella. He and his buddies swapped tales of betting on the ponies.

The Dooleys returned to the Hidden Valley Ranch again the next summer. This time John talked his parents into an afternoon at the historic Saratoga racetrack. John said, "And I went to the races and heard Marshall Cassidy calling the races. And I said, 'You know what? I would love to do that one day.'"

John recognized Marshall's voice over the loudspeaker. It was the same voice he'd heard after school when he sneaked into an off-track betting parlor to practice calling races with his new Betamax tape recorder. He was a sophomore at Moore High School and there were no videos back then of racing. John explained, "Everything was based on the Marshall Cassidy race call. And when Marshall Cassidy said, 'GAINS THE LEAD!' you knew that horse just won."

Mary Ann said that her son is one of the top track announcers in the country because "he has his heart and soul in it." And it all started at the Spa. Mary Ann explained, "That's something he wanted to do. The moment he stepped on the track at Saratoga.... He just looked around and said, 'I'm going to be back here some day. I want to work here. This is what I'm going to do.' That was it."

Back home John became as dedicated about his new-found passion as an Obama campaign volunteer in the fall of 2008. First on the list was to find racetracks near Staten Island. He learned that he and his family had driven right by one each time they'd vacationed on the Jersey Shore: Monmouth Park. John graduated from high school in 1983 and wrote to Bob Weems, the race caller at the Oceanport, New Jersey track. He told Bob about his dream to one day call horse races.

Bob Weems's response set it all in motion. John explained, "He answered my letter and said, 'I'd love to have you come up.' And I would spend almost the entire day with him.... Because of his thoughtfulness, just indulging a

kid from New York, as far as Bob is concerned: sainthood! He was so generous and so open. And every now and then he'd walk outside of the
announcer's booth, and if the phone rang, I'd pick it up. I wasn't sure if I
was allowed to but, 'Announcer's booth!' A kid's dream came through, and
it definitely fueled the fire."

John majored in athletic administration at St. John's University on the
Staten Island campus. He joined Sigma Chi Epsilon fraternity, and was the
disc jockey for Dominating Dooley and the Breakfast Flakes. Rounding out
his broadcasting resume, he was a part-time public address announcer for
the New York Slapshots hockey team.

And on weekends he could be found at the Meadowlands in section
109, row A, seats 1 and 2 with his mom. He said, "I'd bring my tape recorder,
and practice race calls. You'd hear Dave Johnson above, but at the same time,
you'd be calling the race in your mind." Later he'd drag his dad to the Aqueduct fall meeting where it would be "my dad, me, and always Marshall [Cas-
sidy was the announcer for all three New York tracks]. On a cold cold day
at Aqueduct with fifty fans and one hundred pigeons. I would be practicing race calls and just blessed to have two great parents that definitely were
one hundred percent behind me," he remembered.

On Saturday nights while his friends were on dates, John was sprawled
on his parents' floor with his Betamax recording WOR-TV's Charlsie Canty,
Frank Wright, and Marshall Cassidy. And rerecording his version of the race
calls over the original ones from all of the New York racetracks. John
explained, "That's how everyone starts. It makes me wonder how many fans
were born during that era of watching 'Racing from New York.' I am a fan
to this day because of that show."

John Charles and Mary Ann took their support to a new level when
they bought into a partnership for a few racehorses. Mary Ann has happy
memories of owning Thoroughbreds that ran at the Meadowlands, Garden
State, and Philadelphia Park: "When John was just starting out in college I
decided to buy into a partnership so he would have the feeling of owning a
horse. And, lo and behold, a few of the horses came in first and won. He
was thrilled because this way he had the true meaning of what it was
like. He still wanted to be the track announcer and call the races, but
now he had every aspect of it knowing what it was like to go in that winner's circle."

John was a licensed owner, and the trainer was Sal Campo who was
based at Philadelphia Park. John said, "We had some winners. There's a
horse called Four Flora. A horse by the name of Ethereal Moment who actu-

ally became a stakes winner before bucking his shins as a two-year-old. It was a lot of fun.... The best part about being an owner was going to the barn, being in the paddock, and hoping to be in the winner's circle."

His days of owning horses ended when college did. In May 1986, John graduated from college and headed to the Meadowlands. It was the year of John Henry and Bill Shoemaker. And John was interning in the publicity department and learning how to do stats. He was right where he wanted to be. And this led to an internship the following spring at the New York Racing Association (NYRA). By summer he was back where it had all begun: Saratoga. He thrived in the racing atmosphere. Nights closing down the Parting Glass bar were followed two hours later at D. Wayne Lukas' barn getting quotes about Winning Colors, only the third filly to win the Kentucky Derby. "It was a great time definitely working my way up the ladder. But I was a racing fan, not the big gambler," he recalled.

And he met his idol, Marshall Cassidy: "When I finally had the chance to give him one of my race calls that I had completely redone off of the Betamax, he said, 'John, I want you to go practice race calls out on the roof at Belmont, and then I want to hear you call a live race.' I remember Marshall eating a BLT and telling me, 'John, you have a strong voice, and your margins are accurate. I think you have a bright future.' And I never looked back after that."

John was learning from the best. He said, "Marshall is very nice, very proper. I'm glad that I had the chance to work with him. The one thing I learned was the fundamentals first. It wasn't so much the color. It was the fundamentals. Get your names right. Memorize your silks. And Marshall was always so accurate."

That summer John pursued his dream at Monmouth where Lost Code, Bet Twice, and Alysheba were three noses on the wire in the Haskell. He worked hard as the track statistician, and he was living his dream. He recalled, "I was working in horse racing, and it was exciting. The people I met were phenomenal. But I'll never forget the reality of Labor Day. Hal Handel was the general manager of Monmouth Park and he shook my hand. 'John, you did a great job for us this summer. We look forward to seeing you back here next summer.' Somehow it was a long drive from Oceanport, New Jersey back to Staten Island."

The answer to "What do I do now?" appeared when NYRA invited him back for a full-time job. "That was October of 1987, and it started the whole ball rolling. I worked in the press box, and that allowed me the access to practice race calls," John explained. Whether he was doing the morning line odds at Aqueduct, Belmont, or Saratoga, John squeezed in time to hustle up to the roof and practice calling races.

No surprise then that it was during his three-and-a-half years at NYRA that John called his first full card. On September 20, 1989, the *Philadelphia Inquirer* reported the feat: "This afternoon, John Dooley will complete a three-day assignment as substitute track announcer at Philadelphia Park. Dooley, 23, has been filling in while regular track announcer Keith Jones has been on his honeymoon.... Dooley has shown high promise as a track announcer."

John will never forget the first day: "It was a sloppy rainy day, a terrible day. I'd never really worked there. When I called my first race, my hands were shaking. But the second race, I felt I'd nailed it. And I've never looked back."

John asked Marshall to critique more of his calls. Marshall allowed John to call one or two "every now and then, often the last race of the day. You do twelve New York bred maidens [horses that have yet to win a race] at Aqueduct on the inner dirt track, Marshall really schooled me," John said.

But times were changing, and in the fall of 1990 Tom Durkin became the track announcer at the three New York racetracks. Tom told John, "Don't be afraid to add your personality. Add a little bit more of you in your race call."

Looking back, John notes, "What makes a top class announcer is preparation. To me it is the preparation of knowing your first time starter, your trainers, your jockeys, the horses. Preparation is paramount. I learned that from Tom. To see him study and to know exactly what was going to happen during the race."

John credited all of his mentors: "I've tried to incorporate a little bit about what I've learned from everyone. Bob Weems: his humility, friendliness, and befriending people. Marshall Cassidy: the accuracy and being precise. And Tom Durkin: not only the accuracy but the preparation."

In 1991 the *Staten Island Sunday Advance* quoted Tom Durkin, who said, "John has a very bright future.... He's a very good race caller. He's probably a lot better than I was at 25."

Tom was referring to John's new position as the track announcer at Thistledown in Ohio. John was eager to call on a full-time basis, but to his mother, Cleveland was the end of the world! Mary Ann said, "When he took the assignment to go out to Cleveland! Oh! We were losing him at home! It was horrible! But the following week, and that was in the dead of winter, we went out for his Opening Day."

John Gerard Dooley treated his five years at Thistledown like a kid with a scholarship to Harvard. He was young and single, and he was making life-time friends, calling Thoroughbreds, and living life to the fullest:

> I had a great time there, I gotta admit. Thistledown was basically year-round. They would run from March to November. I had a year-round position, and got to know the horses real well. It allowed me to become more descriptive. "Sending a postcard to the others" I think was born there. And "charging faster than a daughter with Dad's credit card" came there.
>
> And when I was in Cleveland I also had a chance to call a diaper derby at the old Cleveland Stadium. These babies were racing for U.S. Savings Bonds. Got to emcee that. The Cleveland Indians had me audition to be the public address announcer at Jacobs Field, but it was just a part-time job, and I'm still a racing announcer, didn't want to give that up.

There were also canoe races to call and animated car races. And in July 1995, John flew to Panama to call the 69th running of the Gran Clasico Presidente de la Republica at the Hipodromo Presidente Remon. It was John's first venture outside the United States. He encountered bomb-sniffing dogs at his feet, and not many people understood his limited Spanish.

John described the day of the race:

> The story behind the race was that they flew me down there to call this race, one of the richest Grade I races in America, for the American fans. Jed Forest was the winner with Rene Douglas, whom I've gone on to call here [at Arlington] for multiple riding crowns. Arlington was going to simulcast the race through Arlington Park to various tracks like the Maryland Jockey Club. It was ninety degrees and one hundred percent humidity. I called from the middle of the grandstand next to the two-person Spanish language crew. It was just me, with my crayon markers, and screaming Panamanians. I'm sweating and calling, "Jed Forest! Jed Forest!" I must have called Jed Forest the whole length of the stretch because I couldn't see because I had people standing in front of me. I remember my great call of the El Presidente del Republica, "Jed Forest! Jed Forest! Jed Forest! Jed Forest!" I got upstairs after the race, and Eddie Royals, our chief steward, said to me, "Well, John, we've got news for you. Nobody heard it." They had satellite problems. At the time Kevin Goemer was the announcer at Arlington, and AP got the race but no race call so Kevin had to recreate it.... My greatest ever race call that nobody ever heard!

No problema! John had enjoyed his all-expense-paid trip to Central America. He acquired a taste for the local beer. And he danced till dawn in the Panama City night club with the publicity director. John said, "I had an absolute blast! Maybe that says something about my personality. I could have put my head between my legs and been just devastated. Instead, 'Cervesa Panama!'"

John returned to Cleveland but he missed the big time, and he missed his mom and dad. In 1996, he returned to the Big Apple: "I had the chance to go back and call winter races. It was too good of a chance. I really wanted to go back home."

In one of his last days at Thistledown, John had a fun time with his announcement: "At River Downs the main track is fast, and the turf is firm. At Thistledown the main track is fast. No turf racing since 1973." Luckily, General Manager Mike McKay had a good sense of humor!

In the 1995 *Staten Island Sunday Advance* article "Big A Means Big Break for Island Native," written by Jeff Mende, John explains how he got his new winter race job: "From what I understand, Durkin and Dave Johnson recommended me to Noe [the NYRA chairman]. That was very generous of them. I owe them a lot."

Tom Durkin is also quoted in the article: "When you get an opportunity to work in New York, it's a big break. John deserves that break. He loves the game, and it shows in his work.... He's enthusiastic about his work and his calls are creative. New York is a perfect fit for him."

Twelve years later, John recalled,

I actually had a great time calling races during those Aqueduct winters. With Tom Durkin spending the winter as the announcer at Gulfstream Park, it gave me a chance to come back home to New York and call again at the Big A.

It could sometimes pose a challenge though during the height of winter. I remember plenty of days when fog, rain, or snow would make it virtually impossible to see a horse, let alone call the field. Of course, a lot of simulcast fans rely on you for a race call. But, it's hard to call what you can't see. So you just struggle through it and hope the weather gods answer your prayers for some sun once in awhile during the inner dirt meet.

I do recall one day in particular though. It seemed like it was a driving rain all day. It was brutal. I felt bad for the grooms, jockeys, and horsemen, who had to endure it all. In the meantime, it had rained so hard, up in the booth, it started to leak a bit. So here is this water dripping onto all of the electrical equipment and wires. Right at that time, I got a call from Tom [Durkin] between races at Gulfstream just to see how it's going. Of course, it was sunny and warm there and here I am jamming paper towels from the men's room into the ceiling to stop the dripping. I remember him chuckling a bit, adding, "Oh my." Somehow I survived that day and eventually would find myself in a warmer climate going down to open up the brand new Lone Star Park in Texas in April 1997.

Friends were astonished that John was leaving New York City and his job as Tom Durkin's assistant. But John believed in the brand-new racetrack at Lone Star Park: "Steve Sexton was one of the people with Corey Johnson that was part of the Lone Star Park Project. I really believed in what they were putting together there. The energy level. The excitement. It was something that I had never seen before. This was fresh, new, young, vibrant. It was very me at the time."

One of John's all-time favorite calls is the Inaugural at Lone Star Park in April 1997: "It seemed as if all of Texas was there. A horse by the name of Iaresharp with Marlin St. Julien won the race. I can remember it like it was yesterday."

John still has his promotional poster of the NTRA All Star Jockey Championship signed by ten Hall of Fame jockeys. He recalled, "Laffit Pincay Jr., Georgie Velasquez, Jerry Bailey, Eddie Delahoussaye, Gary Stevens.... That was fun but definitely a challenge. It was the only time in my career that I called all jockeys in a race. Instead of even mentioning horse names, I called jockey names. It had never been done before. And Lone Star was a new track with the new kid on the block wanting to do something that stood out." In 2008 Trevor Denman would call eight retired jockeys in the Living Legends Race at Santa Anita.

And in 1997 John felt like he had hit the trifecta when he met Heather, a girl at Lone Star who worked in group sales. They got married the next year in Louisville, not far from Churchill Downs. A high point for John was that his friend and fellow race caller Dave Rodman came to the wedding: "He took off nine races to come to my wedding. It was fun to have him there, and I wondered if he was going to call me: 'A quarter to go to get to the pew.'"

Lone Star's schedule enabled John to work year-round. The Thoroughbreds raced April through July. After a break, he called the brief, two-month Quarter Horse meet. John admitted, "I wasn't so interested in that. I'm definitely a Thoroughbred guy. I've called one greyhound race. It was at Phoenix Greyhound Park one day. I was filling in for Luke at Turf Paradise in 2004-5. I said, 'Greyhound home first for all the biscuits.' And I haven't been invited back since," he chuckled. When he wasn't announcing, he worked in publicity or did handicapping.

In 2000 John and Heather divorced, and he got custody of Dallas, the cat. But John has stayed in touch with Heather over the years. He said, "I've always kept my friends close. She was a special person in my life."

Single again, John eagerly accepted an offer in 2000 to announce at two of Chicago's racetracks, Sportsman's Park and Arlington Park. The night before his first Arlington Million, John attended a black-tie affair at Richard Duchossois' estate. Duchossois is the chairman emeritus of Arlington Park. It was an overwhelming week. John recalled,

On a clear day John can see downtown Chicago from his announcer's booth at Arlington Park.

I thought, "Well, I've called a lot of races before. And I've been around a lot of championship caliber horses. This is another Grade I." But really the Million here takes on a new meaning. And you see everything it's gone through. Even when Arlington closed, the fact that the Million persevered and went to Woodbine. And then there was the Miracle Million....

Looking back to 2000, Chester House will always be a special win. The year he won it the Million was a part of the Emirate World Series Challenge which involved the Royal Ascot, Hong Kong, the Arc, and I was calling one leg of it. Chester House is such a special horse to me, and now his offspring are turf crazy! That moment, calling my first Million, was definitely exciting!

John's most memorable Arlington Million was Storming Home in 2003: "It's live on television, and here it is right at the finish so as an announcer, in one breath I'm trying to make a determination, trying to figure out if that happened past the finish line. My first instinct was that it happened right at or on the wire. And as it was ruled by the stewards, they did disqualify Storming Home. But here's Gary Stevens. He's lying prone on the turf course. It was a heart-stopping moment as an announcer.... Then the stewards made their ruling and their disqualification; Sulamani [the declared winner] was a brilliant horse too. He was a Gondolphin horse, the hundredth ever Group I or Grade I winner."

In 2002 at Sportsman's Park John called a relatively unknown colt who was about to take on the world in that year's Triple Crown races: "And they're off in the Illinois Derby! ... There's been no pressure for War Emblem. He's been unchallenged throughout.... And it's War Emblem running to the eighth pole. In front here by five! Repent in a hard drive.... The others well in back of War Emblem who is going to STROLL home in the Illinois Derby. War Emblem and Larry Stirling Junior ridden out to best Repent by seven!"

John described the track: "Sportsman's Park was a grand little track in Cicero, but it went into a partnership that turned it into Auto Racing Meets Horse Racing, and it never took off. A horrible business decision." The race after that year's Illinois Derby turned out to be the last race ever run there even though no one knew it until the following autumn. John explained, "They made the business decision not to run at Sportsman's. Hawthorne [the third racetrack in the Chicago area] absorbed it. And I've never called at Hawthorne. That was the hardest time professionally in my life."

A race caller who is as passionate about the sport as John is wants to be calling races. And January to May of 2003 and 2004 Arlington Park had no live racing. John called a lot of friends, watched a lot of European soccer, and practiced a lot of free throws in the park.

A common thread among all track announcers is the importance of a good racing circuit. Finally John found his when Randy Soth, the general manager of the Fair Grounds in New Orleans, approached him in the fall of 2004. Faster than it takes to eat a dozen raw oysters at Felix's, John accepted the job in the Crescent City. It was a perfect match as the Fair Grounds ran from November to the end of March, and Arlington's live meet was May through September.

But in August 2005, Hurricane Katrina devastated the city of New Orleans. While the elegant French Quarter escaped much of its wrath, the Fair Grounds did not. That year's meet was shortened and held at Shreveport. John called the races from November to February. And then he returned to New York to be with his dad who was dying of cancer. John told his 73-year-old father, "We'll be back in New Orleans." John Charles didn't live to see it, but on Thanksgiving Day of 2006, the Fair Grounds reopened. John had chills as he shouted: "To the cheers of New Orleans, racing is back at the Fair Grounds."

John explained, "It wasn't contrived. It just seemed appropriate. They reached the gate. People started applauding. It was emotional. And Thanksgiving for those people is Fair Grounds, and that is really an incredible city. And I'm glad I've had a chance to be the race caller."

Trainer Neil Howard has listened to John call races both at Arlington and the Fair Grounds. One beautiful afternoon at the New Orleans track he told him, "John, I'm sorry to bother you. I know you're having lunch. I just want to let you know that all of us think you do a fantastic job."

Neil elaborated, "He's absolutely excellent. He's very quick. Very sharp. John is so articulate, and one thing that he does is when a rider is winning a race and going under the wire, he'll refer to the rider and the trainer. 'Another win for Robbie.' It's nice because it illustrates his passion for the game and the people in it."

Dallas Stewart has been training at Fair Grounds since 1985. He pointed out that John adds a lot of flavor to his calls: "He throws a lot of New Orleans sayings into his racing. Very clear. Articulate but not in an annoying way. Straightforward but does have some New Orleans flavor to his announcing, and I think people really like that down here."

One of John's favorite colts was Pyro, who made his presence felt at the Fair Grounds in the 2008 Risen Star Stakes for three-year-olds. John announced, "PYRO! Pyro's coming like a rocket at them! He was last a moment ago. Pyro comes back full __ of __ fire! Pyro! Shaun Bridgmohan for Steve Asmussen.... Well, Pyro's back!"

Yes, John Gerard Dooley is a premier track announcer. But, first and foremost, he is a fan of horse racing. He said, "That was a fun day when Pyro won. It was a very spontaneous call. Definitely when he came back in the Risen Star, it was just a knee-jerk reaction knowing that a lot of eyes were on him, knowing there were a lot of hopes and aspirations going into the first Saturday in May. So instinctively, you're calling a race at the quarter pole at Fair Grounds, albeit a long stretch, but Pyro was last. I think as a fan watching that, whether at home in Staten Island or with Dave Rodman in the Maryland Jockey Club announcer booth, and you looked up and you're like, 'Where's Pyro? He's last!' So I kind of call races as a big fan."

Even if he no longer called races for a living, he would still be a fan. He declared, "No matter where I lived, I would always make a point of going to the track and enjoying a day at the races. I was a fan first. I'd miss the excitement of the job and being able to convey my enthusiasm and passion for the sport."

But John has no plans of leaving the best seat in the house. And his star continues to rise. Breeders' Cup 2005 was held once again at Belmont. John said, "Belmont had me work with Durkin and do all the post parade and pre–Breeders' Cup fanfare. It was the last year that Tom was the Voice of the Breeders' Cup, and I had a chance to work with the person that set the standard for Breeders' Cup announcers. I am definitely a Tom Durkin fan!"

He ranks Breeders' Cup 2006 as the pinnacle of his career:

> Working with Dave Johnson and calling the races for Sirius satellite radio. I was memorizing the field for the Juvenile Fillies, and I remember looking up the stretch at Churchill and thinking, "Wow! Take it all in. You never know when you might have the chance to do it again." Even that one year just having the chance to work with Dave. To see his energy and his preparations! It was just a meticulous telecast! And to be part of this program that broadcast the Breeders' Cup, and that year there was so much excitement between Invasor and Bernardini. [Invasor won the Classic and went on to be named 2006 Horse of the Year.] The fact that Dave suggested me for that, I so wanted to do a good job for him and the rest of the team. I think I just knew that I was part of something unique, dynamic, and special.

John was at the peak, but it had also been a sad year because of his father's death: "Looking up to the heavens, I thought, 'Dad, what you went through was tough. This is what I love to do. Hey, Pop, give me the strength and drive and let me have a great day.' And I felt like he was with me through that day, and I had a spectacular time. Definitely a career highlight."

John admits his biggest superstition: "They could come on the track, and it could be Secretariat in a one-horse race. I'd still do blue and white blocks. When it comes to my markers, I don't care if it's a walkover, I would color that horse in. If not, my binoculars would fall, I'd step on the microphone, something cataclysmic would happen."

Chicago racing fans eagerly look forward to Arlington's three Grade I's in the summer: The Beverly D, the Secretariat Stakes, and the Arlington Million. And one of John's favorites was the 2006 Beverly D. He announced: "And they're off in the Beverly D!" [Turning for home, the favorite Gorella was last.] "Then Gorella is being produced down the center of the Arlington Park turf course. Deep in the final furlong and it's Gorella and Julien Leparoux ... Gorella has become a millionaire filly and she wins the Beverly D!"

John said, "When she won, she became a millionaire mare and gave Julian Leparoux his first career Grade I win! It was a fun race to call with so many high-class horses on the turf."

John has a special regard for the hard-trying geldings. Fort Prado, the gray, seven-year-old son of El Prado, has been a well-loved horse at Arlington Park. Team Block raced the fan favorite into history as he became the first Illinois bred to become a millionaire.

The Tin Man was another extremely popular horse. John said, "He was

Trainer Liane Davis and John host Breakfast at Arlington on Saturday mornings during the summer. Credit: Tom Ferry.

fantastic. And 2006 was Richard Mandella's first ever Million. The Tin Man just showing that heart, and stayed the distance with Victor Espinoza. He was a gelding cut out of the same cloth as John Henry. And having the chance to call him!" John announced: "In the final furlong and a half, The Tin Man trying to see it out. The Tin Man still holding Cacique, Soldier Hollow, and English Channel is one paced. They're coming down to the wire, The Tin Man. It's his million!"

In 2009 jockey Calvin Borel told anyone and everyone that three-year-old Rachel Alexandra is the best horse he has ever ridden. Not filly, but horse. And that speaks volumes since he piloted Street Sense to the Kentucky Derby winner's circle in 2007. John Dooley recognized her turn of foot (capability of speed and acceleration). He called her on March 14, 2009, in the 1¹⁄₁₆ mile Fair Grounds Oaks: "Rachel Alexandra sets the tone in the Fair Grounds Oaks ... Rachel Alexandra continues to dictate her own terms to War Tigress and Flying Spur ... Calvin Borel hand rides Rachel Alexandra ... Rachel Alexandra geared down by Calvin Borel. Rachel Alexandra with a win of quality and class."

Arlington fan favorite Fort Prado at age eight won his fourth Black Tie Affair Handicap on June 20, 2009.

The popular gelding The Tin Man greets his fans before winning the 2006 Arlington Million. Credit: Tom Ferry.

Next to Arlington Park on the corner of Wilkie and Northwest Highway is Jimmy D's Tavern where there is a shot named after J.G. Dooley. And John is philosophical: "While I may never be in Thoroughbred Racing's Hall of Fame, I have a shot named The Voice from Above. It's tropical. I didn't want anything too potent. I've gotta call the next day."

In 2010 John Dooley is very happy with his life. He loves to watch European football. He enjoys history. He likes to travel, and he had the opportunity to call a race at Lingfield Park in England in 2002. In 2008 he went to Dubai, rode a camel, and watched Curlin win the richest race in the world. And recently John combined two of his passions, history and horse racing, when he paid tribute to American soldiers who died in Normandy and saw the Group I Arc at Longchamp.

John never takes a day for granted. He said, "That's what I love about my job. Every day you come in, and there can be a new track record. Or there can be a horse making his or her 100th start like ten-year-old Paul's Dream who made her 101st lifetime start. Or there could be a record superfecta. Or you could have 20–30,000 people here at Arlington for Father's

Day. Every day is a new exciting day. Not every day do you have a chance to call a horse like Curlin or Cigar or Go for Wand or Personal Ensign. But it's the daily routine that I love. Just being able to show my excitement that was generated when a high school kid went to a race course at Saratoga. And twenty years later I can still be like a big kid doing an adult job. And the enthusiasm has never waned."

CHAPTER 8

Luke Kruytbosch

*Luke Kruytbosch: "Down to the final furlong though it's all Barbaro!
Barbaro in front by five, very impressive! Barbaro and Edgar Prado
rolling on to win Kentucky Derby 132."*

*"But it's Proud Spell as she kicks away from the field impressively.
Proud Spell drawing away to romp home in Kentucky Oaks number
134 by five." Luke Kruytbosch called races year-round at Churchill
Downs, Ellis Park, Kentucky Downs, and Turf Paradise.*

He was a man of the people and a shining light at every track where he
announced. His smooth all–American sound seemed to roll off the tongue
like honey butter the moment he declared, "Theeeeeey'rrre off and running." He was only 47 when he died in 2008.

It was easy to feel comfortable with Luke Kruytbosch. His down-to-
earth, no-nonsense persona resonated favorably across the broad spectrum
of the racing industry, from the bread-and-butter race fans, all the way up
to the race officials themselves. After all, in many ways, he was one of them,
cut from the same cloth, if you will.

A graduate of the University of Arizona Racetrack Industry Program in
Tucson, Luke had his sights set on becoming a racing secretary, a job he felt
would allow him to be right in the thick of it, calling the shots as he framed
and filled live race meets.

Luke said, "I thought it'd be great to be a racing secretary, especially at
a track like Belmont, you know, with all those turf courses and different distances you could write. It was just a vague idea, but I wanted to be in the
industry."

As it turned out, Luke would immerse himself in all the form and racing data he could get his hands on but not as a racing secretary. He was to

119

call the shots, not from behind an office desk but from that privileged eye-in-the-sky vantage point known as the announcer's booth.

"I didn't necessarily decide to become a track announcer. I kind of fell into it. I had always paid attention to them. I'd imitate announcers, sports announcers. I used to stay up at night and listen to the AM radio," he explained.

The radio was to prove a constant companion as his family hopscotched around the country. Luke was born in Moscow, Idaho, on May 27, 1961, the same day as world-renowned sire, Northern Dancer. Lucas (Luke) Martin was a mere infant when his family took up residence in Berkeley, California, where his father Carlos was a college professor. Luke said, "My mom was not really formally educated but very very intelligent and could rattle off a *New York Times* crossword. So I was lucky that just from being around them in the house, I'm pretty articulate and have a good vocabulary that's helped me out a lot down the road. Pretty neat. Half the time I wished my dad played pro-football, but now," Luke chuckled, "I appreciate the things he's given me. By osmosis."

Carla, his older sister by five years, rode horses. They both went to horseback riding camp when they were kids in Northern California. Luke admitted, "I'm not a real horse guy. I've worked with horses now, since I've been involved and went to school and looked for jobs and had girlfriends who were trainers and stuff. And I helped them do their chores, but I didn't grow up with horses."

Carla had a different view: "Well what happened was my dad had a contact, or knew, Henry Miller, the rider. So we would go to Henry Miller's little house in a 17-mile drive in Monterey and, there's a golf course there. So my dad used to take us, he would rent a pony and then Luke got on, and the pony threw him, and I guess carried him halfway across the golf course. And so he never got on another horse again," she laughed.

Carla remembered Luke as a very smart and inventive kid:

> Well he had an IQ in the stratosphere, and he had an amazing imagination. I mean he would just go out in our little backyard in Berkeley and he'd have like a hundred little imaginary characters. He'd play in the mud for like seven hours with all these little stick figures and things just concocting imaginary scenarios for them. So that's how you know he was creative enough to develop his crayon coloring. He was just really smart.
>
> He was real even tempered but had that Icelandic personality where when the volcano explodes once every three years, you do not want to be around. Mostly he was super easy to be around and charming but boy, I remember some kids who tried to steal his bicycle. He just ran in and got a kitchen knife.

He was like seven years old, and he was just in this rage. Anyway as a kid he was really sweet, that was just once every three years. Here was this gang of kids, and you'd think most kids would retreat. He was a warrior on the inside. Most people think of him as being really sweet and really kind which he was. Inside when challenged in a big way he would just come out all guns firing.

The second move, to the city of Buffalo, New York, came when Luke was around eight or nine. He said, "I was an A's [Oakland Athletics] fan when I moved to Buffalo, and when the A's were playing, I'd get on the radio late at night. My parents wouldn't like it, but I'd stay up, and I listened to track announcers too. Chic Anderson calling the races."

Moving was one disruption to the family. His mother's alcoholism was another. Carla revealed, "I was the one fighting against my mother's alcoholism. I was always fighting while my brother would just hole up in his room, being the smart one keeping out of it."

His family uprooted again, to McLean, in northern Virginia. Luke enjoyed high school. He said, "We moved around a lot which probably would be a problem for a lot of people, but I always played sports a lot. Everything. Baseball, football, hockey. I was pretty happy in school actually." Luke revealed his creed: "I believe in myself most. I do. Anything I've ever done, I've ended up being good if I've really tried. In sports or anything I was always one of the best."

Carla said that Luke was more adaptable in moving: "He always had a zillion zillion friends.... He was so handsome in HS. He was a football player and I was always getting all these calls: 'How's Luke? What's Luke doing?' It was kind of cute."

In high school Luke became friends with Will Hall. Will, now the sports book director at the MGM Grand in Vegas, got Luke into racehorses. Luke recalled, "We'd go out to Laurel and Charles Town and skip study hall. He was the guy that I went to Saratoga with [in 1980]. My friends and I were like eighteen. It was summer. We drove a Mercury Bobcat up to Saratoga from the DC area. We drove all night. It was about 8:00 in the morning, and we got to Saratoga, and we just went and watched the workouts in the morning. It was classic. And it was Travers Day, and Temperance Hill won it ... I just tried to soak up everything I could about the game."

Luke even went so far as to imagine that he could make a living as a gambler. He studied the *Form* and headed to Hialeah. He lasted a month: "I gambled on the races every day and blew about sixty dollars a week. I had to go home."

Carla said,

He didn't really know what he wanted. Despite his high IQ, he was at loose ends. He didn't have any goals. And he lived in my parents' basement until he was like twenty-seven. But he had always maintained his interest in going to the racetrack. Then I guess at age twenty-seven he thought, "Well what am I doing?" And he decided to go to the racetrack management school in Arizona. And that's when he realized he had sort of a gift at communication, and that's when it sort of took off. He started announcing. He started using his talent. It's an inspirational story to people. There's a huge generation of kids now who can't find jobs and they're stuck in their parents' house and I think it's a lesson not to lose faith in yourself. Sometimes your gifts take awhile to come out.

She added, "There are some people whose life is dictated by Fate."

The University of Arizona Racetrack Industry Program has proven to be quite the dream factory, churning out prominent racing personalities such as Eclipse Award–winning trainers Bob Baffert and Todd Pletcher, former Hollywood Park track announcer Milo Perrins, and Bobby Neuman, the current voice of Calder Racecourse.

Although Luke had dabbled with the idea of being a track announcer, he had never really trusted that he had the right voice for it: "My dad's parents lived in Europe. Actually, my grandfather was an ambassador from Holland to several different countries, to Malaysia, Singapore and later on to Guatemala, El Salvador and Honduras. They retired to Spain, to the Costa del Sol. So my parents would send cassette tapes back and forth and would always make me get on there. 'Thanks for the present, Grandpa' or whatever. They'd play it back and I was like, 'Oh my God!' That was about the only time I heard my voice, so anyway I never thought I had the voice to do it."

The Arizona fair circuit made Luke think twice about just how he really did sound. At that time it was customary for each of the tracks — St. Johns, Kingman, Duncan, Douglas, Safford, Sonoita, and Holbrook — to run two weekends a year.

The father of Dave Eisenbise, one of Luke's college buddies, was a trainer and had a Quarter Horse entered for a race at Holbrook. Luke headed out there with Dave to see how things would pan out, but once on track that day, a strange turn of events took place. The heavens opened up, quickly turning the track to slop, deluging the entire facility and sending fans ducking for cover. It seemed that some late scratches were in the offing, but ironically, one of the first casualties that day was not a horse but the track announcer, who quickly bailed.

When word went out about what happened, Dave piped up on Luke's behalf. The next thing he knew, Luke was on the public address system, and by the end of the day, with the remainder of the card under his belt, he had gone from imitating track announcers to being one. Luke would turn out to be anything but a one-hit wonder.

Luke described what happened next:

> The guy in charge said to me, "You can come back anytime that you want." So I did. I would call the races at those fairs for free or if my friend was running a horse. It was funny because when I started calling races, my roommate, Kevin Colosi, also from Buffalo, had an internship. He's now the Clerk of Scales at Santa Anita and has been doing that for years, one of my best friends. Anyway, he took on an internship at Belmont in the racing office, and I stayed and went to summer school in Tucson.
>
> After I'd called a few races on the fairs, I took a communications class that was voice and diction. You had to speak in front of the class of sixty, and the teacher was a former deejay from Chicago. He told me that I had the best voice in the class so that gave me a lot of confidence, whereas I didn't really have any confidence in my voice, prior to that.

Upon graduating in 1988, Luke was all set to put his penmanship and PR skills to good use, and he headed for the now-defunct Brandywine Raceway harness track in Delaware, where the publicity and the press box awaited him. That was when he received a call from the Downs at Albuquerque, asking him to fill in for a couple of months as their track announcer.

Luke explained, "I had no idea how they found out about me, but they said that they'd heard through the grapevine that I was an up-and-comer. That made me feel good, so I went ahead and took that job instead."

At the same time, another opportunity was in the pipeline. His fellow alumnus, Milo Perrins, had just been appointed as track announcer at Hollywood Park, leaving an opening at Blue Ribbon Downs in Oklahoma.

Luke said, "I went out there and did a ten day try-out. And actually Vic Stauffer ended up getting the job. I was going to go back to the harness track in Delaware where my job was still waiting for me when, a few days in, Vic ended up quitting. They desperately tried to find me, which they eventually did, and so I drove back there to Blue Ribbon Downs and worked there the whole rest of the year."

In early 1988, Blue Ribbon was the lone track running in the state. (Remington Park would open later that same year.) Blue Ribbon boasted an impressive handle for its relatively small size especially on Kentucky Derby Day when it would top the million dollar mark and without simulcast revenue. It was the perfect place for a new announcer to earn his stripes.

Luke recalled, "Believe me, you know, I have listened back to those tapes. I was pretty bad. I was raw. I had no inflection in my voice or anything but you know I got through it OK."

There were, however, a few close shaves. Luke explained, "The horses came out onto the track for this race, a Quarter Horse race when the wind kicks up a little bit. So they're down in the chute warming up when, all of a sudden, this wind really starts to blow, and it takes one of those metal roofs on top of the tote board, takes that off and flies it across the track into the grandstand, crumples up into the grandstand. The tote board falls over, all of the stuff in the tote board flies out all over the place, and the photo finish guy comes out, and he goes, 'Tornado on the ground. Let's get outta here!' I go, 'I can't leave. The stewards haven't called me.' He says, 'Look out the window!' and I see the three stewards running off. That's how green I was, right?"

Fortunately Luke had always been someone who had two feet firmly planted on the ground, and Tornado Alley was not going to blow him over. In 1989 Luke was once more faced with an important decision. There was a fork in the road, one way pointing east to Oklahoma, the other west to New Mexico.

Luke explained, "The announcer that I was filling in for at Albuquerque didn't come back so I had the choice between Blue Ribbon Downs and Albuquerque and Santa Fe, owned by the same people, so I chose to go to Albuquerque. I could have stayed at Blue Ribbon Downs. Maybe I should have, I don't know. But I chose Albuquerque and Santa Fe, because they're both mile tracks."

After moving to the Southwest, Luke found other gigs in the region. Luke said, "In between, I did a couple of other jobs. Tulsa opened up, and I called the first couple of years there and G. Rollie White Downs in Brady, Texas; the state's first track to open in fifty years. Texas passed pari-mutuel wagering after they'd banned it years before and because it was the first to open, it was like a big deal. It's in the middle of nowhere, believe me. Brady is actually the geographical heart of Texas, meaning, if you had a cut-out map of Texas, you could balance it on Brady. It's also the home of the International Goat Cook-Off."

Twelve months later, the announcer's job at New Mexico's premier track, Sunland Park, opened up and astute general manager Harold Payne wasted no time in offering it to Luke. It meant leaving the northern tracks of Albuquerque and Santa Fe, which he did. Since Sunland Park was a winter meet, Luke was now in need of a summer job. He said, "I had worked in the racing office. I'd taken entries at Albuquerque and became the assistant racing secretary at Ruidoso that summer."

Nestled amongst the mountainous backdrop of Ruidoso, New Mexico,

Ruidoso Downs has always run from Memorial Day to Labor Day. Predominantly a Quarter Horse meet, it is home to the nation's first million-dollar race and the world's richest Quarter Horse race, the All American.

Luke liked the good Quarter Horses: "The All American Futurity trial day is one of the best days in racing. They're gorgeous horses. They're well-bred. It's like Saratoga."

R.D. Hubbard, a huge Quarter Horse fan, was the owner of Ruidoso Downs and founder of the Racing Museum adjacent to it. He quickly realized that he had a burgeoning talent spinning his wheels right under his nose and felt it was time to let the motor roll.

Luke explained,

> After the Rainbow Futurity, Hubbard moved me into the announcer position, like the last week of the meet at Ruidoso so then I called the All American [a 440-yard race for qualifying two-year-old Quarter Horses] that year. I really think that was one of my best calls ever. Royal Quick Dash won it, and he was a long-shot. He broke on top, and I called him right away, and I was proud of that. Wire to wire.
>
> Quarter Horse racing is so weird because you can think the inside horse is in front and that this outside horse closed a lot of ground, but that horse is actually in front at that point. It can be an optical illusion from the angle that you are at.
>
> For me, calling Quarter Horse races is 95 percent easier [than calling Thoroughbred races]. The only thing is you'll be in a position where there will be so many horses there at the wire that you may not call the winner. It's the All American on national TV, and there's the chance that you may not call the winner because there's so much going on. But an average Quarter Horse race, during the fall we have a Mixed Meet here [at Turf Paradise], and we'll run one or maybe two Quarter Horse races early in the day. And it's almost like that's a break for me. I don't really have to start trying. Like I said, there's pressure involved in the big races, but normally it's kind of a break. They stay in their lanes pretty much, and it's kind of an easy deal.

Luke would call the prestigious All American Futurity a total of six times.

Luke now had a circuit — Sunland Park in the fall/winter and Ruidoso Downs in the summer — a circuit he would stay at for the next three years. He added the spring meet of the Downs at Albuquerque to his schedule, leaving him about a month off. It was a pleasant change from the stop-start cycle he had come to know.

Luke recalled,

> In those first years there was a lot of time between meets which the average person has a hard time understanding, that you don't have a regular job. I would do this job and that, whatever I needed to.

A couple of years I was a jockey agent, just for something to do. I had a couple of girls that I represented. They did pretty well. I had a good time. I don't think I'm cut out for that though. I can't take the rejection. You're shot down 99 percent of the time.

Elite track announcers are perfectionists, for the most part. Luke constantly strove to be the best race caller he could be: "There's a place called The Wine Cellar, a bar across from Albuquerque. It's no longer in existence. It's now a supermarket. But they would play the replays every night, and I would always go in there almost every night and listen to myself. I would listen to that and critique myself and cringe at the mistakes I made. I want an arsenal of terms up here that I can call upon so that I'm not saying the same thing every time. For every situation I want a big supply of possible ways to describe that thing without saying the same thing over and over."

Pete Drypolcher was the general manager at the Downs when Luke first started. Luke said,

> I could see he was skeptical of me having only called the Arizona fairs. And he came up and stood behind me, and I had them all memorized. And I called them around the track, but he said, "One thing I want to tell you. Stop using that term 'in front' when they cross. We had a guy here who used that for years, and we just think you should use something else." I really appreciated that because it made me come up with all different kinds of things. I usually say how many lengths the horse won by, but I usually say "going away" or "up in time." I might say "in front" once in every one thousand calls. There's nothing wrong with "in front." Some of my favorite announcers have said that, but it made me think of different things to say when they cross the wire.

In 1993 Luke went to work at Turf Paradise: "When I first started, I was the announcer and assistant racing secretary. That was a real grind. I'm glad I did it because I understand the office and pretty much got to know all the people, all the horsemen. There are a lot of announcers that don't know that side of it." And Luke fell in love with his winter abode: "How can you beat Turf Paradise? All winter long, calling the races in a beautiful setting."

The potential for a clash in calendar dates with Turf Paradise was always there for any announcer since the meet ran for five months at the time and was set to extend both ends, brought forward to early May and ending in early October. Three seasons later, Luke was faced with an overlap, but any dilemma in allegiance was moot since both tracks fell under the same ownership.

The common thread was R.D. Hubbard, for whom Luke had first worked at Ruidoso Downs. R.D. also owned Turf Paradise and Hollywood Park, where he was also chairman. In 1996, Trevor Denman, the Voice of

Luke said, "I'm kind of grandfathered in here at Turf Paradise."

Southern California, decided to lessen his full-time load, giving up Holly-wood Park, both its spring and fall meets. Management saw Luke as the per-fect replacement. Luke said that after seven years of "wiling away at the smaller tracks," the break into the big league couldn't have come at a better time.

He admitted, "I can tell you that if I hadn't got the job when I tried out for Hollywood Park, I was seriously thinking of going and doing some-thing else. I really didn't want to be a mid-level announcer for the rest of my career. Who knows if I would have?"

His prayers were answered, and Luke secured the Hollywood Park posi-tion, which effectively parlayed into year-round work since the Turf Paradise job went with it. He explained,

It was basically the same family but it wasn't the same company. Since they owned Turf Paradise, and I was the announcer at the parent track, they pretty much had to let me come and go.
At Hollywood Park I was under a lot of pressure replacing Trevor. So I worked so hard, and I really can tell you that I don't think I made more than a mistake or two over the whole spring/summer meet. I worked hard to not give anybody any ammunition. That was a good thing because I got to be a

much better announcer cuz I had to work so hard at doing it. It doesn't matter. I could be the reincarnation of Chic Anderson or Clem McCarthy, and there are a lot of people that aren't going to like me because I'm not Trevor.

Luke was always wary of getting pigeonholed at one track, and the prospect of a new setting spurred him on. He explained, "I wanted to bounce around. I think it's important to meet a lot of different people. It didn't necessarily help me really early on in my career but it's turned out, if you work for a lot of people, somebody is going to be in the position later on to possibly help you out."

The racetrack program groomed him well. Luke enjoyed an extensive network of racing peers who genuinely connected with him. Having come up through the ranks, there was no guile or pretense to his manner and so much of the respect he had earned came not only from his talent as an announcer but also from having shown himself to be a team player.

He said, "I think a big part of being a successful track announcer is getting along with people. If I were a general manager, I mean I'm pretty nitpicky about my announcers, but I would take a guy who is an 8 on a scale of 10 who is a good guy and would get along with co-workers than I would a 10 and was pleasant. You still have to call the right horse, but somebody might just be a tad better. But anyway, I got along with most everybody I worked with."

Looking back at over 50,000 races that he has called, Luke remembered one in particular that he would have liked another chance to call.

There was a horse, and I was busy. I was doing this and that, and I ended up not paying attention, and I'm calling this horse around, and he's got the lead, a Wesley Ward horse at Hollywood Park. I can't remember the name of the horse but old veteran hard knocker, and I look out at the tote board, and maybe the little red thing wasn't working and, "He's out there 35–1!" Well, it's 3–5! [Luke laughed.] As soon as I said that my mind starts churning. I go, "There's no way this horse is 35–1. He's too good. He's always one of the favorites." So then I look back out. I see the thing flash, looking at the TV I think I see the thing flash, and I go, "Oh, no." I wound up saying it again later in the call so people knew I did correct myself. But it was the last race of the day, and I was so embarrassed. At Hollywood, I'm on the roof, and there's an elevator on the roof. There's a 7th floor, so I didn't stick around like I normally do. Got the hell outta there. Get to the elevator. 7th floor. Boom! Stops on the 6th floor, and there's all these guys from the *Racing Form*, "Hey! 35–1!" and it was like "Ohhhhhhhhh God!" And I was trying to get out of there as fast as I could, and it was like everyone else was on that elevator.

Like several other top track announcers, Luke used crayons to help him memorize the horses. He explained, "I don't know why, but it's evolved over

Luke called from a very cramped announcer's booth at Turf Paradise in Phoenix, Arizona.

the years. If I get up here late, or I'm involved on the phone, and I haven't colored, it's no big deal. I can do it, but it gives me the assurance. Some guys are kind of snobs on it, but my opinion is anything that can possibly help you when you get into a jam, I mean everyone's got a mental block on occasion. And if you can look down and see an orange as opposed to try to look at your program, I mean some guys never look at their program, but you got it there. I have it because I look at it all the time to see who's riding. Sometimes I know who the jockey is just by the way he's riding.... But some guys look similar."

Luke listed his talents that made him a premier race caller: "Memory, vocabulary, natural ability to be able to impart excitement. Normally I'm excited if it's a good race even if it's a $3000 claimer."

And who says it's lonely at the top? Luke said, "He's the only guy who can corroborate this, but a mouse would come out of this socket, and I'd call the race, and the mouse would come out of it in the booth at Hollywood Park. And I'd be calling the race, and the mouse would come up right next to me. And as soon as I stopped calling, he'd run back into the hole," he laughed.

Luke continued to work on his voice. When he did commercials at Sunland, he was told that he sounded like the prominent newscaster Walter Cronkite. Luke continued to improve. He recalled, "I turned out to get much better at the voice-over. When I was at Hollywood Park, I ended up taking these kind of acting classes. I took a couple of them. And they were like eight weeks. I ended up landing a job, a Hertz Rental car commercial. They paid me a lot of money."

And in 1999 he landed The Job: track announcer at Churchill Downs. Luke confided, "The cream will rise to the top. If Tom Durkin was calling on the Arizona Circuit, somebody would find him. And if he was calling at Arapaho Park, he wouldn't be there for long. Somebody is going to find him. You're not going to be in the minor leagues for long if you have the talent." That held true for Luke.

Luke's passion for the history of racing made him a perfect fit at Churchill Downs. He exclaimed, "Just calling my first race at Churchill Downs! Just being in that booth where Chic Anderson was! He was legendary! There was an old wooden chair that is painted black and is almost impossible to pick up. Chic Anderson's chair. 'Do you want a more comfortable chair?' 'NO! That's Chic Anderson's chair. You'd better keep that in there.' I have that in there still. When I interviewed for the job, they took me in to see the Derby movie in the round. I thought, 'I'm going to listen and see what they have to say.' And then I saw that, and I thought, No. This is history." Luke spoke reverently of his experience of interviewing for the track announcer's position at Churchill Downs: "I mean, as great as the Hollywood Gold Cup is, nobody knows what that is when you go to the local market. Everybody knows what the Kentucky Derby is."

Luke would always remember his first Kentucky Derby: "That was very memorable. Just all the pageantry.... That was Charismatic, my first Derby, and I was fairly satisfied with the call." He announced, "But in deep stretch Charismatic has hit the front and Charismatic. Charismatic, Menifee flying late. Charismatic wins the Derby!"

Luke recalled,

That was an amazing deal. The "Old Kentucky Home" and the grandstand shaking. The old booth was pretty much glass. The wall behind you had some carpet on it. It was a brick wall. But this whole wall was glass, glass in front so to the left was the stewards stand so they could see everything you did. To the right were some chairs and outdoor seating. The first week there you don't even feel like it's your own deal, and all of a sudden there are all these people looking right through your work area, and it's kind of disconcerting. My first Derby Tony Terry [Churchill's publicity director at the time], who believe me,

The Twin Spires at Churchill Downs are synonymous with the "greatest two minutes in sports!" Credit: Tom Ferry.

meant this in the best spirit: I'm getting ready to call the Derby. And they're about to go in the gate. I'm getting the horses down and taking my last deep breath. And all of a sudden there's a knock on the back of the window. I'm trying to get no distractions. I'm focused on this so I say, "You know what? I'm not paying any attention." Finally I hear, "Knock, knock." I go, "Maybe my mike isn't working" because, at the time, I was in an enclosed booth and couldn't hear myself come back. So I turn around, and there is Tony waving. Ohhhhhh!!!!!!!

Even without the "help" of the well-meaning publicity guy, Luke was nervous. It was, after all, his first Kentucky Derby to call. He explained,

I get nervous at every Derby somewhat. You call a better race when you've got a little tension. But it's a weird kind of deal; Bernie Hettel who was the chief steward at the time says, "I know it's the Derby, but you know what? When it comes down to it, it's a horse race, another horse race." So I try to convince myself that it is just another horse race. But then again I'm pulled from that by all the interviews. Of course it's different because it's a field of twenty that you just don't see in this country. It's a completely different walk by the stands for the first time. My first Derby, I kind of planned out how I was going to call it, but I didn't plan where the horses were going to be necessarily. I try to have an idea where they're going to be, but I thought, "I'm going to get through the entire field. When they rumble past here, I'll be through the field one time when they hit that." Well Three Ring bumped into Adonis, and that horse that got caught with a buzzer in the Arkansas Derby jumped the finish line, and Stephen Got Even got jostled, and fourteen other things happened that I described, and by that time, I hadn't even gotten through a third of the field.

Luke called the Kentucky Derby ten times. The 2000 running stuck out in his mind. He called, "And here comes Fusiachi Pegasus ... here comes the big horse, Fusiachi Pegasus and Fusiachi Pegasus storming home on the outside ... Fusiachi Pegasus wins Kentucky Derby 126."

Luke said, "I really thought that Fusiachi Pegasus would go on to be a super super star. He's a great horse and a great sire now, but he was a little disappointing afterwards. I thought he'd run better in the Breeders' Cup Classic."

There is no race in the world quite like the Kentucky Derby. Luke admitted, "If I hadn't gotten the job at Churchill, I probably never would have gone to the Derby because it's a big day everywhere else. And it'd be hard to ask Hollywood Park on Kentucky Derby Day when they have their biggest crowd.... Of course, now if I were working somewhere else, I'd make arrangements to go because I think it's such a big great event. All the big days I've been to and, believe me, I have respect for all the tracks I've worked at, but there's nothing even remotely close to the excitement of that whole week, not to mention the day and the day before with one hundred thousand at the Oaks."

He, like Kurt Becker, felt that racing in Kentucky appealed to a young crowd: "Basically, if you want to bring young college guys out, just bring young college girls out. The one thing that is really cool about Louisville and Kentucky, for the most part, is almost everyone knows how to read the *Form*. Almost everyone knows a little something about the races, because they've been going for so many years. If you can get people out in their college years, then all of a sudden, they're a professional with some income, and they remember, 'Yeah, I used to love it.' We're losing our fan base. It's getting older and older and dying out."

Luke admitted that landing the race caller's job at Churchill Downs was the pinnacle of his career. However, there was so much more to the man in the best seat in the house. He reflected, "I think just the body of my work and how I'm thought of. I think I'm thought of very well, both for my race calls and the kind of person I am and how I am to work with, etc. The body of my work speaks for itself, and that's what I'm most proud of."

His peers agree.

In March 2007, Hall of Fame jockey Gary Stevens said, "Luke's a super guy, got a great sense of humor, loves the sport, and is a sensational race caller."

In 2008, Hall of Fame jockey Mike Smith said, "Oh, I love Luke. That's my buddy! Well, he's just a good friend on top of everything. We hang out quite a bit.... But, of course, my favorite call of Luke's would be the 2005 Kentucky Derby."

Trainers praised Luke also: "I think Luke's an excellent announcer. He does a great job, and I like his voice," declared conditioner Bob Holthus in November 2007.

Fellow RTIP alumnus Bob Baffert said in the spring of 2007, "Luke is great. He can call a race. He knows what's going on. I really like Luke. I can have the TV going at a different racetrack, and I hear the voice, I know what track they're at."

Luke's passion was race calling, and his schedule demonstrated that. He explained, "I open Turf Paradise in late September, come back here [Turf Paradise Park] December, January, February, March, and half of April. Go back to Churchill for the spring meet till Ellis opens in mid July. And then do Ellis till Labor Day, have ten days off, and then do Kentucky Downs, and they end on Tuesday. We start on Friday here at Turf Paradise ... I have to take time off from places, leave early and come back late. Turf Paradise is very nice to let me do that." He had less than two weeks a year for a vacation. And he usually spent that at a racetrack.

Kurt Becker remembered, "I was at the DuQuoin State Fair in 2001 or 2002. And I was calling the races there. I looked across the way at DuQuoin one day, and here's Luke Kruytbosch. Out there in his shorts, and he's got a program. And I said, 'What in the world are you doing here?' And here's what he said. He said, 'Well, you know I call at Ellis Park in the summer, and today is a dark day. I saw where they were racing harness horses at the DuQuoin State Fair, and I remember when I was a kid, and they had the Hambletonian here. And I said to myself, 'I have got to go and just say I've been to DuQuoin. Cuz there's so much harness racing history here.'"

Luke said,

Yeah, yeah, I'm a history buff. This is my passion. I love horse racing. I feel like I'm being corny when I talk about passion, but I like a lot of things, you know. I'm really looking forward to the Phoenix Open. That's a lot of fun. Love to travel. Love to spend time with my friends. To gamble. I like to play golf, like to watch sports: Buffalo Bills, University of Arizona teams.

"He's razor sharp coming back from Dubai. Curlin impressively under Robby Albarado come back in the Stephen Foster by three," called Luke in the 2008 Stephen Foster on June 14, 2008. Credit: Tom Ferry.

I like to listen to other announcers too. I really hate it when I go into an OTB bar, and all of the TVs are turned low. I get yelled at when I turn up the sound. If they're inaccurate I don't like them. There's nothing worse than having a guy call your horse, and your horse isn't there. I like Marv Albert, and I like Vince Scully. I like Dick Stockton, and I like Al Michaels. And they're all different. So there's plenty of room for Kurt Becker, Michael Wrona, and Tom Durkin, and Vic Stauffer.

Churchill Downs provided Luke with an abundance of history and race calling. But Luke continued to enjoy announcing at his other tracks: "The best part is you're pretty much left alone to do what you want to do as long as you do a good job. Nobody is going to tell you what to do. There are certain little things in between races, but basically, you're left to be creative on your own. All day long it's up to you to step up to the plate. First of all, you've got to show up on time and then show up prepared and to do the job. As long as you do that, it's tremendous." A highlight for Luke at Turf Paradise was in 2004 when Lost in the Fog ran in his second career start.

Luke announced, "It's all Lost in the Fog. Lost in the Fog accelerates away to lead by five, six with a furlong to go.... But Lost in the Fog ran them off their feet. Lost in the Fog razor sharp to win the Arizona Juvenile by about a dozen at the wire."

Luke knew that even at Turf Paradise, "things like that happen: a good horse or a jockey comes through that turns out to be really good like a Tyler Baze starts out here."

And at Turf Paradise Luke had seen it all and had been there for the call. He said, "I've never called a harness race. I've called greyhounds and, of course, Quarter Horses. And here at Turf Paradise I've called mules and ostriches and camels and pigs and mice and...," he laughed. And Luke called high school football when he was in Oklahoma. And after he became well-known, he called a couple of plays on a Canadian football game on the radio.

Another thing that Luke was known for was helping out others who wanted to become track announcers. He had spent his time in the trenches and could offer advice: "When somebody comes up to me and wants to be an announcer, I say, 'Well, here's what you do: what might help is you come out to your oval track and call race after race after race into a tape recorder. Keep calling until you think you're ok, but you gotta call a lot of races.' Bill Downes, I told him that. Jim McCall, a bunch of guys that have gotten started that way. If you bring me the tape when you think you've called a decent race, I'll listen to it and when I think, you're decent enough, I'll send you to the fair and you call it for free. It gives you invaluable experience, and you can say you've called a race." Another person Luke helped was Mountaineer caller Peter Berry.

On May 3, 2008, Luke called the 134th Kentucky Derby: "Off and running in the Kentucky Derby ... Big Brown has opened up wide by three. The game filly Eight Belles trying to run him down in the final furlong. It's Big Brown. He's now clear. Big Brown and Kent Desormeaux by four lengths.... But Big Brown, Big Brown is a super star, a worthy Kentucky Derby. Big Brown wins by five."

On July 14 Luke Kruytbosch was found dead in his apartment in Evansville, Indiana. He was 47. The day before he had told his coworkers at Ellis Park that he didn't feel well. His death is believed to be heart related.

The horse racing world was shocked and terribly saddened. About 400 people, including Luke's father and sister, attended his memorial service at Churchill Downs. It was fitting that his ashes were spread in the winner's circle.

His sister said that fame and success did not change Luke: "No, never his inner core. It didn't change him but it put so much pressure on him that he dealt with things by withdrawing. He created a world for himself which was a world of racing and it had a lot of positive things for him. And he built that up all by himself, little Lukie.... And I don't think he did it for the fame. I think he did it because he loved the horses. That came through."

She added that there were several factors that made him a top track announcer: "I think it was a combination of high intelligence. It was high. I think growing up in an alcoholic home, my brother became extremely sensitive to emotion. He was always gifted with sensitivity. It's just an artistry. Intelligence and artistry. To be a good track announcer you have to have both. People just think it's easy. It involves both intelligence and quickness of mind in combination with a giftedness of the ability to modulate the way the competition is moving. Plus discipline. He was very disciplined. He understood that there was structure to it. So in terms of his craft, he knew his craft really well. And he had an artistic gift, and he was really smart."

There is no way that Luke will ever be forgotten or replaced. There is a two-year-old colt named Race Caller Luke. And Bob Baffert trains him.

On Opening Day Friday, October 3, 2008, White Spar won the inaugural Luke Kruytbosch Stakes at Turf Paradise. It is a six-furlong race for three-year-olds.

Dallas Stewart won the 2006 Kentucky Oaks with Lemons Forever, and in 2009 his four-year-old gray colt, Macho Again, captured the Stephen Foster at Churchill. He had this to say about the popular late announcer: "Well, Luke was just a joy. He was right there with us, and he did a great job doing the Derby. And there again for the locals at Churchill, he could always add to some races. Not just the Derby but day in and day out, he brought some Louisville flavor into some of the races, and he's sorely missed. He was a very good announcer and did a great job and handled the Derby I thought just terrific."

Jack Knowlton of Funny Cide fame remembered the last time he saw him:

> The late Luke Kruytbosch. Was a very good personal friend. Got to know Luke when Funny Cide was in the Derby. And then the last time I saw him was at last year's Derby.
> We hooked up at the Super Bowl when the Giants went out in Phoenix, and went out to the track with him afterward and partied out there. Some great memories. He was a great guy.

During the fall meet, Churchill Downs held tryouts to find their sixth announcer. Larry Collmus, Mark Johnson, Bobby Neuman, Travis Stone, and Michael Wrona were the finalists, and each called for one week of the meet. "Luke was a great friend to me and every announcer I know," Collmus said. "We shared many laughs together. It will be a bit strange at first to call a race in the booth at Churchill Downs, but I'm excited about the opportunity and look forward to my week in Louisville." [Both quoted on Churchill's website.]

"The thing I admired most about Luke was how he worked his way up through the ranks of small tracks, and never forgot his humble beginnings," Wrona said. "Indeed, he remained a big supporter of small-time racing, and a friend to people at all levels of the industry."

On January 15, 2009, Churchill Downs announced that Mark Johnson from Great Britain would be the new track announcer. He certainly has large shoes to fill.

On January 22, 2006, the author was privileged to talk to Luke Kruytbosch for four hours at Turf Paradise. When asked about his goals and dreams, he responded, "Pretty much to just keep going and maybe announce a little overseas somewhere. That'd be fun to do. Everything has gone pretty well, and I've advanced well in the seventeen years I've been doing it. Keep it going. I hate to set any goal and say, 'Ok, I've done it. That's it. That's life?' The guy I mentioned earlier at Albuquerque asked me, and I said, 'Well one day I want to call the Derby.' That was 1998. Now that I've called eight of them, that's a pretty good deal. It's going to be hard to top that so I'm not going to have any lofty goals. I'd like to be highly thought of and somebody that they can call on."

He was.

CHAPTER 9

Dave Johnson

*Dave Johnson: "And down the stretch they come! With Ruffian in
front now by 2½ lengths ... as they come to the final sixteenth, it's
Ruffian.... It's Ruffian in front!"*

*"And they're off!" announces Dave Johnson. It's the 1984 Ballentine
Scotch Classic on October 13th at the Meadowlands. "John Henry
on the far outside, and he's flying. And down the stretch they come!
The old man John Henry takes command.... Here they come to the
finish, and here's John Henry in front."*

He has the most recognizable signature call in the business. "And down
the stretch they come" is the staple ingredient to many of Dave Johnson's
big-day race calls, and fans remain on tenterhooks waiting for the moment
when those magic words are infused into the mix, symbolic of the buildup
in excitement and the ultimate run to the wire.

There is nothing contrived about how the line and its rumbling delivery came to be. Dave had used the call back in his early years at Fairmount
Park and the now-defunct Cahokia Downs, but it wasn't until he became
the track announcer at Santa Anita in the late 1970s that the phrase took on
a life of its own.

No track announcer has cut through coastal lines like Dave Johnson.
His dulcet tones have reverberated between the two giant racing centers; talk
about East Coast versus West Coast rivalries, in fact rivalries in general, and
Dave has been there.

His first Kentucky Derby call was the unforgettable Affirmed and Alydar match up of 1978. He exhibited both composure and excitement in the
final furlongs as he called, "And DOWN the stretch they come. Affirmed on
the inside takes command again. Believe It is second. Alydar gains ground

138

third.... It's going to be Affirmed. Affirmed and Steve Cauthen are going to win the 104th running of the Kentucky Derby!"

It was the first Triple Crown series beamed to worldwide television audiences. Be it on course, on TV, or on radio, Dave has called the action of *the* most watched races on the North American calendar.

The sandy-haired lad who first took to the microphone by happenstance when an on-course track announcer took ill can still churn them out. As recently as 2005, Dave, along with Bill Finley, his regular Saturday morning cohost, and their supporting talent at Sirius Satellite Radio (Sports Action Channel 127), were honored with an Eclipse Award for their coverage of the XXII Breeders' Cup World Championships at Belmont Park. It is just one in a long list of Eclipse Awards that he started accumulating as far back as 1982 when a local television network show titled *Tall in the Saddle* brought to light the rigors of what it takes to be a jockey.

Dave has been involved in every Breeders' Cup in some capacity, whether it's radio, TV, or the expanded coverage on satellite radio. His last race call was in the 2005 Breeders' Cup Classic that Horse of the Year Ghostzapper won.

Dave says, "No, it wouldn't be the same. Why put an asterisk? No, racing shouldn't change the Triple Crown format." By permission of Dave Johnson.

From 1971 to May 1977, Dave was the voice of the New York Racing Association (NYRA) at each of its three racetracks. He summered in the ever-popular Saratoga and called many champions during the meets at Belmont and Aqueduct. Soon after the ball drop in Times Square, Dave became a snowbird heading down to Hialeah to call the action there. That ended in 1973 when NYRA went to year-round racing.

Dave has always managed to enjoy the best of both worlds. In 1977, the same year that he became track announcer at the Meadowlands in East Rutherford, New Jersey, Dave switched his "tack" to Southern California as track announcer at Santa Anita where he called for seven seasons. In the early 1980s ABC Sports hired him to be the "Voice of the Triple Crown." It was a partnership that would flourish for a quarter of a century, showcasing Dave's talents as both announcer and on-air celebrity.

Tom Dawson, a producer for ESPN, and Dave trace their relationship back over 30 years. Tom recalled, "Dave was always very serious about what he was doing. He didn't leave things to chance. He worked real hard to become a good race caller. He had his technique down and his memorization down and style, and I think he's really the product of hard work and dedication."

Tom said, "More recently when you see Dave on TV it's more in a host role, not as a race caller. But there were a lot of shows that he did when he was both. He would do part of the show downstairs as the host or the co-host, as part of the broadcast team, and then have to call the races as well. So it was double duty that not everybody could pull off."

He added, "He didn't want to just be the race caller. He always wanted to be a part of the broadcast, and he had a good opinion on things and you wanted to get that opinion because he is a great lover of the sport. He taught me a great phrase. The way to identify someone who works in racing who is really a fan: they still go to the track on their day off." That has always applied to Dave Johnson.

After more than four decades and thousands of race calls, Dave reflected, "I'll only stay around calling races as long as I can physically do the job. I think some announcers stay on longer than they should. I think I still can call a decent race. I've listened to my call of Barbaro's Kentucky Derby on radio which was ok, and we won the Eclipse Award for Sirius for the Breeders' Cup of 2005. I called all eight races on the radio that day. So I can still do it. If I slip to the point where I believe or my producers believe that I shouldn't call, then I won't call."

Wish to take a walk down memory lane? Chances are that a Dave Johnson call might do the trick. Just head to Louisville's Kentucky Derby Museum and you'll soon discover how prolific his body of work is. During the 1995 Pimlico Special, for example, he called, "Can anybody catch Cigar?... And DOWN the stretch they come! Cigar with Jerry Bailey going easily on the front end. He's in front ... Cigar! Smokin through the stretch takes it by two lengths!"

Fast-forward to today and this true golden oldie may take more of a backseat now than in his heyday, but he remains polished and pertinent. His undying passion is the fuel that keeps the spark alive. He admits to being semiretired, but in 2007 he was a guest announcer at the Meadowlands on five Tuesday afternoons.

Dave said, "I would say that the three of us, Trevor, Tom, and I changed the face of announcing from what it used to be of calling, just doing a chart and never using a jockey's name or the meaning of a race. The WHY, that's another thing. You can tell how a horse won, but I think that Tom and Trevor and I revolutionalized ... I'm much older than they are. I opened the door I guess. And then Trevor is just magnificent in terms of laying out a race early on and setting up what could happen. And Tom is just the master of the verbiage.... We're really friends. There's no jealousy or animosity with the three of us."

Opening doors has never been a struggle for Dave, who has always managed to recognize opportunity when it knocks. A native of St. Louis, Missouri, Dave got his foot in the door at his home track, Cahokia Downs.

Racing runs in his blood. Dave recalled, "My grandparents, my mom and dad, my uncles and aunts, we were all $2 bettors. I remember my grandfather poring over the *Racing Form* between races. He even had a little magnifying glass — you've seen those guys at the track — and he would announce, 'Can't beat the favorite!'"

One of four children, Dave is now the elder statesman. Donna, with whom he is extremely close, lives in Atlanta and is seven years younger. Debbie is his junior by 11 years, and his brother Drew, a radio personality and production manager for a station in St. Louis, is 17 years younger.

Dave said, "I marvel at the love in my family.... Constant communication. Then I see other families. They don't talk to one another. It's really a shame. My brother and I email each other all the time. Even living in separate cities, we're still very close."

Dave reports in 2010 that his mother Mary is 93 and still "with it." His father Jay died 43 years ago. He was a steelworker on the open hearth in a steel mill in Grand City, Illinois, right across the river from St. Louis. Jay made sure his children were well provided for and had a good education. Dave explained,

> I went to a Catholic school. I wasn't a great student. I mean, I got through, but it wasn't easy. When I was in third or fourth grade, the principal called my home one day and my dad answered. The principal said, "You know, it's just amazing. Dave is not the sharpest kid in the class. But you know everybody likes him, and he likes Show and Tell and gives speeches. But now in arithmetic, the nuns are teaching fractions, and Dave is just unbelievably good. Not only does he understand it right away. But he's showing the other kids. And I've never seen another kid take on and teach the other kids in the class

about fractions." Well, of course. 3 to 5. 9 to 5. 5 to 2. Well, of course I knew fractions! I had been seeing them on a tote board since I could see the light bulbs! So that was a part of the racetrack background that the school didn't understand, but, of course, my dad did. And that was so much fun.

He was just a wonderful father who provided for his family and loved the horses and my mom Mary.

As fate would have it, Jay would not live to see the illustrious manner in which his elder son's career would unfold. Dave had been toying with a few career possibilities, from teaching to politics to law, once he had abandoned fanciful thoughts of becoming a jockey. He explained, "In 1959 I went to the freshman orientation at the University of Missouri, and one of the questions was if you could have any job in the world, what would it be? And what did I write down but I'd like to be a racetrack announcer. But I never pursued it. It was just a fantasy.... I was in a position at that point where I was going to get my liberal arts background, and I was either going to go into law or politics or both, or teaching."

Dave began to gravitate toward law and in the early 1960s signed on with his uncle's law firm working summers and Saturdays while going to night school. It turned out be the right move for all the wrong reasons. The law firm had a box at Cahokia Downs. Dave said, "It reads like a B-grade movie script, but it's absolutely true."

In 1965 on a Friday night in mid–June, Dave was in the firm's box in the clubhouse watching the first race when the call of the announcer, Todd Creed, just stopped. Power failures were not that uncommon at the time, so everyone thought it was a problem with the speaker system. That was until Dave noticed a stretcher being rushed past. He recalled,

> I asked the usher for our box what had happened, and he said some guy had been taken ill, oh, the announcer. Soon after, a strange voice came out on the P.A. system — I later found out was the steward — and he said, "Ladies and Gentlemen, our announcer is ill. We're going to shut the microphone off. Please watch the tote board. Thank you, and make your bets early."
>
> I thought, my God, you can't do that. I knew the General Manager. Everybody called her Miss Ann. So I went over to her office and said, "Miss Ann, I could call the races for you." It was funny. I was an American History major, and it was very easy for me to memorize the ten points of the Yalta Agreement or things that I needed to. So I knew that I could memorize a field of horses. I don't have a photographic memory, and I forget to buy milk, but this was a very easy thing, and I knew I could do it.
>
> She said, "Just a minute," and she calls the stewards on her phone. I'm standing right at her desk. She says, "I've got a young kid here. I know who he is, says he can call the races. What do you think?" And she says, "Ok.

Thanks anyway." And she says, "Thanks, Dave, but the announcer's son is going to fill in for his dad for the rest of the card." I said "Ok." So I just went out to my box.

Mike, the 17-year-old son of Todd Creed, did take over, calling the second race. But he tried to do it with two spotters. Dave explained,

The spotters he used were the electrician and the bugler. He wasn't really the bugler. He was a musician who had to be hired to put the needle on the Victrola to play the call to post because it required a union man to be there if you were going to actually play the call to post. The electrician told me about it later as we became great friends. He said that Mike stood in the middle, and the electrician stood on one side, and the musician on the other, and the horses broke from the gate.

He turned on the microphone and it was like, "That's Blue Boy going to the front." And another voice says, "Nah, that's not Blue Boy." And a third voice says, "I think it's the five." See, I'm in the stands listening to this. Well the entire five furlongs race was nothing but an argument between these three guys as to who was in front. As soon as the race was over Miss Ann sent her daughter Barbara out to my box, and I can remember it like it happened yesterday. "You're next." That's what she said. "Dave, you're next." I went up and called the third race.

A modest Dave claimed the horses stayed pretty much in a line throughout, but he was through it without a hitch, no spotters required. Dave continued,

Then the phone rang, and the electrician said, "That's your phone." And it was the president of the track who was the majority owner, Colonel George Edward Day, a real character, with a voice that had been wracked with cancer, the kind deejays mimic. "Would you stay and do the rest of the races?" And I said, "Oh sure. This is great!" After the races, the phone rang again. They invited me over to the office for a drink. They said thank you for helping us out but that Todd was in the hospital and would be staying overnight. They asked me if I would come back and do it again tomorrow, and I said I'd love to, at which point Colonel Day pushed twenty-five dollars across the table to me, and I thought, "How long has this been going on?" So I called the races the next night, got another twenty-five, and thought how lucky I am.

Todd and I became friends. Upon his return, he came down and saw me and thanked me for being there for him. He had no backup. The following winter of '66, he called me from California and said, "I'm taking the job at Aksarben, Nebraska." And he said, "I'm not coming back to Cahokia or Fairmont. If you want, why don't you put your name in?" So I did.

The rest, as they say, is history. Dave was hired at both Cahokia Downs and Fairmount Park racetracks. At Fairmount, he called both Thoroughbred and harness races and also became publicity director. It conducted a spring and a fall meet. His days at the law offices were over. Dave exclaimed, "I never looked back! The law firm was work. The racetrack was great fun. I made a decent living, and I was with friends."

Throughout Dave's childhood, Fairmount Park had been a destination, a safe cradle, where his entire family got together and had fun. Dave's first visit to the track was when he was six months old.

His mother, Mary, was the one who taught Dave to read the *Daily Racing Form*. He was only four. They were riding on a slow-moving train from St. Louis to New Orleans at the time to join his father who had enlisted in the army. By the journey's end, Dave had the hang of it.

Dave recalled, "When my dad came back after the war, we'd go out to Fairmount Park. My mom told me a story that there was a huge guy in a big white suit like Sydney Greenstreet in the next box ... talking loudly about a horse in a race. I'm five years old sitting there listening to this and all at once I say to him, 'That horse has no chance of winning. He's never been farther than a mile and he has the worst jockey at the racetrack on him.' I was a tout!"

Dave was a fan first and has always had a feel for betting. He admitted, "I don't bet every race I call, but I certainly do play. And that makes me a fan. I was a fan before I was an announcer, and that in turn makes you more than simply a technician. I always understood the significance of a horse or a jockey and was the one who started counting up a jockey's wins. Someone going for their third win of the day, I'd put it in my call." The years at Cahokia Downs and Fairmount Park went without a hitch. Well, almost.

There was that one embarrassing moment, the one call that an announcer would take back if he could. Fortunately, Dave can look back and laugh at it now, but at Cahokia Downs back in 1966, it wasn't quite so amusing. Dave explained,

Remember, Cahokia Downs was a very small racetrack, what they would call a bullring in circumference. And one night they were running a 1⅜ mile race, and it started on the backstretch where they usually started the five furlongs races which were the backbone of their racing at Cahokia Downs. They broke from the gate and as they turned for home, I looked at the jockeys on the two front runners and they both had the brakes on. I thought, "Oh my God! What is going on here?" The thought that went through my mind was that each jockey had bet on the other jockey and they didn't want to win. I made the most dramatic stretch call.... I shut off the microphone, hung it up and said to that same engineer that was there that first night, "Omigod! I think that was a fixed race! I can't believe it." And Steve said, "Dave, they're going round again." Oh my God. I put the microphone back on and said, "I'm sorry, Ladies and Gentlemen, this is a mile and three eighths race." If I would have had a bed upstairs in the announcer's booth, I would never have left. I took such a razzing, and I feel sorry because some people tore up their tickets, and those two horses were nowhere to be found at the finish. It was just an awful mess.

There was no need to apologize after that. Dave was making a decent living and could easily have stayed on. St. Louis was home, and Dave was doing something he loved, surrounded by a tremendously supportive family. It had been a year since his father, Jay, had lost his battle with a terminal illness, and Dave was still working at the track but no longer living at home. His mother, who had been a stay-at-home mom until then, learned how to drive and got a job. There was change in the air and having left the nest, Dave was about to spread his wings farther than he had imagined. "I was born and raised in St. Louis and was twenty-nine before I found out that I was allowed to leave," he claimed, half jokingly. Dave recalled,

In 1970 there was an ad in the *Daily Racing Form* for an announcer at Hialeah in Florida so I sent my tapes down. Bill Fisher who was the General Manager at the time hired me off my tapes. So I became the track announcer at Hialeah in January of '71 at which point NYRA needed to replace "Cappy" [track announcer Fred Capposella]. New York Racing had a mandatory age retirement at sixty-five. But if you were a department head, you could stay until sixty-nine. Well Cappy, when he was sixty-five, didn't want to retire so they made him the department head of the announcing department which was himself.

The timing was perfect. If he'd retired at sixty-five, I wasn't around. I was just in my early years at Cahokia and would never have been chosen to replace him at Hialeah. But the fact was that he stayed on until he was sixty-nine and then retired from Hialeah in the winter of '71, and then he mandatorily had to leave NYRA in '72.

One day they sent Pat Lynch, the Vice President down to Hialeah to listen to me. Pat told me a funny story before he passed away. He said he walked in and saw an East Coast bookmaker in the paddock back there and said to him, "How's this kid calling the races?" and the bookmaker replied, "When this kid says the horse is in front, he's in front." Pat listened to me call one race and then suggested that NYRA hire me as their announcer. I went to New York in 1971 as Fred's assistant, and that was one of the most wonderful years of my life because I loved Cappy.... He was just a wonderful human being.

Dave continued,

He was a role model in terms of being a human being. I had already been calling races for eight years, and I did not use his style at all.... You know he never mentioned the jockey's name, and we were not allowed to call the finish back then. They didn't want the result to get out of the confines of the racetrack. It was a really strange time.... So there alone are two story lines that pretty well hand-cuffed an announcer.

I was the one that originated crayons/flair pens. That's me. Oh, yes. Well, Fred Capposella would take his program, and he would take a red pen, and he would circle the words "purple" or "yellow." I thought if you're gonna circle the colors, and it works for him, why not use the flair pens. So I started to make the caps and the arms ... I didn't teach Luke [Kruytbosch], but I am 100 percent sure that I am the one that started that.... As they come on the track, as you're making the colors and putting them on your program with the name of the horse, it's a wonderful stamp of recognition. I don't need to do it. I've called them for eight years without it. But it's a wonderful system.

Anyway, Cappy and I became great friends in the year that I was his assistant and then he retired in '72, and I became the New York announcer.

Remember too, in my days in New York, and calling all of those Triple Crown races, we didn't have colored saddlecloths. I think colored saddlecloths are a terrific thing for the patrons, especially the simulcast patrons because they can see that if you bet the #1 horse, you're looking for the red saddlecloth. You may not be able to hear the announcer, but you always know you've got the 1, you got the red. I just think they're great, and they're beneficial for the announcer too. But before that, you identified the horse using the colors that the jockeys wear and that's of the owners. And up at Saratoga (which shows it's much easier to remember than it is to forget) in a Bernard Baruch Stakes race at Saratoga, Mac Miller sent out a horse for Charles Engelhardt in each race. Red Ransom was one of them ... I had Red Ransom running in two successive races, because I hadn't forgotten. You have to wipe that race out of your mind.

His own tricks of the trade served him well. Dave Johnson quickly became a household name in the industry. His seven-year stretch in the Big Apple bore witness to some of the most emotional Thoroughbred moments of our time. Dave was not the only star to debut in 1972. On the Fourth of July a strapping chestnut, the third offspring of 1957 Preakness Stakes winner Bold Ruler, the greatest sire of his generation, burst onto the scene. Secretariat. And Dave got to call the colt in his very first race. Secretariat was impeded after the start and finished fourth. He would never finish that far back again.

With seven victories in nine races that could have been eight but for disqualification, Secretariat became the first two-year-old to be voted Horse of the Year. One of those victories was on September 16 at Belmont when Dave called him in the 6½ furlongs Futurity Stakes: "Secretariat moving up on the outside.... There goes Secretariat with a rush on the outside getting the lead. Secretariat now in front by a length. Swift Courier toward the inside second. Stop The Music moving up on the far outside. Seventy yards from the finish it's Secretariat in front."

Pundits were not surprised that the 1973 Triple Crown was at his mercy, but nobody could have possibly envisioned the manner in which "Big Red," as he was affectionately known, would triumph.

Most racing fans are familiar with Chic Anderson, the CBS race caller, who described the legendary three-year-old in the Belmont Stakes as "moving like a tremendous machine" to the television audience. Dave was the voice on the loudspeaker that day, and what fans at the track heard was his stirring rendition of the phenomenal margin of victory that Secretariat was extending with every stride. Dave recalled,

> I called him in front by twenty-five lengths. And I don't think I'd ever called a horse that far in front before in a Thoroughbred race, maybe a steeplechase, but never a Thoroughbred race. So I was pretty accurate at the 16th pole to call him twenty-five considering he was still lengthening his margin of victory as he was drawing away from the field. The greatest horse I've ever seen was Secretariat winning the Belmont. In terms of a racehorse, you bring any horse in the history of the sport to him on Belmont Day, and he beats them. That's how good he was that day. The whole Secretariat story and the people surrounding it, was just a wonderful part of my life.
>
> He had the good fortune to have been ridden by Ron Turcotte and trained by Lucien Laurin, and they just made a helluva team.

Dave announced at Belmont Park on October 8, 1973, when Secretariat demonstrated his power on turf in the Man O' War Stakes: "Into the final furlong Secretariat has the lead by three. It's Tentam second. Past the sixteenth pole. Ron Turcotte aboard Secretariat. Secretariat in front!

Dave also recalled, "I went to Canada and called his last race at Woodbine for CBS radio when Eddie Maple rode him." It was the 1⅝-mile Canadian International Championship Stakes, and Secretariat won by 6½ lengths raising his career earnings to $1,316,808. Dave said, "It was a great couple of years. And you know, I was around for Riva Ridge also."

Riva Ridge was another freakish galloper trained by Laurin, 1971 Champion Two-Year-Old Colt with earnings of more than $500,000 that many consider may well have won the 1972 Triple Crown had it not been for a heavy rainstorm at Pimlico Racecourse that led to a muddy track for the Preakness Stakes that year. He ran fourth but rebounded in the Belmont Stakes to complete two-thirds of the Triple Crown, only to be upstaged by his stablemate, Secretariat, 12 months later. And Dave called both horses when they ran against each other on September 15, 1973, in the Marlboro Cup Handicap: "On the outside Turcotte takes Secretariat up now taking the lead by a length. Riva Ridge is second. The rest of them far back as they come into the final sixteenths of a mile. On the outside it's

Secretariat. Secretariat in front by two. Riva Ridge second ... Secretariat, in front!"

In 2000 Dave anchored an Eclipse Award–winning ESPN Sports Century special, titled "Secretariat" that pays homage to the champion and remains one of the most inspiring documentaries on the Sport of Kings. Secretariat's Triple Crown success, the first in a quarter of a century, had managed to put horse racing on the cover of *Sports Illustrated*, and the industry was on a high. But a mere two years later, fans had a bitter pill to swallow.

In 1975 at Belmont Park, in what was billed "The Battle of the Sexes," the beloved filly Ruffian, the only undefeated three-year-old that year, with a record of 10–0, took on the colt Foolish Pleasure, winner of the Kentucky Derby. It turned out to be a match race. Ruffian had led the field every step of the way when disaster struck. A hushed silence befell the Belmont crowd. Ruffian, the apple of the eye of every racing fan, broke down helplessly.

Dave remembered, "Foolish Pleasure running down the track to the far turn and Ruffian being pulled up and [Jacinto] Vasquez trying to brace his shoulder upon her flank." Dave played himself in the 2007 made-for-television movie *Ruffian*. He said it was very difficult having to relive the filly's last race: "It's like opening up a wound. It was a very tough time. Wonderful horse. Good memories. And then one of the most tragic days of my life. That, and when I was calling Barbaro in the Preakness on radio, would rank as the saddest moments. With Barbaro, my thoughts immediately shot back to 1975."

The undefeated 2006 Kentucky Derby winner, Barbaro, who broke down shortly after the gates opened in the Preakness Stakes, lost a courageous battle with a series of ailments in January 2007. Dave said, "I really thought that Barbaro would win the Triple Crown. I think it'll happen. I hope it happens in my lifetime again. I hope to get to see it."

There has not been a Triple Crown winner since Affirmed in 1978, who came hot on the heels of the great Seattle Slew in 1977, and although Dave was behind the microphone calling the action, it was not as the New York track announcer. He explained,

> I left New York racing in 1977 over a contract money dispute. To make a long story short, I was doing commercials and a television show for the Thoroughbreds and the trotters on Super Station WOR, and they basically wanted exclusivity but they didn't want to pay for exclusivity. It would have meant a pay cut of over 35 percent. Back in the '70s there wasn't the big money that people throw around now, but a 35 percent pay cut was not something that I

was willing to do. It just rankled me. I said, "If you want to pay me to be your exclusive voice, I'll call your races and make your commercials and go to Lions' Clubs."

They basically said, "Oh no-no-no, we just want you to stop all of that outside work and just call the races, but we're not going to pay you anymore." Well that was the easiest decision I ever made in my life. So I left New York racing and immediately was hired by Santa Anita and the Meadowlands.

Actually, I was interviewed and hired by Santa Anita before I even left New York racing. They'd hired me, and we made a deal ... I was there seven years. I started in '77, left after the 82–83 season. I had a situation where I had quite a bit of voice-over work in New York. I was basically flying cross-country every other week. I would fly [back to New York] after the Sunday races, work Monday, Tuesday, Wednesday, and then fly back for the Thursday card.... Santa Anita didn't want to make up for the lost income that I would have from voiceovers....

[Sonny Werblin] knew of my work from Saratoga, and I was very friendly with his whole family including his son Tom. Sonny was the owner of the New York Jets, and the one who signed Joe Namath to the $400,000 contract. He was an incredible sportsman. He owned half of Monmouth Park [New Jersey] at one point. In 1977, he was Governor Byrnes' pick to put the Meadowlands on the map. So he hired me there.

Even though his passion lies with the Thoroughbreds, Dave became well acquainted with some of the greatest harness horses in the nation. In addition to its Thoroughbred meet, the Meadowlands is the premier harness track in the country and home to the premier harness race, the Hambletonian. Dave joins Tom Durkin as the only other person to have called both the Kentucky Derby and the Hambletonian to a national television audience. Dave said,

I've been very blessed to have that association having called it a couple of times with ABC Sports. I had a twenty-five year association with ABC. We also did the races on a network called the Sports Network which originated out of Canada but broadcast all over the world.

It's very humbling when I think about the Kentucky Derby or the Hambletonian to think that long after I'm gone, somebody will press a button somewhere and that my call will come out, and that in some way is the oral history of that race. And that long after I'm gone, those calls will be floating around the universe. It's a wonderful feeling, but it's very humbling to know that this is one of the legacies I leave, and I'm so proud of that.

And it is not just the old guard who fell in love with Dave's Kentucky Derby calls. Modern-day training legend Bob Baffert, a three-time Derby winner — Silver Charm (1997), Real Quiet (1998), and War Emblem (2002) — is a huge fan.

Bob said, "He was great. I love the way he called the Kentucky Derby because you get used to a certain guy's style. There are twenty horses, and it's hard to get it right. But when they turn for home, everybody's waiting for him to say, 'And down the stretch they come!' and the crowd just goes nuts and you need that."

His friends and family are tremendously proud of Dave and not simply because of his achievements in the racing industry. He is clearly a fabulous brother and son. Given the age difference between him and his siblings, they have a tendency to see him as a kind of father figure, an image that appears to have strengthened as they all got older, especially to sister Donna. She explained,

> My mom and Dave kind of held the family together throughout my father's illness. My mother really kept our family together with laughter. We joked about everything. We are a really close family and have a great sense of humor. We e-mail each other constantly with continuing jokes that we add on to all the time.
>
> He was so funny, the way he would tease me about my dates. We all teased each other. I went out with a fellow one time that was overweight quite a bit. When I came home, from the date, Dave had a beach ball with a belt around it on my bed that said, "Nice meeting Ed." We've all fought weight our whole lives so it wasn't anything we were not familiar with. We were terribly irreverent.

Donna adores her older brother. She said, "He was always so good to us. Oh gosh, I remember him taking us all to New York for the first time. A trip for all of us after my father had passed away. And he took us to Acapulco, because he went to school in Mexico."

Dave had been in Mexico as a scholarship student at the University of Mexico where he spent a year immersing himself in Spanish. He lived with a Mexican family and really absorbed the language. He also spent one summer in Miami, living with his aunt and selling tickets for an airline company. He also roofed houses in the mornings and went to Hialeah in the afternoons. Later, he attended college at Southern Illinois University in Edwardsville.

Dave loves the performing arts and at one time he pursued theater and diction. He said, "My grandfather and grandmother were blackface comedians. They were on the Orpheum Circuit, along with their whole family. My mom was a dancer. My uncle was a ukulele player and a dancer. It was called The McLeod Troop on the Orpheum circuit. This was back in the late '20s, early '30s so when you think about the breeding lines, here I am with a great love of Thoroughbreds and the performances of my side of the family with vaudeville. There's only one job in racing that combines those two, and that's the track announcer."

Dave's already accomplished career rose to new heights at Santa Anita. He became identified with sensational horses, such as the 1978 Santa Anita Handicap winner and crowd-favorite Vigors and the 1980 Horse of the Year Spectacular Bid. Dave also became known as the man with the phrase, "and down the stretch they come." Dave recalled,

It came about at Santa Anita in the late '70s. The sound system there was the same sound system that was in the Marx Brothers movies. Look at the infield, and you'd see these poles with cone-like speakers coming out of them ... Santa Anita did not own it. They rented it from a sound system, and it was cheaper for them to rent it every year because it would have been very expensive to rewire. Anyway, there was a second and a half delay between the time you said something in the announcer's booth and it came back over those cones. You had to block out what was coming back at you. Very tough.

So when I was calling races at Santa Anita, in order to really be heard over a big crowd I had to underline it, to put a rumble in it. And there was a big old gray horse named Vigors, and he brought out these big crowds when he was going up to the Santa Anita Handicap, the Big 'Cap, in the prep races. He had this very eye-appealing way of running. He would wheel to the middle of the track, drop his head, and he would just smoke home past everybody else, and the crowd would go wild. So in order to be heard over that, I would always underline that and project whatever I was saying once they turned for home.

But I noticed on the evening news when I would say, "and down the stretch they come" that I could be heard over the crowd. No matter where I said it, that's where the TV stations picked up their call for their shows.

And then I noticed that people started to say it back to me, and it was not forced or planned. I have tapes of me calling races at Fairmount Park and Hialeah in which I said that, but I didn't put the rumble underneath it. There was no emphasis like I have now.

One time I was in Atlanta visiting my sister and her family, and we just decided to walk down from the second floor of a mall to the main floor, just my sister and I. And as we passed a guy, he said, "and DOWN the stairs he comes!" Never stopped, no autographs, just the line, and disappeared.

Celebrity status can bring with it some odd reactions from race fans, just ask track announcer Tom Durkin, the current voice of New York Racing. One day at Belmont Park someone said to him: "Wait I know who you are. You're not Dave Johnson."

Dave can identify with that. He said, "After I left New York Racing, somebody came up to me and said, 'Didn't you used to be Dave Johnson?' That's true. It happened in front of Bloomingdales in 1977."

Trainer Neil Howard said, "Dave is a great friend of mine. I always thought Dave was a very very good race caller and very articulate."

Hall of Fame jockey Mike Smith added, "Oh, Dave Johnson I absolutely love! Man he's famous for that ["And down the stretch they come!"] And he's just a great human being too. He's a wonderful wonderful man. I think the world of him, you know?"

Dave remains instantly recognizable for his now-famous line, but racing is not the only field he works in. Dave is in many commercials, both on camera and as voice-over talent. He has also been a spokesperson for Mobil Oil, a New York furniture outlet, Bayer Aspirin, AOL, Desenex, and AT&T.

Dave said, "I started doing commercials soon after I got an agent, and I got an agent after I'd been doing the WOR Channel 9 racing show in New York. One time, I went to the casting director. He was having the casting call and he said, 'It's a race between two mops and one of them has been in Spic and Span, and what we want is for you to sound exactly like the guy who calls the Kentucky Derby on ABC.' And I said, 'Well, I am the guy who calls the Kentucky Derby on ABC.' And he said, 'Oh, that's great.' I didn't get the job! Another sportscaster got it. I thought for sure I was going to get that one. So, it's a zany business, the whole racing, television, commercials. I'm in a zany part of the world."

Dave also had small roles on several popular TV shows, including *Fantasy Island* (1981), *Diff'rent Strokes* (1981), *Magnum PI* (1982), and *Tales from the Darkside* (1984) as well as in movies, like *Phar Lap* (1983), *The Longshot* (1986), and *Moving* (1988).

Dave has always kept busy and harnessed his strong entrepreneurial spirit. His sister, Donna, traces this back to his formative years: "He was always making money. I remember him putting me in a wagon when I was little, going to the park, and selling watermelon slices. He was always involved with organizing something. He was always in charge of everything. He was well liked. I think people were a little envious of him because he was wise beyond his years."

Dave began to exercise some of that wisdom by investing in the theater. His first Broadway investment was in 1983 in a comedy show titled *Noises Off*, and it turned out to be very profitable.

Dave said, "I made a good amount of money. However, I also got the financial statements every week, and I saw just how outrageous the costs were and that when you have a hit, you really have a hit, but that the costs of running a show are enormous."

That first investment enabled Dave to get his feet wet so that by the time a similar opportunity came his way, he was ready to take the plunge.

When asked what he believed in most, Dave said, "Myself. Well, I *do* believe in myself." Credit: Lisa Photo, Inc.

His connection was a great friend of his, Rocco Landesman. Dave had known him from St. Louis through the racing industry. Landesman is the owner of six Broadway theaters known as the Jujamcyn Theatres.

Dave explained, "Rocco had been touting the idea of making a musical out of the 1968 Mel Brooks Oscar-winning classic movie, *The Producers*, which is one of my favorite movies of all time.... *Noises Off* was a comedy, not a musical, so when he started talking about making it into a musical, I thought, 'Well I'll get back into the investing on this one.' So I did and from day one everybody says, 'Oh, what a slam dunk it was.' But you know, 90 percent of Broadway musicals close and lose money; it's a huge gamble."

It turned out to be the best gamble of his life. Dave already enjoyed a lucrative income as a track announcer, but that was nothing compared to the return on an investment in a Broadway hit.

Billed as "the biggest hit to land on Broadway in years," *The Producers* took home a record-breaking 12 Tony Awards in 2001. Dave said, "It's a mega hit, and after that everything else is just additional income. It's like I hit the Pick Six.... It has given me the kind of cushion to my old age that I'm really thankful for."

Neither fame nor fortune has changed Dave, however. He still lives in the same apartment building that he has been in since 1973 and has his favorite routine: "I go to my favorite coffee shop and read the papers early in the morning. Then, I may have an audition or run some errands or whatever and then come back to my apartment in New York. What a great life! I may watch a little Saratoga from my office, bet on a couple of races. Sunday I usually head to an OTB [off-track betting facility], play with my buddies, and have lunch."

Dave has been generous with his earnings from the Broadway megahit. He bought an apartment in New York for his mother, paid for family trips to Europe, and even helped put his cleaning lady's children through school.

Dave serves on the boards for the Don MacBeth Memorial Jockey Fund, which assists injured or disabled riders and their families, and for the Thoroughbred Retirement Foundation, which helps place racehorses in a loving home after their racing careers are over.

Dave explained, "The Disabled Jockeys' Fund is one that Charlsie Canty and I did some work for. New Vocations in Ohio is another. Sometimes I'll do a benefit, and the fee will go directly to them." Charlsie teamed up with Dave to anchor the Triple Crown broadcasts on ABC television, and they have remained close friends ever since. Dave said,

> The people are the best part. In any job, the biggest kick you get are the human associations. That is what makes the SIRIUS show so wonderful. I'm working with old friends. Bill Finley and I have been friends for twenty-five years.
>
> My producer Ed Pappas is another one. I met him about twenty-five years ago too. It's really wonderful when you can make a career with your friends.

And for Dave, the "human associations" with family are the most precious. He has, in particular, a deep connection to his mother, Mary, who fittingly is afforded the closing words: "Everybody always says if you do something with your life that you really truly love, you're going to do a good job and I believe that ... he's very personable. His disposition, it's a wonderful happy disposition. He faces life in a wonderful way."

CHAPTER 10

Robert Geller

Robert Geller: "The world record holder of the biggest streak in history. Peppers Pride by five!"

"All in the gate. Locked up. And away and racing!" Thus begins premier track announcer Robert Geller's calls. Robert enjoys the best of two worlds: five late spring and summer months at Emerald Downs and four winter and early spring months at Sunland Park. His answering machine explains: "I've got the Northwest and the Southwest covered."

Robert Geller has called races in Australia, Hong Kong, the United States, and Canada. For six and a half years, he was the English commentator for the Royal Hong Kong Jockey Club. When he arrived in 1989, the ICAC [Independent Commission Against Corruption] was cleaning up the image of racing at Sha Tin and Happy Valley racetracks.

Robert explained, "I'd heard on the news that there had been some huge scandals there involving jockeys and trainers. By the time I had come in, they had appointed a completely different administrative leader, a British army general named Major Guy Watkins, and his job was to clean the image up. There had been a bad taste left about Hong Kong that everything was corrupt."

Robert loved the international aspect and, for him, it was all about the announcing. However, racing only took place two days a week. Robert explained,

> They had to find ways of utilizing me, and I had to find ways of understanding what was required of me. So I was in that unique position of trying to put the nice cover on Hong Kong racing for them, and with that came an advent of international races that they had never had.
>
> It's a very high profile world. You take an Oaks Day, a big race day, and

make that your standard day. That's how it is [in Hong Kong], and that's the hard part of Hong Kong because it becomes tiring to maintain that level of intensity on something that may not warrant it.

However, the racing was quickly moving from unraced horses, called subscription griffins, to some of the best horses in the world. Those regular race days attracted 30,000 fans. And on the big occasion days, there would be between 50,000 and 60,000. That was due, in large part, to racing being the only legal form of gambling in the entire country, other than the lottery also run by the Jockey Club.

There was a chasm between the administrative world of the Jockey Club and the backstretch workers. And Robert was caught in the middle. He explained, "I was very naïve, and I understood that I had to please the Jockey Club because I was in their system. There's just a lot of animosity sometimes with people who are on the backside of racetracks, not for any other reason than they just want to have their own identity. Hong Kong was tricky because they were spoiled." The jockeys and trainers were given their very own apartments and interest-free loans on their fancy cars. Robert continued, "They were given the world, but they would still complain.... Those were the things that were hard for me ... to understand where they were coming from."

Yet on the positive side, Robert thrived in the high-energy city. He said, "Hong Kong is a very exciting city. It was such a wonderful experience to be living overseas. It was wonderful to learn the culture and to go deeper into that." Robert, who had already reached an advanced level in French and who had studied Hebrew all 12 years that he had attended Mt. Scopus, a Jewish school, could make himself understood in Cantonese. He had more in common with his Hong Kong Chinese friends than with his bosses in the Jockey Club. He explained, "I had a very hard time learning how to live with such excess of wealth [of the ruling British]. Lots of these people weren't that talented. Yet they were substantially wealthy. And some people who were in the Hong Kong society were living in small apartments trying to make a go of it. They were doing draftsman jobs and doing the best that they could. And my heart went with them, because I was someone who didn't like to see that imbalance, and I was kind of torn."

Robert Geller was born on July 31, 1959, in Birmingham, England. When he was only three and a half years old, his family immigrated to Australia where they settled in the cosmopolitan city of Melbourne. His sister Yvonne was 11 and his sister Karen was six. Robert's father, John, worked as a lady's fashion manufacturer in the "rag" trade. His mother, Ann, was a stay-at-home mom for most of his childhood.

There is racing history in the family. Robert's paternal grandfather owned a dog track. And his maternal grandfather was a bookmaker in Brighton, England. Robert was four years old when he went to his first race. It was in Melbourne, and to this day, he remembers everything from that day: "A horse that I fell in love with straightaway was called Future.... I've got a picture of Future who won a couple of top-class races and was a very game horse. He ran second all the time. I loved that horse."

Karen explained the family dynamics that involved horse racing:

> Our parents had trouble settling into Australian life and gravitated towards the races, a leisure activity that reminded them of England. The entire weekend was devoted to the sport. On Friday nights our parents read the racing paper and made selections for Saturday. Early on Saturday morning the racing form show was blaring out of the radio, with our parents paying complete attention to the tips. And no child was able to interrupt it.... We were in the car by half past ten, heading for the track to "get a good seat." Saturday was spent at the track, and Saturday night was spent commiserating and watching a show on television that was hosted by the top race caller in Melbourne, Bill Collins. Sunday morning was spent watching another television show that reviewed all the races from the day before and gave tipping forecasts on the horses to watch at upcoming meetings.

Karen continued,

> If you didn't like racing, then you were really saying you didn't like Mum and Dad. They were so heavily identified with racing that they took it very person-ally. They talked about jockeys and trainers as if they knew them intimately. Of course they didn't, but we held these people in high esteem and occasion-ally obtained their autographs and boasted about them as if we had just met the Prime Minister or Paul McCartney. When I owned up to not liking racing, they were very disappointed with me, and I found myself on the outside too [along with Yvonne who had reluctantly gone to the races, but rebelled and sat there with a radio earpiece and listened to pop music]. Robert kept his loy-alty to their interest, and in those days it was a way of having their complete attention.

Robert remembered, "It was a safe place for me ... an escape. My sis-ters were quite bored with it. I wasn't bored. I was totally into it."

He was so into it that he would even stay up at night with his radio. He said it was "turned up ever so slightly so as not to wake anyone and lis-ten to the live radio broadcast of the Epsom Derby with Bert Bryant. I was really into horse racing, and I knew as a child that that interest was very much a passion in my life." Robert, like Australian Michael Wrona, began his illustrious career in track announcing by calling races from his bedroom floor boards. Robert explained, "I would create a racetrack, and I just pulled out little cars and little toys and rolled the dice and every time there's a different plank; six planks might have been a furlong. And I called the races as a kid so it was always there." Karen said that her little brother called races every day while she and her sister did the dishes.

It was not a happy household. Robert's father was an angry and rather bitter man. And his mother was controlled by her husband and she relied on her children for her happiness. On top of that, Robert knew at a young age that he was gay: "My father was extremely homophobic. I came out to him at twenty-one by which stage he was ready to receive me as a person.... He had to go through a lot of grief about his own value system. But as I was growing up, no, he was not helpful in that way. That's ok. We worked that out." His father died in 1986 when Robert was twenty-six. Robert recalled, "He came through for me. In fact, he turned his world and thinking around a lot. My sisters were always, 'No big deal.' But it was a big deal for my parents."

So was education. Robert's parents were not financially well-off, but his father sacrificed a great deal so that Robert could attend an expensive school. He graduated from the Lincoln Institute of Health Sciences in 1980 with a degree in communication disorders in speech pathology. He worked for two years with children and adults who had cerebral palsy. According to Karen, "He became a trusted and exemplary speech pathologist at St. Vincent's Hospital in Melbourne working with car accident victims and brain injury patients. He was compassionate and committed in this work."

However, during the years he worked in his medical career, Robert was still following his dream of calling races. He said, "I knew my heart was not satisfied if I never gave it a shot. My transition was sort of from part-time hobby to practicing part-time to eventually getting into a switch from career paths which took ten years."

Talk about dedication and persistence! Robert often drove several hundred miles to a country track to practice his calls. He said that Australians encourage young people to practice, and he had been able to call harness racing trials for a couple of years at Marong and Sebastian Harness tracks as well. And for four years Robert called the harness racing trials at Kilmore Harness Club, which was the second main harness track in Victoria. He was interested in every single aspect of horse racing, and he took a course to be a bookmaker's clerk, also known as a penciller, run by Melbourne bookmaker Anthony Doughty. Robert explained,

The penciller writes the bets down so as someone comes up to bet, the book-maker sets the odds and does the board. And someone comes up and says, "I'll have ten on the nose on Wonderboy." You write all of the horses' names in, and with Wonderboy, you write down the bet 20–10, and you add it up, and you put down ten dollars, and it's supposed to pay off thirty. And the next bet comes in, and you have to basically keep tab on all of the bets as they come in. At some point the bookmaker will ask, "How much am I standing to lose on this?" and according to that, he might bring the horse down in price, or he might put the horse out depending, and you have to keep the book up. And then you have to pay them out. You mustn't make mistakes! It wasn't city track pressure, but there were times when a rush would come, and there were some big coups. Top gamblers would come down the line, and they'd put four or five people in their little posse together, and they'd hit all of us at once. And we'd all get caught for a lot.

Robert was penciling the day he got to call his very first race at the age of 22. He was at the bush track in Alexandra, and the regular announcer had not shown up. A call went out to find someone to take his place. Robert exclaimed, "My heart started beating. Omigod! I've been waiting for this opportunity."

The bookmaker was not nearly as eager for Robert to call his first race as the nervous and nervy Robert was. He didn't release him to call until the last minute. Robert recalled, "I ran from my bookmaking stand to the race stand which was just a rostrum, just stood there, and it was really late to learn the colors. And they were about to go off, and I had nowhere to balance. I had binoculars, microphone, book, and it was a bit of a disaster. I really hadn't had enough time. I walked off from that, and they were like, 'Oh, good try, good try.' Damn!"

Robert knew he could do much better given the proper time to learn the horses' names. He asked for and got a second chance. He noted, "I went back two races later, and it was really good. I knew I could do it! It was the first moment where I was confident that I was not fooling myself."

Australian racing is different in many respects from American racing. There are no "meets" like in America that last for 60 or 90 consecutive days. The city tracks hold their races on the weekends, with possibly another thrown in on Wednesday. Therefore, if a race caller wants daily work, he has to travel out to the rural tracks.

Another difference concerned radio and nonradio work. Robert explained, "The radio work was very elite. There were only four or five people who were used, and they covered all of the TAB or totalized agency board tracks. So I used to do what is called non–TAB meets which were the lower level."

In 1984 Robert got his first official job in Wangaratta, but it was for calling races only ten days a year. But it was a start. In 1983 Robert had called one race on the ANZAC Day card at Seymour Racing Club, and in 1984 he called one race there again. The following year he called the entire card. Robert pointed out, "I had little experiences here and there. But I got that job in Wangaratta, and then from that it opened up the northeast circuit. And there are four provincial tracks — Wangaratta, Tatura, Benalla, and Wodonga — in that circuit. And they all ended up employing me over the next four or five years. So I became a regular weekend worker."

Racing had its high and low points during those years. Robert recalled, "A first-time starter was leading in the stretch at Wodonga. It kind of stumbled and tripped; the winning post was made of wood, and it just skewered itself. It was just hushed, complete hush. Silence. I've never seen anything like it ever again."

Another time Robert was calling a race in Seymour: "It was going really well, and I swear to God, the jockey goes off like a sack of potatoes after the wire. And I'm like, 'He's not getting up.' The next thing they're running over with the emergency to bring him back to life, and I'm, 'This is just unbelievable.' He had died, and they [the stewards] said, 'You have to make an announcement.' And I said, 'Well what am I supposed to say?' I was pretty inexperienced, and they told me what to say, and I said it."

Robert drove hundreds of miles from the racetrack at Wangaratta to Wodonga, Tatura, and Benalla; the tracks were miles from Melbourne. He said, "I was obsessed. You have to be in order to do that sort of nonsense. But it was wonderful." He also covered morning race trials at Yarra Glen and Geelong racetracks, just outside of Melbourne, and throughout the summer months also enjoyed a regular gig as course commentator at the popular picnic meetings of Woolamai and Wonthaggi race clubs located along the picturesque southern peninsula.

The popular Bill Collins, who retired on Easter in 1988, contacted Robert about a position as the second-in-line race caller behind Bryan Martin, who had taken over as the number one at the racing industry owned and run radio station, 3UZ, previously 3DB. Robert said, "Bill Collins accompanied me in the interview, but the position went to Terry McCauliffe." He was later offered greyhound announcing on the network. He was calling greyhounds for the radio station, working as the weekend announcer in the circuit, but he still hadn't broken into calling the Thoroughbreds. Robert admitted, "I was getting a foot in the door, but I was thinking, 'Greyhounds? I don't like greyhounds.' But I'd previously taken myself out to greyhound trials anyway, gaining some experience with them at a little track called Melton Kennel Club."

Robert began calling greyhounds on the air for the Sale Greyhounds TAB meetings and before long was being asked to fill in when needed for Melbourne's leading greyhound race caller, Ron Hawkswell, at Cranbourne Greyhounds, the second largest track for dog racing in the state. He would also endure the long drive and often terrible weather to get to the Shepparton Greyhounds on last-minute notice from the station. By now Robert had just about given up his dream of becoming a full-time track announcer: "My best job was at St. Vincent's Hospital in the neurosurgical unit. I was working with cancer patients, car accident victims, stroke patients. And I thought, 'It doesn't matter if I never get a job in the racing field, because I'm kind of comfortable.' I was at that point where I had accepted it, because I had given up."

However, Robert was destined to become a track announcer. It was at this time that he learned there was a job opening in Hong Kong for an Australian race caller. Robert was offered the position and he accepted immediately: "It was huge because it was leaving the country. But there's a big part of me that loves to travel. I used to think as a kid, 'How will I ever resolve this? I want to do racing, but I want to travel.' I never knew how I could marry the two."

He also ended his medical career: "I decided to let go of the speech pathology, because I went so far with that. So much time ... but [the job opportunity in Hong Kong] came out of nowhere, and I had worked for this all along." Robert knew he had to follow his heart.

Robert has called races for two decades, and one of his most memorable was the Hong Kong Gold Cup in 1990. He recalled, "It was the most exciting finish I've ever seen in a horse race. It was incredible. There were four horses head to head, and a fifth one is coming. And it comes through the pack, and they go to the wire, and I'm like, "I know that that horse got up, but I'm trying to remember if I've got the right name.' I think I learned a lot from that call. It really helped me. I wasn't necessarily happy with the call because I could have been more instant with it, but I was just like a fan who was almost thrown by it because it was almost unbelievable.... Yeah, I did call the winner, Starlight, right."

Many announcers would have been content to remain in Hong Kong and call races at the prestigious tracks for the rest of their careers. But after six and a half years, Robert was becoming dissatisfied with his lifestyle: "It's not a place that has middle ground. You've got all these wonderful hotels, and you've got very high profiles, sort of high-end living where people like to spend a lot of money. And then you've got simple living; market life where people don't really spend much at all. And so your life was very extreme." Robert struggled with the expatriates who swarmed into the city, made extreme amounts of money, and departed. He struggled with the excesses. And he struggled with being a gay man in a city that was not receptive to gays: "A lot of Chinese men are in the closet, and I was very uncomfortable about coming out. I was insecure about it in Hong Kong because it was a very old-school, old-boy network."

The racing was beginning to burn him out too: "Unless it was as big as Texas, it wasn't important. Well, I didn't like that. That was hard on me. But I also handled it because I played the game. 'If you want this to be as big as Texas, I'll make it that big.' The problem is then you can get addicted to that. And I got into my comfort zone there. When I got ready to leave, I was afraid to leave. I had to start paying my rent again, because they [the Jockey Club] pay for that. I had to start proving I can call races where I don't know all the horses, because in Hong Kong they were often the same ones. The Big Occasion Days I handled, but I was tired of it. It was wearing me down."

Robert instinctively knew that if he was going to leave race calling in Hong Kong, it had to be soon. He bravely did just that. In 1995 the Jockey Club loaned Robert to call a race in Vancouver, British Columbia, Canada that they were sponsoring, the Royal Hong Kong Jockey Club Stakes. While calling the race at Hastings Park in Vancouver, he heard that racing in Washington State, which had come to a halt with the closure of Longacres in 1992, would resume in 1996 at Emerald Downs in Auburn. He called the track, offered to send them his tape, and met with vacationing investors who recommended him to Emerald Downs president Ron Crockett. He landed the job.

Robert reflected on his move to Emerald Downs:

I could come to somewhere like Emerald which might be considered small, and somehow see that as bigger. Because bigger in prestige and space and money does not buy you happiness unless that also is where you resonate. I could bring myself to something here at Emerald that was more like a team building a new track with no guarantee of success and take the skills that I had learned from Hong Kong and apply them here.

Once I came to Emerald Downs, I didn't know how long I'd be here. Ron Crockett said, "Just give me a verbal agreement that you'll stay at least two years." And it's been fourteen. I really feel like it's a team, a very strong connected team. It runs itself like an A grade track. It might not be perceived as that. It's probably perceived as a B grade track. Who cares? It's trying to bring its level up all the time. We want to have a turf track.

I've been the signature voice of this track, and I never thought it would last that long. That was partly what attracted me. When I saw this place I thought, "It's totally new. I can put my complete freedom of expression here, and there's nothing to compare it with." I was very nervous about it. I'm a very insecure person when it comes to starting things off. I never have any confidence in myself, but after awhile when I find out what I need to know, then I can stride out just fine.

And stride out he does! Robert's sister Karen said, "He has mastered so many things in the racing game and can do it with his eyes closed. I believe he has a photographic memory and tremendously good judgment for a photo finish.... His main mastery is within himself.... Now he gets up, goes to the track and gives his best, then leaves and gets on with the rest of his creative life."

Robert feels that concentration is really important: "The only time I put notes on the page is when it's a sloppy track. I always make sure I've got the gear changes and color changes, colors of horses. Because they do have a lot of sloppy tracks at Emerald, and it gets quite hard when you have a lot of deep closers. So those things are really crucial to have. Sometimes you're just looking at a shadow roll. I'm strong visually, and I think that's part of the intellectual fun of it: that you can just match it quickly."

There is a lot to be said for experience. Robert explained, "When you do not remember a horse, like as a novice, you start off and you just panic and there's a pregnant pause. But when you get experienced you know when

Robert Geller has been Emerald Downs' only track announcer.

you've missed a horse, and you just quietly go back to the one you know while you find the horse that you missed, and then bring it in as if it was nothing. And there are moments you still know that it's not as big to the public as it is to you. And all of those things give you an anchor."

Robert continued, "I really love to try to read a race. That's to me the challenge. What I mean by that is they might have gone a furlong, and I think, 'I can tell who's going to win, or I certainly can tell who isn't going to win.' And sometimes it's very gratifying because I can see a horse at the back, and I know that horse is going to be right there. And you can pick it up early. And they're the calls I like. That is just a wonderful moment; you can see the way the horse is settled, the way the rider is holding the horse, and the speed of the race. You know that that's going to change later."

Many racing fans do not realize that track announcers must find a circuit that has complementary dates. For instance, Keeneland has a spring race meet that lasts for three weeks and another one in the autumn that runs for three weeks. Saratoga has a summer meet. Belmont runs a spring meet and one in the fall. And Aqueduct races in the winter, thereby giving those lucky fans in New York year-round racing. Emerald Downs, located in Auburn, Washington, with a spectacular view of Mount Rainier, runs from mid–April to October. Robert needed to find work for the other half of the year. Enter Sunland Park Racetrack & Casino in New Mexico.

Stan Fulton owns the Sunland Park Racetrack and Casino which runs from mid–December until the middle of April. It has been a good fit for Robert, who began calling races at the Thoroughbred–Quarter Horse meet in November 2000. Robert said, "I was wanting to get a winter job, and it took four years. And it came to fit. The calendar is so much of everything in the United States. I got a job in Sunland, and now I have the two that coexist very well." Recently, however, the meets have overlapped in the spring.

Robert arrived at Sunland as it was taking off in a new direction. He felt that it was all part of a pattern for him: "Hong Kong was trying to come into this international thing. It was on the upswing, on the way to upgrading itself. And we were all starting from scratch trying to build.... It's taken a long time, but I think Emerald in that last two years has gone right up over a hump, and it's going to go forward. And at Sunland I came in right at the time that the casino was starting to take off. I feel like I really am learning that one of my gifts is to know how to bring something forward. That is a very unique experience, because there's excitement, there's uncertainty, and you just don't know where you'll level off."

Calling the short Quarter Horse races was a new challenge for Robert:

"It's just really exciting to call because it's so fast. It sharpens you. And you have so many photo finishes in Quarter Horse racing, because it's shorter. I think they're tougher to call in Quarter Horse racing so sometimes I'd stay out of them. But I'd often call them and put my neck on the line.... The odd thing I never understood is it's the shortest distance, and they allow the longest names. Go figure."

Sunland's prestigious WinStar Derby is a 1⅛ mile race for three-year-olds. In 2005 ESPN's well-respected commentator Randy Moss hailed Robert as "one of the greatest announcers in the country."

Sunland has not been successful yet in getting the needed votes to make its WinStar Derby a graded stakes race. But it has attracted good horses to its course, and in 2005 Thor's Echo won the WinStar Derby. Robert announced, "It's been a match in two. Thor's Echo, Southern Africa, stride-to-stride as they turn.... But Thor's Echo just led, Southern Africa on the outside knuckling down again. Thor's Echo and Southern Africa, it's a test of stamina.... But it is Thor's Echo's Day!"

In 2006 Robert said, ""I swear to God, around the first turn I thought the race was over. What was I going to say? I know Wanna Runner can win." Not only did the colt win, he set a track record. He called, "It's going to be Bob Baffert, Mike Pegram, and Wanna Runner. Wanna Runner, a scintillating win ... four lengths."

Thor's Echo went on to win the Breeders' Cup Sprint in 2006; Wanna Runner set a track record. However, in 2008, the WinStar Derby remained ungraded, and Robert felt that was unjustified: "It greatly angers me to think that someone sitting in his ivory tower can turn around and just poo poo it because it doesn't seem to have status. And yet, why were all the top jockeys [Tyler Baze, Corey Nakatani, Aaron Gryder, Garrett Gomez] in the country flying in? Why were trainers Tom Amoss, Steve Asmussen, Doug O'Neil, and Bob Baffert here? These guys understand there's been a real shift here, and that's why they support us." In 2010 the WinStar Derby became graded.

Robert's loyalty to Sunland Park was apparent as he pointed out why the WinStar Derby deserved to be a graded race: "It's about bringing a racing community in the region of New Mexico on the border of El Paso in a somewhat obscure part of the country that has brought itself up from a very very small bush track to a track that can now offer purses almost to the equivalent of Arlington. It's about offering the community in this region who love the WinStar Derby the chance to have this race graded and legitimately put itself in what I believe is the road to the Kentucky Derby."

Robert called Peppers Pride, five-year-old mare, on March 23, 2008, in the Sydney Valentini Handicap at Sunland. She nailed her 15th win that day and on April 26 at SunRay Park and Casino, she tied the record of 16 consecutive wins shared by Citation, Cigar, Mister Frisky, and Hallowed Dreams. Peppers Pride's storybook ending on the racetrack occurred on December 14, 2008. She raced six furlongs in the New Mexico State Racing Commission Handicap at Sunland, and Robert gave the great mare a great call: "She is now in striking range on the outside but she's still three behind. Top of the lane Negotiablafections two and a half. Here comes the mighty Peppers Pride MOWS her down in the blink of an eye, and she is unheralded. She's going

Peppers Pride now resides at Taylor Made Farm in Kentucky. Credit: Tom Ferry.

to go into another dimension. This will be number nineteen. The world record holder of the biggest streak in history. Peppers Pride by five!"

On January 15, 2009, trainer Joel Marr informed Peppers Pride's fans that she had been retired. Robert said, "I felt honored to have the privilege of calling her win what was her final race. She had also broken the million dollar mark when she went to her nineteenth consecutive win. And actually in calling that race, as I did have a chance to call her several other times, her manner of victory was the most impressive that I had seen in all of her career. So she ended on a high note."

In 2010 she was in foal to Distorted Humor. Robert added, "More importantly is the reality of what it did to New Mexico where she had raced at every track circuit, and I want to just say that people who knock the situation of the quality of the opposition that she ran against are missing the

Robert (right) visits the backside often; here at Emerald Downs with trainer Dave Bennett and 3YO "Mork."

point…. The incredible wisdom of her trainer was to place her where she belonged. And he also realized that when you get a horse who is dominant in a division, how rare it is to find a race written that allows her to actually run regularly."

Robert pointed out, "She won at a mile as well as at six furlongs and lower distances, and that proves that she's got many gears. And why was she so successful? Because her margins of victory were very narrow in most instances. That shows that she had something called 'heart,' and that's what won her the fans."

Most racetrack announcers have other duties and opportunities to interact with horses. At Emerald one can find Robert hanging out on the backside talking to trainers and filming short segments for Comcast on Demand. He puts his love of writing to good use penning a different script each week.

"Mork, the Racehorse" was a segment about how racehorses are named. Mork's actual name is Raging Nono. As a three-year-old, the colt was on the local derby trail for trainer Dave Bennett, and he was eager to talk about the course commentator at Emerald Downs: "He's a character. I very much enjoy his race calling, because he will just come out of the blue sometimes with a comment that you don't expect during a race. Recently it was the Raging Nono thing, and he was waiting for a run, and he was very unlucky not to win. A lot of people wouldn't say that. They would just call a race. He's very colorful."

Another responsibility is handicapping, and Robert thrives on it: "Oh I love to handicap, love, love, love handicapping. Think it's a wonderful challenge, and I think the more you do in any area, the more you love the sport. I love to pick value. I'm very bored with favorites. So my niche is to look for the little unsung hero coming up, and I'm good with that. That's my strength. I have no tolerance for the rational, can't do Beyer figures, can't do speed indexes, don't understand it, don't really care to, but I can tell in the paddock. You look at a horse. I can feel when it's ready to go. The other day I told my camera man, 'This horse: I've got a vibe. Look at him. He's going to win. I just know he's going to win.' And he won!"

Robert took a horse husbandry course run by Riverina College from Wagga Wagga, New South Wales, when he first started out in Australia. He admitted, "I wanted to try to learn everything. I still have those books that I will refer to that teach about pigeon-toed horses, conformation, and Roman noses." He even mucked out stalls and learned how to age a horse by looking into its mouth.

In Washington he has gone out to horse farms and assisted in foaling. He said, "We were filming, and Nina Hagen runs a very good operation, El Dorado Farm. And she said, 'Come stay the night.' We were waiting for the water to break and, of course, you wait and wait and, 'Oh, I give up.' And then it happens! We were right there, and I helped the foal stand. It was pretty amazing."

The most up-close and personal part is owning a racehorse. Robert joined a syndicate and found himself part owner of Asummerforwindy. She raced every year at Emerald Downs until she was seven. "She turned out to be really reliably game. She was not a world beater, but she won I think four times, and she placed a lot. We had a lot of fun."

One graded race that Robert calls is the popular Grade III Longacres Mile at Emerald Downs. In 2003 the speedy Skyjack won it. Robert announced, "But what a powerhouse effort by Skyjack. Skyjack by six."

And in 2008 Wasserman, the hometown favorite, won and the crowd went wild! Robert called, "But here comes True Metropolitan. True Metropolitan down the outside. Wasserman. Tropic Storm in front a length and a half. Wasserman. True Metropolitan ... Wasserman takes the lead. True

Track announcer Robert Geller (right) joins publicity director and anchor Joe Withee in the paddock. Both have been the backbone of Emerald Downs since its inception on June 20, 1996. Courtesy of Duane Hamamura.

Metropolitan fighting back. Wasserman in front and WASSERMAN in a photo!"

In the spring of 2009 Robert was the only announcer to call Mine That Bird as a three year-old before the Triple Crown races. On March 29, the little gelding ran in the Sunland Derby. Robert announced, "Joining them to make a line of three is Mine That Bird.... Battling away is Mine That Bird. Kelly Leak trying to put them away holding on. Mythical Power in second but Kelly Leak goes on to win the Sunland Derby by a length.

Mine That Bird came in fourth. Not getting much respect in the Kentucky Derby, the son of Birdstone went into gate number eight at odds of 50–1. He came out of the Derby the winner, by over eight lengths. Both he and Sunland Derby gained respect, especially after the bay's second-place finish behind Rachel Alexandra two weeks later in the Preakness.

Co-owner Mark Allen was still numb the day after the Derby, but he was loyal to his New Mexican roots. When asked about Robert, he did not hesitate: "Oh he's the best. He's the best announcer going right now. He's articulate, and he's just got an excitement in his voice that makes everybody happy."

To be a top-class announcer, Robert said, "Well, top-class is a perception, but in my opinion, to be the best that I can be, especially as you have a lengthy career, you have to find ways to be fresh to it all the time. I think people know when you start to get stale or burned out.... Occasionally you need to step back from it. Maybe every few months look back on your work.... The job should just be a reflection of the way you live. And I do like to see my life as just ongoing. I feel like I'm the same person on the mike as off. That's important to me, because I don't want to be an image."

Robert Geller is a content man. He confided, "I had two very significant relationships and some wonderful opportunities to have partners in my life. At the same time, I'm very comfortable being a single man. I get up every day, and I go to work, and oh! It doesn't feel like work at all, and it's just a pleasure. So I wake up every day, and I'm like, 'Oh, work. How fun!' And I think if you follow your heart and your passion, you are a happy person."

CHAPTER 11

Trevor Denman

Trevor Denman: "And it's all Curlin in the Race of the Year for Horse of the Year. It's Curlin in an absolutely stylish performance! Curlin and Robby Albarado win it easy."

"All set for the Grade I Santa Anita Handicap. And awaaaaaaaaay they go," growls Trevor Denman. On March 3, 2007, the popular gelding Lava Man wins his second Big 'Cap in a row! "Lava Man has to call on all his class.... But Lava Man is too good, and Lava Man and Corey Nakatani win The Big 'Cap."

The year was 1982 and visiting South African commentator Trevor Denman decided to hang out in Los Angeles for a couple of days before returning home. He had been at the Bay Meadows Racecourse in Northern California where, as he'd done the year before at Aqueduct Racetrack in New York, he added his voice to an international race-day cast.

His Aqueduct call had gone well so Trevor was eager for a repeat performance when the venue switched to the West Coast. Bay Meadows management had responded, "We can't pay your airfare, but if you want to show up here, yeah, we'll let you call a race." As it turned out, he called two.

The Thursday before his weekend departure from LAX, Trevor headed to Santa Anita Park. Other than the rain, a rather unexceptional midweek race card was headed for the books. Until the nightcap, that is. Earlier in the day, Trevor met racing secretary Frank Kilroe. The Arcadia Handicap would later be renamed in Kilroe's honor. The Frank E. Kilroe Mile, a Grade I $300,000 turf classic run each March, is a race that continues to take on Breeders' Cup significance.

Trevor recalled, "I asked Frank, 'Do you mind if I call a race?' He said,

'I've got no problem with it, but the man to talk to is Alan Balch.'" He was in charge of that department, and he let Trevor call a race. And the feedback was positive.

Trevor continued, "I came back Friday just to watch the races when they sent one of the guys from the office and said, 'Hey, if you want to call another race, you're more than welcome.'" Trevor needed little persuasion and announced one more time before catching his plane back home. His refreshing style and unique sound pricked the ears of Santa Anita race fans.

Daily Racing Form columnist Jay Hovdey remembered, "Bill Kolberg was one of the publicists at Santa Anita Park and Del Mar ... and ended up in South Africa in 1981 or '82, and he discovered Trevor and came back to California extolling the virtues of this young South African race caller." Now the higher-ups saw for themselves what he was about. Trevor's visit had left quite an impression, so much so that two weeks later, back in South Africa, he received a letter in the mail indicating that if he was looking for employment, Santa Anita would give him a job. Such an endorsement paved the way for what was to become a turning point in North American announcing. Trevor said, "Call it serendipity, I don't know. I was in the right place at the right time."

Track announcer Dave Johnson, the voice of Santa Anita since 1977, was moving to Meadowlands in New Jersey, creating an opportunity for Trevor.

After his two promising visits to the States, Trevor was eager to leave his homeland. Life in South Africa remained volatile. Prime Minister P.W. Botha and his all-white regime had ruled with an iron fist since 1978. Now they were coming under increased international pressure from antiapartheid organizations worldwide that were calling not only for the withdrawal of overseas investments and boycotts against South Africa but also for the release of Nelson Mandela. The wheels of change were in motion, but the country was still a decade away from ending apartheid.

The article "That Vivid Voice" by Jay Hovdey in the summer 2006 issue of *Del Mar Scene* quotes Trevor as saying, "One of the reasons I wanted to come to America in the first place was because of my opposition to the South African government. I did get one hate letter, and I was surprised. I no more believed in apartheid than the person who wrote the letter."

Having successfully tested the waters, the Pacific Ocean was now calling to him. This time, Trevor would be packing his bags for good in a move that would make him a permanent fixture in Southern California, one of the hottest racing centers of the nation.

The youngest of three boys, Trevor is a natural announcer. One could say it runs in the family. His older brother, Eric, followed him into commentating in South Africa and recently retired after 30 years of race calling. His brother Alan lives on a farm in Ireland with his wife and three children. Trevor seems to mirror them both, marrying his love for animals and nature with an uncanny ability to describe a horse race.

Soon after his birth on September 24, 1952, Trevor's parents Doug and Sheila moved from Germiston, located about 20 miles outside of Johannesburg, to the principal port of Durban. Trevor described Durban as "a lovely, little city.... It was racing crazy. I believe *everybody* in Durban went to the races! I got hooked at five years of age, and it was all downhill from there." With the region home to three racecourses — Clairwood, Greyville, and Scottsville — some of his fondest memories are of trips to the track that fueled a childhood dream to become a jockey.

Clive Barker, the renowned soccer coach who led the South African national team to its only African Nations Cup title in 1996, first put the idea into Trevor's head. His reality check came at age 14 when the jockeys' academy turned him down due to his size. The decision did not completely preclude Trevor from riding since it was still possible to purchase a day license, which is exactly what he did.

Trevor explained, "You could buy a license just for a day in a small center that was about four hundred miles from where I lived. Because it was such a small country, there were very few jockeys. So if they had a ten-horse field, they might have eight jockeys so you could buy a license for a day."

Although Trevor continued to ride competitively on the smaller circuits for awhile, the writing was on the wall. The jockeys' academy proved to be right. Eventually, Trevor did get too big, reaching five feet, seven inches. This may not seem very tall against the general populace, but in a jockeys' colony where height and weight are everything, it was certainly up there.

Trevor realized that it worked out for the best: "I was a cinch to be a jockey. Absolute cinch! And it didn't happen, and it was absolutely fantastic that it didn't happen. I would say from sixteen to about twenty-five, being a jockey is great, but after that as you develop, I think you tend to leave that world behind. I have no regrets and I'm very, very happy. I believe in adepts, and I think my adepts guided me to not be accepted as a jockey."

His adepts, what others might term spiritual guides, were hinting at a bigger plan that Trevor was beginning to tap into. The academy's loss turned out to be horse racing's gain as Trevor switched his focus from riding to what he deemed to be the next best thing: announcing. The journey began like it had for most other novice announcers — calling races into a tape recorder. Trevor recalled,

> Gerald Lee was the General Manager of Greyville Racecourse in Durban. Greyville was South Africa's premier track at the time. I took him tapes of races I had called from an apartment overlooking the track when I was fourteen years old. I kept bugging him for four years until his assistant announcer up and left for a more lucrative job in another province. I am sure he smiled under his breath when I went for my first interview as a fourteen-year-old kid, with a tape recorder confidently tucked under my arm, but he had the foresight and courage to give me a shot when the opportunity arose.
>
> At eighteen I went to the track for an audition and was told I would only be calling the races into a tape recorder for the day. However, after race six Mr. Lee came to me and said, "Son, you are up. Go upstairs to the announcer's booth and call the next race live." It was great, because I did not have the chance to get nervous!

The duel between Charm School and New Gold had nothing on the epic battles Trevor was destined to later describe but being his first live race, those horses are forever etched in his memory. Trevor continued, "I called the race and then was hired for the job as assistant announcer. He took a big chance because the Powers That Be at that time [1971] were very stodgy, influential old men who would not have taken kindly to a kid messing up their hallowed racing. Mr. Lee would have had a lot of explaining to do."

Looking back, Trevor reflected, "In South Africa when I was growing up, racing personalities were treated much like football or baseball personalities in America. It was a big deal. So just getting into horse racing was a dream in South Africa. When I started going after the announcing job at age fourteen, I wasn't really concerned with the money aspect. Being offered the job of race calling was like being offered the job to do Monday Night Football here."

It was fortuitous that as Trevor was breaking into the industry, one of the true masters of the craft was navigating its waters. They say to be the best, you learn from the best, and the best was the legendary Bill Collins.

Regarded as the best race caller Australia has ever produced, Bill announced a record 34 Melbourne Cups. What few Australians know is that Bill had a huge following in South Africa too where he was a guest commentator five times for their Spring Carnival of racing. Trevor recalled,

> He's dead now, but he was the guy I mostly focused on and looked up to. I didn't really try to copy or emulate him in his style, but he was the guy that had the biggest impression on me. I met him when I was about eighteen. He was an absolutely fantastic guy!

Clockers' Corner gives Santa Anita its distinctive flavor in the early mornings.

The Australian announcers relied so heavily on speed. The tracks are so big. And you've got invariably a twenty-horse field. And that was the same in South Africa. And they just went for speed, the old-fashioned announcers, to get through the field. They went through the field as fast as they could, would then go back to the leader, and get through it again. And Bill was the first one that really brought a little description into it … not just rattling off names. It was a case of "The quicker you were, the better you were…." That really doesn't make any sense. That's illogical. Because maybe the fans can say, "Wow! That announcer is fast!" But for the poor guy in the grandstand it's like, "What is he talking about?!" It's mumbo-jumbo; you can't even understand him. Even if you can, you just catch your horse's name, and it goes on. There's no margins. There's no pace. There's no description of what's going on. I think Bill Collins was the first guy who really changed that.

Bill's magic rubbed off on Trevor, helping him lay down a solid foundation and spurring him to set his sights high. Five years later Trevor became the number-one announcer for the region. During the ensuing eight years, the Kwazulu-Natal circuit would provide the springboard to an internationally acclaimed career. With field sizes anywhere up to 20 on a regular basis and distances ranging from 800 to 3,250 meters [4 furlongs to just over 2 miles], racing was akin to other Commonwealth countries such as England and Australia, conducted on turf with less emphasis on speed than in the United States and more on stamina.

From the lush, left-handed turf course of Clairwood with its long 600-meter [three-furlong] straight to the uphill run-in of Scottsville, Trevor was experiencing it all, including the big occasion race days. They were highlighted by none other than the Durban July Handicap, South Africa's premier horse race, run at Greyville the first Saturday of that month and open to all ages over a distance of 2,200 meters [11 furlongs].

The race Trevor had grown up watching religiously as a child was now his to call. The first July Handicap with Trevor on the mike was won by local hero, Jamaican Music. Six years later Trevor was still in Durban to call the 1983 July Handicap won by the Argentine-bred Tecla Bluff. However, he had put out feelers to the United States over the previous two years and with the Santa Anita offer pretty much a done deal, his calling of the classic would be his last rendition.

When Trevor arrived in the fall as track announcer for the Oak Tree meet at Santa Anita, it was not too late to catch the John Henry wave. In 1983, the eight-year-old gelding ran in the Oak Tree Invitational. He finished second, beaten half a length to Zalatai. It would be Trevor's one and only time to call the iron horse, and the record books show that John's final chapter was to have a fairy-tale ending. Named 1984 Horse of the Year, an honor bestowed upon him three years prior, John Henry became the second horse in U.S. history to repeat in nonconsecutive years.

There may have been some resistance to the new sound and style but that soon melted away. Even Hall of Fame trainer Ron McAnally, conditioner of the great John Henry, admitted to having felt wary of the change at the time: "I was introduced to him in the paddock when he first came by Bill Kolberg. He said, 'This is going to be the new race announcer,' and I sort of gave him the cold shoulder," Ron chuckled. "Then once I started hearing his race calls, I said, 'Boy, this guy is the best,' and I've felt that way ever since."

Trainer Vladimir Cerin has known Trevor since he arrived at Santa Anita. He remembered, "When he first started announcing races here, he'd come to the barn area almost every morning and talk with the trainers and owners. He just wanted to get 'the lay of the land,' as they say."

Vladimir was very impressed with how quickly Trevor learned the horses' names. He said, "You know what is absolutely amazing about Trevor?

I've sat or stood with him in the booth. We usually talk about soccer, mostly American soccer. And he'll say, 'Excuse me, Vlado.' And he'll look at the horses for the first time as they're loading into the gate and memorize them all in the minute and a half to two minutes from the time the first horse is loaded to the last horse. And never miss a beat."

At the time North American race fans had some exposure to announcers with foreign accents due to guest announcers, but for the most part, they remained unfamiliar with the more descriptive, cerebral style that typified race commentators in Australia, South Africa, and Britain. If distracted by an accent, fans might not be receptive to a full-time foreign announcer. Santa Anita was mindful of the possibility that Trevor's accent might be a problem. Trevor explained,

> You could really put it down to maybe a dozen words; key words that you would use in racing like filly, lass, dance; horses that had "dance" in their names. With my English, it was the long A, the long E, and the long I, so I would be calling "filly" almost like "fully." Bill Shoemaker was riding at the time and it sounded like I was calling him "Bull" Shoemaker. The "I" came out like a "U."
>
> So Alan Balch, Director of Marketing, came up with the idea of an elocution teacher. You don't have to do the whole language so that you come out talking totally different. That would be like an actor, taking three months to do it. That's not necessary. Just the key words. So basically, that's what I did. This guy worked with a lot of movie stars, and he took me on. I probably had somewhere between six to twelve hours of elocution.

Trevor knows that people don't like change. If they couldn't understand his accent, they would give up listening to him. He exclaimed, "It was a major difference coming from South Africa to here. A *huge* difference!

He continued, "Keep in mind, I came here in '83 and in those days we still had the speaker system that was installed back in 1937, and it was in the infield. The speakers came back at you. It was a few seconds delay, and man, it distorted a lot. That was one of the problems I faced. If you listened to the call on television, you could understand everything, but if you listened over those antiquated speakers, it was a little tough."

In addition to Trevor's natural affinity for the job, he had a sensitivity in bridging the gap between what American race fans were accustomed to hearing and where he wanted to take them, almost like an internal compass that allowed him to gently guide his audience.

Typically, American announcers rode on emotion to bring a race call to a boil, conveyed through a change of inflection, rising volume, or both. It is apparent in Trevor's calls in his first season that his paced delivery and deliberate emphasis when spotting horses fell within the comfort zone of his listening audience. Trevor was then able to add in the next dimension, infusing a call with insight, picking up on those telltale signs that indicated how a horse was travelling and nearly every time, his comments were right on the money. Nor was there a reliance on signaling fractional times to indicate the pace of a race.

DRF journalist and now longtime friend Jay Hovdey, who has taken delight in covering Trevor's American career since day one, recalled the mood well:

> A lot of racing fans were surprised when he would start anticipating things for them rather than telling them what had just happened or what was happening in real time. He would say things like, "This horse is going very well." or "This horse is being asked for something." In other words he would add that second, third, or fourth layer of depth to the appreciation of what was happening out there rather than just call numbers and lengths. That's what set him apart from the instant that he started calling. A lot of people had to get used to it because our American style is very much "Native Diver by a length." ... But Trevor comes along. He's accurate. He's dramatic. He has a great voice. And he's telling you something that no one's ever told you before.

Even the downward lilt to his signature opening of each call, "And away they go," initially a little outside the box, soon sounded just right to his converted fans like trainer Ron McAnally, who said, "You know, he's with his accent and it is unusual — 'And away they go!' — and he can almost pick up a horse at the half-mile pole before the race is over and almost invariably pick out that horse, and that horse will win, even though he's back in the pack someplace."

By stepping up the quality and content of his calls, Trevor forced the bar higher for himself, but he would not have it any other way. He said, "You know, if I just wanted to get up there and say, so and so is first, so and so is second, so and so is third, and they come to the eighth pole and so and so takes over, I would have no pressure. Probably I wouldn't be at Santa Anita. That would be like joining the dots and painting a picture. Well, anybody can do that. But if you take a few chances and you stick your neck out on a few things, you put pressure on yourself. "

Trevor's call of the 1987 Santa Anita Handicap showcased his race calling ability: "Snow Chief going along easily at the rail, and Snow Chief now tugging Pat Valenzuela to the lead ... Broad Brush is looming dangerously in fourth.... And Ferdinand's got his ears pricked and going beautifully under Bill Shoemaker on the outside. Broad Brush coming to take him on.... But it's Ferdinand and Broad Brush coming to the wire together in the Big 'Cap.''

Californians began to romance their new-found star, opening up doors that no previous track announcer had been afforded, handing him the keys to the entire Southern California circuit. After two full-time meets at Santa Anita and one meet as an assistant track announcer, Trevor also became the voice of Del Mar Racecourse and Fairplex Park in 1984. In 1991 he added Hollywood Park, which gave him a year-round gig that brought him a fan following.

Before he knew it, an official Trevor Fan Club was in the making, reflective of his rapid acceptance on the West Coast. Trevor bobbleheads and Trevor T-shirts followed. The East Coast has always been seen as more traditional than the West and, according to Trevor, there is some truth to that. He explained,

> When I first came out here for some bizarre reason, there was a very condescending attitude towards announcers. It was probably born back in the '30s ... I know of one big time executive on the East Coast who believed we shouldn't even have announcers. He's retired now, but he totally scorned them, had disdain for them.
>
> I also know of a journalist who wrote an article on me for a magazine. It wasn't a feature article. It was only about half a page long, and he was told by the editor, "That's way too much to dedicate to announcers." It doesn't bother me, but it was disrespectful.... In contrast, in England their great announcer of the past few decades, Peter O'Sullevan, was knighted by the Queen. Thus the Queen equated Sir Peter O'Sullevan with Sir Paul McCartney. A little difference in attitudes!

Retired Hall of Fame jockey Gary Stevens has nothing but admiration for Trevor: "He can see a race as a jockey sees a race. He predicts things happening." And one of Gary's favorite calls is the 1988 Santa Anita Derby. During that race, Trevor announced, "Winning Colors still doing it effortlessly out on the lead.... Gary Stevens going to the whip left-handed, just one crack though. It's Winning Colors turning in an absolutely outstanding performance. We're looking at one exceptional filly who'll be carrying the hopes of California all the way to the Kentucky Derby. What a winner that one was! Winning Colors! Magnificent in victory!"

And the filly did carry California's hopes right into the winner's circle on the first Saturday in May at Churchill Downs. The third filly to win the Run for the Roses retired in 1989 and lived most of the next two decades at Gainesway Farm. On February 17, 2007, she was euthanized due to complications from colic. She was 23 years old and carrying a foal by Mr. Greeley.

Whatever resistance non–West Coast tracks may have initially had to a foreign voice was beginning to soften. Keen to move with the times, Pimlico Racecourse in Maryland, home to the second leg of the Triple Crown, the Preakness Stakes, broke with tradition, appointing Trevor as track announcer for the 1989 summer and 1990 winter meets. Destiny certainly handed Trevor a golden opportunity to showcase his talents. With nearly 75,000 races now to his credit, he deems the 1989 Preakness his most memorable: "If I were backed into a corner, it would definitely be the '89 Preakness — Sunday Silence and Easy Goer. You know, they hooked up at like the ¾ pole. They were never more than a head apart. It was Pat Day and Pat Valenzuela, two of the best jockeys in the world. Two of the best horses in the world. How do you beat it? You can't. And they came down to the wire like that. I would say it was the quintessential horse race."

Since Trevor announced to on-track fans only for the 1989 Preakness and not to ABC's television audience, where Dave Johnson got the call, Jay Hovdey believes that not enough people heard Trevor's thrilling blow-by-blow description of that stretch duel. He recalled, "It should be broadcast from the rooftops every year or shown to clinics.... It was just out of this world. And he did call the winner too. Trevor doesn't blink. He doesn't flinch. If there's a winner to be called, he calls it! Even if it's a nose, he doesn't hedge. If he hedges, you might even want to bet that it's a dead heat." Trevor was sure on the money that Preakness as he declared Sunday Silence the winner by a nose over Easy Goer, just as the racing charts later showed. Trevor called, "And here's the race we've been waiting for! Sunday Silence on the outside. Easy Goer at the rail, head and head coming to the eighth pole. Sunday Silence and Pat Valenzuela. Easy Goer and Pat Day. Head and head through the stretch. What a horse race this one is! Easy Goer and Sunday Silence going nose and nose in the Preakness. Sunday Silence. Easy Goer. Here's the finish. Sunday Silence wins it by a nose!"

The following summer, Trevor returned to Hollywood Park. A very private man, with a daughter from his first marriage, Trevor found true love the second time around with Robin. They met at a restaurant in Los Angeles. Trevor said,

> Neither of us knew we were both in racing. Robin was an official clocker at the racetrack. She had just moved here from Minnesota and didn't know too many personalities in racing here.
> She knows a lot about horse racing. She's been a fan and actually was in horseracing for awhile.... Anytime she listens, if anything's not right, she'll tell me. She keeps me sharp.

Robin said, "Husband bias aside, Trevor is the best announcer in the world right now. He is often referred to as a legend, and he hasn't even stopped calling races. Most legends happen after death. Not Trevor. He is considered a 'Living Legend' in both South Africa and America. I am extremely proud of his tenacity, perfectionism, professionalism (he wears a suit and tie every day to work) and instinctive insights into the races as they unfold. He is like an artist painting a picture in a matter of seconds. I often listen to his race calls with my eyes closed and can visualize every move that is being made."

Del Mar Scene reported, "Denman has described a bounty of classic California events, including 23 Santa Anita Handicaps and every Pacific Classic at Del Mar since the race was inaugurated in 1991. 'The first one always sticks out, when a very popular Best Pal won the race,' Denman said."

Here's that call: "Best Pal is coming after him now. Twilight Agenda, but here comes Best Pal. Best Pal gonna catch him at the wire. Best Pal has got Twilight Agenda, and Best Pal has got Valenzuela!"

When the time is ripe, Trevor will not hesitate to amplify a finish with much-anticipated phrases, like "they'd need to sprout wings to catch him" or "so-and-so looks as if he just jumped in at the quarter pole" and "moving like a winner," staple announcer expressions that he has turned into his own.

And he has no trouble keeping his race calling fresh. He admits, "Each time they go to the gate I go back to being a youngster again. The adrenalin pumps as though I was seeing the race through my teenage eyes, when *every* race was treated as though it was life and death."

Trevor is in his element when the match-ups that everyone hopes for materialize, like in the 1997 Santa Anita Derby between the two giant-hearted gray colts, Silver Charm and Free House. The winner, Silver Charm, would go on to capture the first two legs of the Triple Crown that year, and his Hall of Fame trainer Bob Baffert revels in the drama of Trevor's calls whether his horse is involved or not. Baffert said,

> He's best when you have two good horses that you can see is like a two-horse race and he has this thing: "It's so-and-so jockey on the inside," and he builds it up like this is the match we've been waiting for. And then it unfolds.
>
> He knows how to get the crowd into it. Any of these good horses, Silver Charm, Lava Man [2006, 2007 Santa Anita Handicap winner] when he sees the horses are running their race, he really builds it up, like "Here he comes" and the minute he says it, you can hear the whole crowd lighten up. When he said, "Lava Man is picking it up. He's making his move," the whole crowd, you could just see them start to get excited. And so to me, you want an announcer that gives you goose bumps.

Baffert fantasized, "If I owned a racetrack, I'd want Trevor. He'd be my first pick. I like his style. He tells it the way it is. He unfolds it. He makes it exciting. Whether it's a ten thousand dollar claimer or a stakes race, he makes it very exciting and enjoyable for the two dollar bettor."

Trevor agreed: "In every race there is a person (perhaps a few) who is treating the race, even the third on a Thursday afternoon, as his Kentucky Derby. I respect and can feel his emotions."

With only a break of three weeks a year, the rigors of such an intense and high-profile schedule were beginning to take its toll on Trevor. By 1996, Trevor was in a secure position both professionally and financially to lessen his load, and to safeguard against burnout, he decided to relinquish Hollywood Park.

Those close to Trevor, like Jay, who knew of his interests beyond racing, were not surprised. Jay said, "When he stepped away from Hollywood Park so that he could be a little fresher, spend time on the road, at his farm, with his family and his wife, it probably saved his life, his sanity. Because you can't do what he did. He was calling the whole circuit in California. No one had ever done that before."

For the first time in years, Trevor could enjoy some peace and quiet. In 1996, he and Robin purchased a dairy farm in Minnesota, a haven where he could retreat, bury his head in his books, and catch up on his favorite sport, soccer.

Trevor's marriage to Robin goes far deeper than any racing connection. It has been transformative and one of the highlights of his life. With a rich, ever-evolving mind and a solid work ethic, it is no wonder that he has been able to reach his goals. It all, of course, goes back to his upbringing.

Trevor explains, "I think work ethic was the main thing. We couldn't shirk any issues. There was no whining. You couldn't just say, 'I can't do that, or I don't want to do that.' My parents weren't harsh at all, but the best way to put it was, no whining. Get out there! Do it!"

Trevor's father, Doug, was in the fencing industry. Trevor remembered, "He had terrible war memories from fighting in the Second World War. He was injured in battle at El Alamein, and it affected him greatly." Trevor was only 14 years old when his father died.

He said his mother Sheila "dedicated her life to her three boys." Now in her nineties, she suffers from Alzheimer's disease.

Trevor recalled, "I was very determined. I set goals and was lucky enough to have them happen. I mean, a lot of people set goals and they don't get there, not because they're no good but because they didn't have luck on their side. Unless those adepts are looking after you, you can forget about it."

Those adepts have sure played a big part in Trevor's life. He said, "I haven't missed a day's work in thirty-eight years. And that's not a brag. I mean it's not because of me. Somebody up there is taking care of me: the adepts."

Don't be fooled. It is not as though Trevor has left his well-being up to chance. Both physically and mentally, he has taken active steps to align his lifestyle with his philosophies. By exercising his responsibilities, it makes sense that he feels supported on the invisible plane by his adepts. He explained, "I don't believe in harming anything, and I'm obviously a vegetarian. I do not harm anything intentionally. If I walk out the door and accidentally stand on an ant, gosh, I can't help that, but if I see the ant and I stand on it, that's wrong. So I would say I base myself on harmlessness as far as I can."

Having gained respect from his peers for excellence at his craft, Trevor uses it to impart some of his personal awareness in the professional arena. Robin said, "What I am most proud of is his compassion for the horses, and the changes he has made in racing regarding the whip and educating the public on what happens to horses after they are through racing. We both are active in raising money to save horses from going to slaughter."

Indeed, Trevor is on the board of three horse racing retirement funds: CERF (California Equine Retirement Foundation), Tranquility Farm, and Pegasus Foundation. Hovdey said, "Any cause that he becomes associated with is significant in horse racing because of his name and reputation." Not surprisingly, he is against two-year-olds racing.

In Southern California, Trevor has gone out of his way to educate others on the use of the whip, warning against excessive use and encouraging jockeys to loosen their reliance on it in a finish. It is easy to find examples of top riders who, through balance, timing, and horsemanship skills, have prevailed over opponents who resorted to heavy use of the whip. Trevor was once a rider himself, and that fact gives him added credibility, but his underlying message stems from his love and respect for the Thoroughbred itself.

He pointed to England's philosophy: "I just wish we would learn from the English how to use a whip in a race. The English jockeys are so much more humane, and the results are still the same. We are barbarians when it comes to treating our horses right. Speak to any foreigner about our jockeys, and they wince when it comes to their brutality with the whip."

Ron McAnally said, "One of the best riders that I have ever seen in my life, and I grew up with him, was Shoemaker. Shoemaker very seldom used the whip. He'd hit a horse a couple of times if it didn't respond, then he'd put it away. But he had terrific balance ... and he never really used a stick that much. So I agree with Trevor 100 percent."

Trevor called Shoemaker in the 1988 Big 'Cap: "Alysheba takes the lead but Bill Shoemaker and Ferdinand immediately up to take them on on the outside.... What a race this is! Just what the fans wanted! Ferdinand and Alysheba! Alysheba's holding on at the rail. Alysheba and Chris McCarron win the Big 'Cap by about a neck in the end."

Vladimir Cerin, whose Student Council beat The Tin Man in the 2007 Pacific Classic, is a close friend of Trevor. Cerin said, "Horses do run from pain. I think if they had less pain, they would still perform equally well as they do now. And you wouldn't have those deep welts and cuts. I would have to say that Trevor and Robin have had an effect on the racing industry in that sense. They have alienated some people, but on the other hand, the state vet now examines horses after the race. And if the horse has welts in places that he shouldn't, and there seems to be abuse of the whip, you can check the CA Horse Racing Board, and there have been numerous fines."

One jockey who has no problem with Trevor's whip policy is Hall of Fame jockey Mike Smith. In 2008 he rode the two-year-old filly Stardom Bound in the Breeders' Cup Juvenile Fillies, and she won easily. Trevor was impressed with the gray daughter of Tapit in the Mile and a 16th Oak Leaf Stakes Grade I for two-year-olds on September 27. He called, "And Stardom Bound, the grey, now winding up about eight wide but here comes Stardom Bound ... she leaps forward. Through the stretch they come in the Oak Leaf, and look at Stardom Bound. What an impressive performance today ... Stardom Bound just overwhelms them, hand ridden by Mike Smith takes the Oak Leaf."

Mike said, "It's nice that someone actually cares. I use a different style of whip than most people do. I call it a pillow whip, very very soft at the end. I can hit as hard as I can, and it doesn't hurt. It makes a lot of noise."

However, in the Breeders' Cup Ladies Classic on October 24, 2008, Mike didn't touch classy Zenyatta with his stick. Trevor announced, "Mike Smith shaking the reins at her, and Zenyatta is starting to move now. Here comes Zenyatta. She's caught about five wide, but she's coming gamely ... Grandstand-side Zenyatta. She knows she's in a race today, but just look at her. Zenyatta on the outside now strikes the front, and it's Zenyatta coming away ... Zenyatta's going to come home to score. Undoubtedly now a living legend! Zenyatta nine for nine!"

Trevor pointed out, "A Thoroughbred racehorse is one of the most magnificent animals in the world. When they're running down the backstretch and they're just running on their own and there are no whips involved, they don't stop running. They're running willingly. It is just a magnificent picture."

That is why, for any true racing fan, the breakdown of a horse during the run is undoubtedly the toughest pill to swallow. Trevor explained, "The worst part is a breakdown, horses breaking down, THE worst part. You cannot become callous and say, 'Oh, it's part of the game.' I just detest that. That's a coward's way out. That's like saying slavery is part of life or child exploitation is just a part of life. It's not as though you can stop breakdowns overnight but, my gosh, you have to try to do something about it. I think these new track surfaces are going to be great."

Racing is more conscious than ever of the need to minimize the stress on the structure of the horse, especially their delicate hooves, and any undue strain on their ligaments. In 2007 the California Horse Racing Board passed a bill that required five major racetracks in the state to convert their track from traditional dirt soil to a synthetic surface. The types of synthetic surfaces are cushion, tapeta, or polytrack. Despite some early problems, the data so far suggests there is a reduction in the number of breakdowns.

Trevor said, "The best part is just seeing a Grade I race with three or four great horses under the best jockeys, none of them being abused and fighting it out to a tremendous finish. That's the highlight of racing."

Trevor conceded that change can be a long process:

> You just have to know that things take time. Then there are the three R's: rejection, reflection and recognition. The first one in human nature is rejection. Whenever you come up with something new, they'll just look at you. So when I first brought that up about the whips, it was a blatant NO. Wow! But they definitely got past that stage.
>
> Now, they're in the reflection part. And reflection just means they're thinking about it. And then the final R is recognition when they say, "Oh yeah, that's right. That's right!" And you see it happen all the time! It's rejection, reflection, recognition. We're definitely through the first phase. We're in the second phase right now. Have they totally accepted it? No, it's too soon. So these things take time.

Trevor managed to cushion his positive message inside a heavy dose of realism. His mantra has always been for a more humane world and now more than ever, the racing industry must move in that direction if it is to attract a younger audience.

Trevor explained, "There are a number of reasons why it is that animals in sport are nowhere near as big as they were one hundred or two hundred years ago. Animals in entertainment are not big anymore. Circuses are almost nonexistent. Zoos are radically changed or on the way out. There's been a huge metamorphosis in people's attitude towards the treatment of animals that I would say started around 1970. But things take time. I would say the next generation of kids is just not going to be into horse racing unless it is far more humane."

Trevor thought about the most significant change to racing that he has witnessed. He said, "Definitely off-track betting, and now the Internet. It has changed racing completely as far as atmosphere goes. Sports need crowds at the action, and unfortunately, racing has lost the crowds."

And though Trevor keeps a watchful eye on the future with a vision for his own life beyond racing, for now he remains one of its brightest beacons. In 2006, Trevor reached a pinnacle in his already magnificent career. The television rights for the championship races were awarded to the ESPN network, and it invited Trevor to be the voice for Breeders' Cup Limited.

For the previous 18 years, Trevor had been one of the talents on the NBC broadcast, working on location by the rail to offer a

On November 7, 2009, Zenyatta strutted into history as the first female to win the Breeders' Cup Classic, and Trevor matched her brilliance with his call, "Zenyatta coming flying on the grandstand side.... This — is — un — be — lievable! Zenyatta! What a performance, one we'll never forget! Looked impossible but it is Zenyatta, still unbeaten...." The great six-year-old mare has won *all* sixteen starts (as of April 9, 2010) beating Personal Ensign's record.

Hall of Fame jockey Mike Smith and Stardom Bound in the post parade for the 2008 Breeders' Cup Juvenile Filly. Credit: Cheryl Hecht.

succinct recap of each race, using his magic marker to highlight interference, key moves and riding tactics, as the tape rolled on the monitor in front of him. His comments were a breath of fresh air to viewers as they were able to learn from his horsemanship knowledge and easily follow his poignant presentations. Under the ESPN format, Trevor would no longer be stationed down by the rail, but right up in the best seat of the house, the announcer's booth.

Trevor was never one to be flustered by the big occasion. The Santa Anita Handicap, the Pacific Classic at Del Mar, or the Santa Anita Derby, the three giants of the southern Californian stakes schedule, are all testament to Trevor's composure, his ability to trust the moment.

Like a coin toss, sometimes the big races live up to their promise and sometimes they don't. Jay believes Trevor's ability to not get in the way of the race is a great quality. He said, "There is no artifice to him. He doesn't prepare catch phrases or anticipate an outcome and then be caught surprised when something else happens."

Trevor allows himself to feel the adrenaline rush and transmit it through his call to the fans. He said, "I think it's human nature [to get nervous]. If you didn't, I think there'd be something wrong, you know. Not that you don't get up for the smaller races but for the big races, you have to have the adrenaline pumping. Just seeing the horses in front of you gets you excited ... I always liken it to a dart game. If you play darts, you always want to get the highest score. Let's say you want to hit a 20 every time. You don't throw for a three or four. You want the big ones. The Big 'Cap, the Breeders' Cup, that's the bull's eye. You go for the bull's eye, so yeah, you've got to get excited for those."

For Breeders' Cup XXIII, Trevor was excited but not overwhelmed, safe in the knowledge that having successfully coped with the pressure of the Big 'Cap, there was no reason to imagine the Breeders' Cup as any different. In fact, some announcers will argue that it becomes easier to relax into a rhythm when there is a series of elite races rather than only one that magnetizes all the build-up to it.

Trevor received some mixed reviews about his first Breeders' Cup at Churchill Downs, but that was inevitable because before he opened his mouth, many race fans already believed that Tom Durkin, who had called every race since the first one in 1984, was the only announcer for the job.

By Breeders' Cup XXIV, at the more intimate Monmouth Park, race fans had had more time to accept that Durkin was no longer the announcer. Trevor had successfully weathered the fallout and rose to the occasion for the expanded two-day version, closing the program out with a stirring description of Curlin's monstrous Breeders' Cup Classic win.

This time the unbelievably bad weather was Trevor's only major challenge. He recalled,

> Those two days at Breeders' Cup were quite an experience! Especially the Friday. I can honestly say they were the worst conditions I have ever experienced. A strong rain storm with the wind blowing directly into the booth. We had to open the windows (large pull-back windows, not small, easy to open ones) while the horses were loading into the gate, and then the rain was hitting the lenses of the binoculars as the race was progressing. So, the image of the horses during the race was like driving a car in a rain storm without wipers. As one can see from watching the replays, the field at the top of the lane looked like one big mud ball! Fortunately, I was well prepared and managed to get through it all. Saturday was far from ideal, but compared to Friday, it was a breeze!

The 25th Breeders' Cup was held during the Oak Tree meet at Trevor's home track, Santa Anita. He celebrated the successful two days. He said, "I think it was one of the best Breeders' Cups ever! Number one because no

Tiago exercising before his third-place finish in the 2008 Breeders' Cup Classic.

horse even got a bruise on his foot. Every single horse came back perfectly sound, which is a rarity with that many horses running."

Trevor is someone who many would say has lived the American dream, whose work as a pioneer in his field has taken him to the very top, blessing him with celebrity status and financial freedom. He now chooses to put his energy into those areas where he feels he can make a difference, where it is worth reaching out or going out on a limb. He and his wife, Robin, sponsor seven orphaned children in South Africa, their donations ensuring they have food and water. He and Robin returned from a visit in 2006, vowing to expand their involvement.

Trevor said, "As far as personal goals go, the only desire I have that I haven't done yet is to go and help little African kids. Obviously I grew up in Africa, and I always feel that people here say, you should help Americans first but the problem being that Americans have the chance to make it, provided they have a brain cell and are physically fit. Any single human being in America can make it. No one dies of malnutrition. Even the most down-and-out guy's wearing Nike shoes and a jacket. Africa? Woohoo!! Totally

Trevor called the great fillies and mares Estrapade, Royal Heroine, Bayakoa, Paseana, Lady's Secret, and Zenyatta.

different. Those poor little kids don't have a chance. So that's one thing that I've set that I will do, and it's not just hot air. It will happen, but the timing has to be right."

He is quick to say just what he likes about his life today: "My wife, Robin, and I are soul mates after twenty years. I feel I have achieved something in life, and I am looking forward to giving a whole lot back to life once I retire."

Trevor wants to be remembered "as someone who looked out for the horses. Even if my ideas are ridiculed, I know they are ethically correct. The day will come when people will see it my way. William Wilberforce, the great abolitionist, dedicated more than thirty years of his life to erase slavery. He was ridiculed and mocked his entire life and died never seeing his vision come to be. The Anti-Slavery Bill banning slavery was passed thirty days after his death.... He has been a guiding force in my life."

Appendix

Do you think there will be another Triple Crown winner?

DURKIN: "Oh, absolutely. We wouldn't be having this conversation if Real Quiet had bobbed his head a tenth of a second earlier or later. And if Chris McCarron hadn't outfoxed everybody with Touch Gold by putting him on the lead and then just appearing out of nowhere and basically cold clocking Silver Charm coming from out of his view. And maybe if Charismatic hadn't taken a bad step at some point."

BECKER: "Yes, it will happen but, wow! Lord only knows when ... I believe that God created these animals, and I believe like the rest of them, that they ultimately answer to Him. I think that whenever in His good grace He looks down and decides it's time for this to happen, it will happen. And boy! What a great day that will be for the sport!"

RODMAN: "I've almost given up hope. It just seems like horses are maybe a little more fragile now. Maybe the blood lines have been raided by foreign interest. Well maybe the last three or four years I've given up hope.... But if it happens, I hope it happens while I still have a chance to say, 'Yes, I did call a horse that won the Triple Crown.'"

WRONA: "Yes. Despite the growing fragility of the breed, I think there are too many horses that have gone too close in the last decade for there not to be another one. I think it will happen."

WALLACE: "Sure, somewhere along the way. That's why we keep the dream alive. We've come awfully close these last coupla years. I think Smarty just had a kind of muscle failure, and probably it was the mile and a half that did it."

COLLMUS: "I certainly hope so. But we've come close so many times.

It's really a lot harder now, because horses don't run as much, and they space their races, and you get to that Triple Crown where they're spaced the same way they've been for a million years ... and the horses aren't prepared to do that anymore where they were before."

DOOLEY: "I hope so. As a racing fan who just happens to be a track announcer, I think that it would be great to see a Triple Crown.... I agree with what Kent Desormeaux said after Big Brown lost the Triple Crown: 'It shows how special those prior Triple Crown winners were.' I think it takes a very special horse to win the Triple Crown. I hope to see it as a fan. I'll stay optimistic."

KRUYTBOSCH: "Sure there will be. I don't like all this talk about changing the format. All that does is slap the connections of all the great horses in the face that have done it. That have gone through the grind.... I don't want to see a Triple Crown winner just to see it. Some of these horses didn't win it for a reason.... I want to see a Triple Crown winner come back and be a Seattle Slew or Affirmed as a four-year-old and be one of the best, if not the best, in the country that everybody has to shoot at.... Remember when they were blaming Jerry Bailey for making Smarty Jones lose that race? There were people writing into the *Form* about Jerry Bailey not being a sportsman. Well, nobody ever said anything about Laffit Pincay on Sham pushing Secretariat in 1:09.04 for six furlongs and trying to make him lose, because he didn't lose the race, right?"

GELLER: "Well, here's the reality. I came to the States in '96, and I have seen so many close calls. Like all of us, I seemed to be on this wave when I first arrived of, 'We're right on the brink!' And on it went with Real Quiet, Silver Charm, Charismatic, War Emblem, Smarty Jones.... By the time it got to Smarty Jones, I'm like, 'I know I'll never see a Triple Crown winner in my life.' I'm sure it will happen again, but whether I'm alive to see it."

DENMAN: "Ah, yeah, eventually there will. I don't know if it's just being random. You know, randomness is an amazing thing, isn't it? Thirty to forty years with nothing, and then who knows, you might get two back-to-back. I do think there will be one, because they will come around to where one stands out head and shoulders above. Perhaps one of the reasons there hasn't been one for a long time, is the set-up of the Triple Crown. I don't know why, but horses 150 years ago could run more often than they can now.... The people who are against having a longer Triple Crown [more weeks between the races] say it sorts the wheat from the chaff, which sounds like a very good saying, but it's an absolute platitude. Horses are dying for a platitude."

What are the tricks of your trade?

RODMAN: "In a large field, or any field, identifying horses with one distinguishing characteristic. That's the first thing I think of. The horse: silks, or color of jockey's helmet, or blinkers on the horse. I always try to look for one distinguishing mark."

KRUYTBOSCH: "Have a good memory, but you need a better ability to forget ... I do the crayons some. I almost hesitate to call them tricks. There's one thing that people don't know when they first start, and I want to thank the people that told me about it. When you first start, you're buying all this time because you really don't know who these horses are, and the Cardinal Rule of Announcing is you want to say the horse's name first, and then what the horse is doing second.... That shows you know who that is, and you've done your homework."

DURKIN: "You know, repetition is the mother of learning. There's no real trick. Sometimes late in the day I will have to use some types of ... devices like images and things like that. But I don't like using images because it just takes longer for your mind to process.... You try to get to know the horses on a first name basis like you know your friends."

DENMAN: "None! I think riding racehorses and mixing inside the racing world from a young age have given me a very good insight into how horse racing actually operates. I could probably call a baseball game if coached, but the intrinsic feeling would not be there."

GELLER: "Concentration is really important. No, never do crayons. Don't find that helpful because that to me would just confuse me. As the horses come out, I'll just go through them. I like to have as little on the page as possible."

Who was your favorite racehorse?

WALLACE: "Over the long haul, now, the horse that I've been able to have the most enjoyment with was Smarty Jones. My first great mare was Susan's Girl. I had a race that I called when I was subbing for Chic Anderson at Churchill Downs where a horse passed her in mid-stretch and actually got a length and a half on her, and she came back on and caught that horse.... There's a mare that will never say quit, and she ended up having a great career."

COLLMUS: "Cigar, for sure. But I was a huge Holy Bull fan. Holy Bull was here for the Haskell, 1994. He was stabled here so I had a chance to go into the backstretch and see him a few times. I remember going back there, and you would yell his name out ... 'Hey, Bull!' and you could be outside the shedrow, and he'd come storming to the front in a snap. He knew his name.... He was a great horse."

DOOLEY: "Personal Ensign. I covered her so extensively during that campaign, working for NYRA. It's my all-time favorite Tom Durkin race call. I was at the far end of the Aqueduct press box, leaning with every stride, willing Personal Ensign to get up."

KRUYTBOSCH: "Pole Position. One day there was an allowance race, and I was at Bowie Racetrack. Dave's Friend was like 4–5, and Pole Position was like 2–1. Dave's Friend was a great sprinter, one of the best sprinters in the country. Pole Position was the fastest horse out of the gate. Dave's Friend spent the whole time trying to catch him, and he never could, and he went seven furlongs in about 1:21 and change. I was twenty. There live ... Pole Position could go long too."

GELLER: "I love Afleet Alex. When that happened in the Preakness, that's so memorable. More than distance. I don't care what opposition you're running against. If you can do that, that's a horse with heart."

RODMAN: "Xtra Heat was probably my favorite filly because she was a local rags to riches story, a $5000 purchase. Xtra Heat racing in the fog in the Barbara Fritchie. Total fog. It started off as a rainy, foggy, cold drizzly yukky day, and then the fog just got lower and lower and deeper and deeper as they went to the gate to the point where you couldn't see a thing. Just a glimpse of shadows running, and she emerged from the fog in front, but I really wanted to play up that race and make it special, but there really wasn't any way during the body of the call. You couldn't see it! Her emerging from the fog has to be one of my fondest memories of calling in Maryland. She emerged from the thick blanket of fog to capture her twenty-fifth career stakes win with Rick Wilson up."

DURKIN: "I'd have to put Cigar, just that winning streak, and he was a pretty good draw, and a lot of people followed his career, went to see him race. And he was probably a little more popular than people give him credit for."

DENMAN: "I only called John Henry once, right at the end of his career.... He's still one of the greatest of all time. Everybody likes the underdog to come out on top, and he certainly was. And, you know, he was a scraggly-looking little horse. He wasn't expensive. He was a gelding. He had nothing going for him. And he was just such a tough individual. I think he ran in a really tough era when there were a lot of good horses around. And they carried big weights, and you could almost say he never ran a bad race. So he's definitely one of the best of all time."

WRONA: "Makybe Diva. No horse had ever won three Melbourne Cups.... The thing that Kingston Town, Makybe Diva, and Cigar [Michael's favorite American racehorse] have in common is longevity in their careers. She was six when she was retired."

What was your most memorable race, or
saddest, or one you'd like to have back?

WALLACE: "The match race with Doctor Who and Explosive Girl. Round Pond and Happy Ticket. When you get the stars, hook one another right from the beginning, and it's like nothing else mattered that was going on out there.... It turned out to be just spectacular. Azeri and Take Charge Lady.... Those are among the top races. If you had to put your finger on one, it's impossible.

COLLMUS: "The '96 MassCap which was Cigar's second one ... probably Invasor's Donn was the most impressive race I've called, but I don't think anything will match [Cigar's MassCap]. Nothing's even come close!"

KRUYTBOSCH: "Oh, I believe that Sandpit won that race.... I'm up there [Hollywood Park].... The stewards say, 'Listen. We have no power. We're going to have to run the race [on the turf]. These are million dollar horses. The gate was mechanical. It didn't need the power so they get out there.... I thought just in case, I'm going to call the race. I know it's not going out, but I'm not going to sit here. So I call it aloud. All of a sudden I could hear myself come back at me, and that was about the half mile pole. And the funny part was soon as I could hear myself coming back at me, all the phones started ringing with people wanting to tell me, 'Hey! You're back on!'"

JOHNSON: "It was the 1989 Preakness Stakes with Sunday Silence and Easy Goer. That was the best race because what you had was a gigantic stage, two superstars, great horses terrifically trained, and super jockeys with so much at stake and just nose to nose for the last quarter mile. The excitement of the race itself; I get chills thinking about it every time I go back Memory Lane."

DOOLEY: "At Thistledown, there was an owner, Mr. Ray Feldman, I can see to this day: yellow silks, green sleeves. And I was talking to someone, and the race ran, and I thought I'd called a great race. Well I'd confused one of the horses with the other. One was She's English, and the other one was European Lady. So I swapped the two during this race. Otherwise, it was a great call besides the fact that one horse was at the barn, and the other one ran."

DURKIN: "Nothing compares with Go For Wand [in the 1990 Breeders' Cup Distaff]. Because it was right there. Right in front of you. And it was just like this tremendous race leading up to it. Just ghastly.... Having to call the next race, [the Breeders' Cup Mile] was very hard to concentrate."

WRONA: "There was a multiple horse fall at Golden Gate Fields. One of the horses somehow found his way either through or over a gate leading through a corporation yard to the parking lot to the road outside to the off-ramp of a freeway. He proceeded along in the wrong direction; a runaway horse on the freeway! There was an out-rider taking off after him, and I could follow it all through my binoculars. The classic is that one of the other horses was called Take to the Road. It would have been perfect if that was the horse that actually did take to the road!"

KRUYTBOSCH: "Yeah, it was a long time ago at the Arizona Oaks, and there was a horse called Arizona Irish. Bart Hone trained it, and it was coming down the stretch about to win easy and broke a leg. That's a sad deal. Some of the happier moments are when a horse will suffer heat exhaustion and will be down on the track and everybody is holding their breath, and all of a sudden he gets back up. You hear the crowd go crazy."

GELLER: There was a race when I was in Australia at a smaller track where a horse was so far ahead, and I just couldn't remember who it was, had no idea. And this one's five in front, six in front, and I'm almost like I'd better not look at my book. It's so embarrassing, but I got it after the wire."

Where do you see horse racing in ten years? What could help it?

DENMAN: "Probably the same as where it is right now. It's taken a massive transformation in the last thirty years because of off-track betting, but it won't change in the next twenty years, I don't think. This generation is fine. The next generation is fine. When you start getting into fifty to one hundred years, I think its time has come."

JOHNSON: "I think television is tied into it. It's a major catalyst here, and it's not just a theory. All you have to do is look at history. In England two of the most popular things to bet on are snooker and darts. And the reason is because they were put on television. In the United States it's even more dramatic. Look at the explosion of poker. I think that it could have been that way with horse racing, but the industry had a terrible view back in the '50s thinking that if racing were on TV, people wouldn't go to the track. What a stupid thing that was! They really blew it! They blew it at the highest levels! For instance, the Swaps/Nashua Match race in '55. Absolute national interest. The Seabiscuit/War Admiral that was on the radio. Didn't they realize that if they put it on TV it would become an event? If TV would have taken the bull by the horns in the '50s and '60s and shown the sport as it was at Hialeah and Santa Anita and the lead-up races to the Triple Crown, not just the Triple Crown.... I think the question mark is whether the industry will embrace television even more.... I think everybody will have satellite radio in their cars and their homes, and it's a niche I think we could promote. I hope that the television industry and the racing industry can come together and become really good partners and show what television did for poker, television can do for racing."

DURKIN: "It's in the hands of the politicians, You know, I'm concerned about the brittleness of the breed. But I'm probably more concerned about the politicians. I don't hold them in anything but very little regard actually."

DOOLEY: "So many young people come out for Breakfast at Arlington [once a month in the summer], and they stay for the races afterwards. We have a Junior Jockey Program, and if one out of every ten or one hundred of those kids becomes a racing fan, that will continue. It's important for there to be places like Arlington, Belmont, Saratoga, Del Mar whether you're a hard-nosed handicapper or a horseman or just a casual fan. I think when fans come out to Arlington, it breeds a love for the sport. And as long as there is that passion, I think there will be Thoroughbred racing for many years to come."

BECKER: "The sport is going to be strong, and, the Lord willing, it will be that way across the board, not just for the top end.... The pageantry and splendor of horse racing continue to give the sport timeless appeal.... Let the world see that we have fun.... When the filly She Says It Best won the Alcibiades, there was a throng of twenty or twenty-five owners in the winner's circle that were laughing and smiling. That's a promotion for horse racing."

WALLACE: "I have no idea because the world is moving so fast. There are so many changes that have come: photo finish, speed ratings. We do need some heroes to last for awhile to help us maintain our place in the sports page. Our challenge is to keep people coming to the races."

COLLMUS: "That's a tough question. The game has changed *so much* in the last ten years. This whole thing with slot machines. I'm not a big fan of that ... I think you really have to focus on the horse racing."

GELLER: "That's a very hard question. I don't know. Let's just say I work for two independents. I'm one of the last people to do that. Mr. Ron Crockett, independent. Stan Fulton who runs Sunland, independent.... All I can say is that independence is a good thing because it's unique to its region. It's fueled by passion."

WRONA: "The small fields are the biggest problem with California racing. There's no two ways about it. But we're kind of isolated out here in California regarding where we draw horses from. I'm not sure how to fix the problem."

What advice would you give an aspiring race caller?

RODMAN: "I don't encourage it, and I don't discourage it. They'll decide whether they have a passion for it. You have to have a passion because there are fewer and fewer tracks. And it's very hard to make a living."

DENMAN: "You know, I've always said to new announcers, 'If you make one mistake, don't let it bother you because then you'll make two mistakes.' You've got to just let it go, and go on like it never happened. And you primarily find that if you do make a little blur along the way, people generally are not going to draw attention to it. But if you go back and try to make this major correction, then it does become, 'Gee, what's going on here?' The less attention that's paid to it, I think the better. You're only human. You're going to slip up. And if you do, just go on with it. Just make sure you don't make the second mistake."

JOHNSON: "Well, it's very difficult now ... I think they have to get a job at the track. And then work their way into a situation where they're given a chance.... But there is nothing that beats going to the track calling race after race after race."

BECKER: "I would advise him to focus more on the need to gain experience than on any other consideration. And he should never decline the opportunity to get experience at the microphone, even if it's not what he or she initially desired. For example, if you want to be a Thoroughbred announcer but a harness track needs help in the booth, by all means, call the trotters and pacers and build your resume."

DOOLEY: "Practice. I love coming up with new expressions and phrases and watching racing from over in Europe. And listening to other announcers. As you know, I'm a big fan of Dave Rodman. But most important, being accurate."

What do you believe caused the death of the
great Australian racehorse Phar Lap?

GELLER: "I was too young so it's all hearsay to me. The only part that resonates to me is the Tommy Woodcock part. Woodcock was the strapper [groom in Australia], and he was the young lad who nursed Phar Lap through his death.... Woodcock's leaning was that they [bookmakers or the underworld] did it. He was a pretty truthful man."

WRONA: "Well actually a story came out awhile ago that pretty much exonerated the Americans from the poisoning thing. It has been a long held grudge Down Under where and, rest assured, 'Oh, the Yanks, they poisoned Phar Lap.' But I've never known what to think until recently when I read that the new evidence is that he was not poisoned. At least not deliberately, and by nobody other than his own strapper . You'll never convince a lot of people Down Under though."

Should track announcers be in the Official National
Thoroughbred Racing Hall of Fame?

WRONA: "That's a great question. Yeah, I think so. I think they make a contribution. There's no Eclipse Award for race calling. There are plenty of awards for journalists. And photographers even win awards. So on that basis there should be some recognition. I'd be on board with that."

RODMAN: "Well if you read the Mission Statement, it doesn't say anything about track announcers. My answer is no unless one of us wins the Derby, the Preakness, or the Belmont. It's the RACING Hall of Fame. It's not the announcers' Hall of Fame."

GELLER: "Yes, absolutely. I think there are amazing people that have made announcing something people identify with. Absolutely. I'm sure Trevor Denman will be in the Hall of Fame, because he was the first to bridge the gap between overseas style and the American style ... Dave Johnson or Tom Durkin. Those people are identified with and held in high esteem."

KRUYTBOSCH: "Whether it's at Saratoga or not, there should be some Hall of Fame. Chic Anderson. Definitely Tom Durkin down the road. Bob Weems. A lot of other guys including Clem McCarthy, was awesome in his day. I mean that's ridiculous that they're not in there. There should be other categories like track managers. I mean Matt Winn and the Kentucky Derby, the great race that it is. There's no place for him in the Hall of Fame. That's ridiculous. Look at Cooperstown. They have the great broadcasters in there."

COLLMUS: "Yes, absolutely. I think so. We're a part of the game that the public gets a chance to see or, at least, hear. I don't see why not."

WALLACE: "Maybe. There have been a few that have been worthy of that, I suspect. Capposella in New York should be. He was the voice of racing for a lot of generations at a time when racing was real big. And Clem McCarthy. And Chic. Of the modern announcers the only one who rates up there is Tom Durkin. There is something about him that is really memorable."

BECKER: "If Tom Durkin doesn't end up in the Hall of Fame, that's a black eye on the sport."

DOOLEY: "Yes. I think there should be a special broadcast section. I mean the Fred Capposellas of the world or Dave Johnson. Tom Durkin was the Voice of the Breeders' Cup, and as the person that brought that to life for two decades, I think there should be a special section in there for that."

JOHNSON: "No, I don't think so. If they're going to do that, they'd have to put in Capposella and Joe Hernandez. So do you also put in the greatest admissions manager and the greatest marketing director?"

DENMAN: "Of course they should ... I mean somebody tell me why! [Some say there's no need for announcers.] They're not important enough! But that just seems really really bizarre! If they don't think we're contributing to horse racing, wow! They are so far overboard!"

DURKIN: "No. No, not at all."

Interviews and Bibliography

Author Interviews

Mark Allen, May 3, 2009, in Louisville, Kentucky.

Bob Baffert, March 4, 2007, in Arcadia, California.

Carl Becker, June 7, 2006, by phone.

Kurt Becker, October 10, 2005, in Lexington, Kentucky; August 2008 by e-mail.

Dave Bennett, June 2006, in Albany, Washington.

Michael Blowen, May 4, 2009, in Georgetown, Kentucky.

Vladimir Cerin, March 4, 2007, in Arcadia, California.

Karen Cohen, June 2006, by e-mail.

Bob Collmus, December 2004, by phone.

Larry Collmus, August 4, 2007, in Oceanport, New Jersey; January 6, 2008, in Hallendale Beach, Florida.

Tom Dawson, September 7, 2006, by phone.

Robin Denman, April 13, 2007, by e-mail.

Trevor Denman, March 2, 2007, in Arcadia, California; April 13, 2007, by e-mail; November 19, 2008, by phone.

Michael Dickinson, April 3, 2008, by phone.

John Dooley, June 18 and 19, 2008, in Arlington Heights, Illinois.

Mary Ann Dooley, July 25, 2008, by phone.

Tom Durkin, August 9 and 10, 2006, in Saratoga Springs, New York.

Robert Geller, June 15, 16, and 17, 2006, in Auburn, Washington; March 17, 2008, by phone; January 19, 2009, by phone.

Greg Gilchrist, March 25, 2008, by phone.

Bob Holthus, November 14, 2007, by phone.

Jay Hovdey, February 12, 2007, by phone.

Neil Howard, April 7, 2008, by phone.

Dave Johnson, July 28, 2006, by phone; August 7, 2007, in Manhattan, New York; January 2008, by phone.

Mary Johnson, September 6, 2006, by phone.

Carla Kruytbosch Kirkpatrick, June 9, 2009, by phone.

Jack Knowlton, May 3, 2009, in Lexington, Kentucky.

Judy Wallace Koenig, November 27, 2008, by phone.
Luke Kruytbosch, January 22, 2006, in Phoenix, Arizona.
Donna Johnson Kunz, September 7, 2006, by phone.
Sally Collmus La Hart, December 5, 2007, by phone.
Ron McAnally, March 5, 2007, in Arcadia, California.
Bill Nader, September 7, 2006, by phone.
Bill Peters, March 19, 2006, in Hot Springs, Arkansas.
Josh Pons, April 19, 2008, in Baltimore, Maryland.
Beth Ann Durkin Ptacek, September 11, 2006, by phone.
Tim Ritchey, March 22, 2006, in Hot Springs, Arkansas.
Dave Rodman, April 17 and 18, 2008, in Baltimore, Maryland.
John Servis, March 22, 2006, in Hot Springs, Arkansas.
Mike Smith, April 9, 2008, by phone.
Gary Stevens, March 4, 2007, in Arcadia, California.
Dallas Stewart, March 4, 2009, by phone.
Marty Walker, November 25, 2007, by phone.
Terry Wallace, March 17 and 19, 2006, in Hot Springs, Arkansas.
Carol Wrona, September 29, 2008, by phone.
Julie Wrona (now Arbagey), October 17, 2006, by phone.
Michael Wrona, April 20 and 21, 2006, in Berkeley, California; March 6, 2008, in San Francisco, California; March 7, 2008, in San Mateo, California.
Wayne Wrona, July 2006, by e-mail.

Bibliography

Alvarado, Rudolph. *The Untold Story of Joe Hernandez: The Voice of Santa Anita.* Ann Arbor, MI: Morris, 2008.
Cairns, Steven. "London to a Brick On." *Australian Bloodhorse Review,* 1994.
Crossley, Liane. "5 Minutes with Terry Wallace." *Thoroughbred Times,* January 19, 2008.
De Martini, Tom. "5 Minutes with Larry Collmus." *Thoroughbred Times,* June 23, 2007.
Durkin, Tom. Keynote address, induction ceremony at the National Museum of Racing and Hall of Fame, Saratoga Springs, New York, August 7, 2006.
Georgeff, Phil. *And They're Off!* Lanham, MD: Taylor Trade, 2002.
Harris, Russ. "Back Injury Puts Wilson on Shelf for Several Weeks." *Philadelphia Inquirer,* September 20, 1989.
Haskin, Steve. *John Henry.* Lexington, KY: Eclipse Press, 2001.
Hillenbrand, Laura. *Seabiscuit: An American Legend.* New York: Random House, 2001.
Hovdey, Jay. "That Vivid Voice." *Del Mar Scene,* Summer 2006.
Klingaman, Mike. "Swing and a Miss." *Baltimore Sun,* May 16, 2009, www.balti moresun.com/sports/horse-racing/bal-sp.punch16may16,0,3269051.story.
Leonard, Connie. "A Fond Farewell of 'Voice of Churchill Downs.'" Wave 3, July 21, 2008, www.wave3.com/global/story.asp?s=8710432.

Lowe, Jeff. "Five Minutes with Trevor Denman." *Thoroughbred Times*, February 3, 2007.

Maharaj, Ash. "Personality of the Week: Trevor Denman." SAHorseracing.com, June 25, 2006.

Mende, Jeff. "Big A Means Big Break for Island Native." *Staten Island Sunday Advance*, November 19, 1995.

_____. "Islander Named Ohio Race Caller." *Staten Island Sunday Advance*, February 3, 1991.

Nack, William. *Secretariat: The Making of a Champion*. New York: Da Capo, 1975.

Rogers, Darren. "Select Group of Five Guest Announcers Will Be Featured During Churchill Downs' Fall Meet from Oct. 26–Nov. 29." Churchill Downs, October 2, 2008, www.churchilldowns.com/news/archives/select-group-of-five-guest-announcers-will-be-featured-during-churchill-downs-fall-mee.

Scaravilli, Chuck. "Dooley Truly Enjoyed Trip." *Daily Racing Form*, July 9, 1995.

Simon, Mary. *Racing Through the Century: The Story of Thoroughbred Racing in America*. Irvine, CA: Bowtie, 2002.

Smitha, Frank E. "South Africa and the End of Apartheid." MACROHISTORY and World Report, www.fsmitha.com/h2/ch34-sa.htm.

"South African Courses and Course Records." www.sahorseracing.com/racecourses.asp.

Thoroughbred Times, "Pimlico to Re-enact Seabiscuit–War Admiral Match Race." *Thoroughbred Times*, May 13, 2003, www.thoroughbredtimes.com/national-news/2003/May/13/Pimlico-to-re-enact-Seabiscuit-War-Admiral-match-race.aspx.

Times Staff, "Horse Runs onto I-580 After Crash at the Track." *Times*, November 23, 1998.

Woolfe, Raymond G., Jr. *Secretariat*. Radnor, PA: Chilton Book, 1974.

Many times I used the following helpful sources: www.bloodhorse.com, www.breederscup.com, www.drf.com, www.equibase.com, www.ntraracing.com, www.oldfriendsequine.org, www.pedigreequiry.com, www.wikipedia.org, and www.youtube.com. The forum that I belong to at www.thoroughbredchampions.com offers a wealth of information on all aspects of horse racing. Many racetrack media guides, programs, and track websites were also invaluable.

Index

Numbers in ***bold italics*** indicate pages with photographs.